Pro-Life Activists

in America

MEANING, MOTIVATION, AND DIRECT ACTION

Carol J. C. Maxwell

CAMBRIDGE
UNIVERSITY PRESS

PUBLISHED BY THE PRESS SYNDICATE OF THE UNIVERSITY OF CAMBRIDGE
The Pitt Building, Trumpington Street, Cambridge, United Kingdom

CAMBRIDGE UNIVERSITY PRESS
The Edinburgh Building, Cambridge CB2 2RU, UK
40 West 20th Street, New York, NY 10011-4211, USA
477 Williamstown Road, Port Melbourne, VIC 3207, Australia
Ruiz de Alarcón 13, 28014 Madrid, Spain
Dock House, The Waterfront, Cape Town 8001, South Africa

http://www.cambridge.org

First published 2002

Printed in the United States of America

Typeface Goudy 10.5/13 pt.   *System* LATEX 2_ε [TB]

A catalog record for this book is available from the British Library.

Library of Congress Cataloging in Publication Data
Maxwell, Carol J. C., 1950–
Pro-life activists in America : meaning, motivation,
and direct action / Carol J. C. Maxwell.
p.   cm.
Includes bibliographical references and index.
ISBN 0-521-66044-0 – ISBN 0-521-66942-1 (pb.)
1. Pro-life movement – United States.   2. Abortion – United States.
I. Title.
HQ767.5.U5 M372   2002
363.46′0973 – dc21   2001037929

ISBN 0 521 66044 0 hardback
ISBN 0 521 66942 1 paperback

*For Bruce, Ian, Clinton, Collin, Jim, and the friends
who have brought such light, contentment,
and joy into my life, as makes a woman rich.*

CONTENTS

ACKNOWLEDGMENTS

I marvel at the trust and generosity of the activists who shared their memories, thoughts, and feelings with me so that this book could be written. I must thank them first. I am grateful to Sigma Xi for their Grant-in-Aid; it covered all the research expenses I incurred in gathering data for this book. I also thank Cindy Kronauge for providing National Abortion Federation data to me at a time when it was not broadly disseminated. The violent events of 1993 made providers protective of such material. I send my thanks to the research librarians at Washington University, St. Louis University, and Northern Arizona University for their help in tracking down information over the years; I deeply appreciate their services.

I am grateful to John Bowen, first for the gentle and creative way he eased me toward the dissertation research that underlies this book, and then for the clear, kind, and insightful comments he made on drafts of my thesis. He was a good guide, who never dampened my interest or undermined my confidence. Contact with my committee members – Bob Canfield, Jean Ensminger, Richard Fox, Jack Knight, and Marilyn Friedman – was all too brief, but very encouraging. I particularly appreciated their enthusiasm for the analysis, as it unfolded. But these are deep wells, and I would have drunk more from them, had time permitted. I delighted in the friendship, mentoring, and collegial encouragement shown me by Philippe Bourgois, Dave Knowlton, Dave Edwards, Karen Brison, and Steve Leavitt – and thank them for it. The trust and respect I have for these scholars has drawn me back to them for help with later research. I cannot estimate the thanks I owe Mary Child, my editor at Cambridge, who worried about misunderstandings and pointed out wording that could have been misconstrued, given this hot-button topic. My thanks, also, to Jennifer Carey for her careful project management.

I do not understand why Ted Jelen allowed himself to become my unofficial, but tirelessly loyal mentor (and coauthor), but I am exceedingly grateful that he did. I thank him first for his unwavering friendship and collegial support, and second for leading me through the world of statistics. I especially appreciate his spending weekends on the phone with me, exploring questions that arose from my data through quantitative analysis. More than that, though, I am indebted to him for reading the near-final draft of this book. His criticisms were invaluable. I am also very grateful to the anonymous Cambridge reader who commented on my dissertation and, later, the first draft of this manuscript. Thank you for understanding how important your words were, and for taking the time to couch your valuable suggestions in praise of my work.

I will always be grateful to Rose Passalacqua for chiding me when I wrote "ugly sentences." Rose did not read this manuscript, but her lesson went deep; as I read, I try to weed out ugliness, and I always think of Rose, then.

I am especially grateful to my brother, Jim, Miyako Inoue, Roosevelt Peabody, and Carey and Sue Loomis (yes, Daniel, Lizzy, and Jason, too) for their enduring friendships. They have nurtured me. Most of all I must thank Bruce, my husband, who was so very tired of my working on this project, but cleaned the house and bought the groceries anyway. Thank you for wanting me to do well, and for making it possible. There at the top, too, are my sons, Ian, Clinton, and Collin. The joy you take in my accomplishments is a pleasure with few equals. It makes me want to do more, better.

CHAPTER ONE

CHOOSING INCIVILITY

Let us never cease from thinking – what is this 'civilization' in which we find ourselves?. . . Where in short is it leading us?
— Woolf 1936:62–3

You can't possibly run a control group, can't look at this like any other study. We're more complicated than paramecium – and we lie!
— An activist in my sample

In the mid 1970s, abortion clinics in the United States experienced their first sit-ins, orchestrated by activists who eventually came to call themselves "rescuers." These activists added a new dimension to the anti-abortion movement generally termed "direct activism." Since then, pro-life direct action has been either feared or dismissed as a manifestation of religious conservatism, the work of a relatively homogeneous group. My first encounter with these activists challenged both presumptions and suggested, instead, that an unexpected array of private motivations underlay a fairly uniform mode of public expression. Intrigued by the apparent complexity of this phenomenon, I embarked on two years of field observations to provide an anthropological account of this social movement. By taking this approach I found that, not only was individual motivation within the group I encountered diverse, but the movement's sociological composition and the basis of members' ideological commitment to direct action shifted over time. While mass anti-abortion sit-ins are not currently occurring, a close understanding of this movement offers valuable insight into both activism and motivation, more generally.

1

My first observation occurred early one frigid February morning in 1989, outside an abortion clinic in St. Louis. I set off to accompany two fellow graduate students, Miyako Inoue and Ma Qi, making field observations as part of a class assignment. We three linked our arms tightly – half against the cold, half to be sure we were safely together – and set off to observe Operation Rescue in action. This nationwide organization had arrived in St. Louis to lead local activists in a blockade and demonstration at the most prominant abortion clinic in our vicinity.

We found a crowd of about 100 men and women picketing in front of the clinic; most demonstrators were approximately 20 to 50 years of age, white, and perhaps best described as middle class. A wall of policemen stood baracading the clinic doors, silent as a queen's guard, as we three approached the slowly circulating mass of picketers. These activists, heavily bundled against the cold, eagerly responded to our inquiries and freely discussed their motivations. We first spoke with a small, elderly Jewish woman wearing a very large, bright yellow Star of David sewn to a band around her arm. (She was the only Jewish pro-life direct activist I ever encountered.) This woman explained that she attended the event in defiance of her rabbi because she felt a personal responsibility as a Jew to picket, equating legal abortion and the Holocaust. Clearly, other activists' motivations would differ. We moved among the picketers, listening to their stories one by one. Eventually a volunteer clinic escort kindly asked us if we intended to be arrested. When we assured her we did not, she directed us away from the driveway just as activists began to prostrate themselves in front of incoming traffic. Police began removing and arresting the demonstrators as we left. We must have looked uncertain and confused. As we turned to go, a tall woman acting as a "sidewalk counselor," took charge of us, mistaking our trepidation for concern over a problematic pregnancy of our own. After speaking with her until our feet grew numb, we withdrew to a warm restaurant and tried to sort out our observations. The one message that came through clearly was that these activists were diverse and their motivations were complex.

In this book, I will try to explain variation within the pro-life direct action movement by illustrating diverse motives for adopting direct action and explaining how such differences bore on individuals' persistence in the movement, their withdrawal from it, and the consequent redefinition of this activism. Pro-life direct action was conducted by successive waves of activists with relatively distinct demographic characteristics, tactical strategies, and objectives. Over time, the movement teetered between two precipitous footings. On the one hand, direct activists' intensity and rigidity threatened to isolate them from other pro-lifers and stultify their movement. On the other hand, the expansion needed to sustain the movement required tactical and, so, ideological dilution that evicerated the impulses underlying commitment to such radical measures as breaking the law and risking arrest. That is, people inclined to accommodate conflicting demands, weigh consequences against imperatives, and consider options outside their primary choice were unlikely to adopt direct action.

By the early 1990s, an estimated forty thousand individuals had participated in sit-ins at abortion facilities and related locations in the United States (Ginsburg 1993:564). Most had no previous experience with direct activism; this political involvement was a dramatic, portentous episode in their lives. These men and women described intense, wide-ranging motivations for their participation, motives not captured by analyses of conventional anti-abortion activism (which revolve around women's issues, such as "the felt contradiction between mothering and other kinds of labor in this society"; Ginsburg 1993:581). From their detailed quantitative analysis Cook, Jelen, and Wilcox (1992:64) concluded that,

> Differences in education, region, and family structure all help explain some of the variation in abortion attitudes. However, the explanatory power of such demographic variables is rather weak . . . What is needed is a more detailed analysis of the reasons people have for their abortion attitudes.

In doing the research that underlies this book, I wanted most to understand the thought processes and circumstances that lead people to participate in direct action. Such personal experiences become both interesting and useful when they either voice the universal, or expand our understanding by articulating an unseen dimension of it. Accordingly, I interviewed people about their personal experiences of the decision to join direct action (as activists defined it) regardless of the number of times they had experienced this decision process. I spent two years (September 1989 to August 1991) making field observations in St. Louis, Missouri, Wichita, Kansas, and Washington, D.C. I began audiotaping long, semistructured interviews with activists during the second year. Altogether, I taped interviews with 80 direct activists. (Appendix 1 provides a detailed description of the sample.)

I began with field ethnography in order to learn how direct action had developed and to identify the range of activities and attitudes involved in this activism. After the first year of field observations I felt I had a good enough sense of what was being done, and what had been done in the past, to identify the groups I needed to sample and the outsiders I should include in order to represent the scope of direct activism in St. Louis. I verified individuals' participation through my own observations and the consensus of their peers. In identifying their own peers, activists directed me to essentially everyone currently sitting-in (or actively demonstrating), as well as many people who sat-in only once, and a few people who never sat-in, but were considered integral (or endemic) to local pro-life direct action by the activists themselves.

The definition of direct action not only was contested, it was chimerical. Activists debated its nature by recognizing or refuting its varied parts. For example, a given individual might laud picketing as an indispensable aspect of direct action one day, then later denigrate it and insist that only sitting-in qualified as direct action. I coped with this changeability by interviewing people who engaged in all the different activities described as direct action, while seeking out people who engaged in those activities most consistently defined as "rescue." Consequently, my sample cut across the activists' informal hierarchy of involvement to include a cross section of people who participated in pro-life direct action over time.

I relied on three sources to gather a snowball sample (a type of sample that builds outward in many directions as each member identifies more prospective interviewees). Those three sources were: referrals, publications, and personal observations. Since direct action organizations did not keep membership lists, I identified potential interviewees by networking through local pro-life organizations and asking individuals I encountered during field observations to name the direct activists they knew. I asked past and current direct action leaders to refer me to both active and former rescuers. To a one, leaders resorted to their personal telephone directories to supplement their memories. Periodically, I asked leaders for more referrals. This worked best when we were discussing past events; then leaders were able to recall activists they had not previously mentioned. To supplement leaders' lists, I contacted people named in a local rescue newsletter and asked them to interview. I also asked each interviewee to refer me to other people who had rescued. Interviews were open ended and allowed activists to reflect on their rescue experiences and the circumstances surrounding them. The interviewees appreciated this format, called the people they recommended to me, told them

I would be contacting them, and set aside their fears. Periodically, I com-pared my list of interviewees to people named in past injunctions to see how complete my sample was.

In this way I interviewed people associated with the three major pro-life direct action organizations that formed in St. Louis. To these I added most of the people regularly protesting at abortion clinics but not affiliated with a group, and a random sample of people who came to clinics intermittently to protest. I suspect that, numerically, the least well-represented organization was the first group organized in the area, which was composed of college-aged activists and seminarians. However, I did sample from among the various segments comprising this early group. That is, I interviewed people from this cohort who had been young when they sat-in and their middle-aged companions; liberals and conservatives; Catholic, Protestant, and seminarian; those who contin-ued in direct action and those who returned to conventional activism, or left activism altogether; leaders and followers; male and female.

I stopped seeking new interviewees after leaders of both current groups said I had interviewed people even they had never heard of, and that I "must have talked to everyone," including people they thought were essential to include, "If you want to talk about rescue." In the end, the St. Louis sample included a cross section of the people who had initiated, altered, and sustained the movement, as well as those who were currently embodying it.[1]

Most people I asked to participate heard about the interviews from friends before I contacted them, and had already decided to interview. Many people told me this decision was difficult because they feared they did not have anything of value to say or that they were inarticulate (generally groundless fears). Most people said they decided to interview because they felt misrepresented and wanted a chance to accurately depict their activism, explaining that their cause was critically important and should be understood.

I interviewed most activists in their homes, mainly because many of them were no longer sitting-in, and so were not to be found at abor-tion clinics. Interviews often lasted many hours longer than anticipated,

---

[1] Seven people declined to interview. Two people refused because they felt their roles were insignificant; another two said they resented the idea of being studied. One man declined because he felt my affiliation with Washington University would force me to write a biased thesis, and another person declined because she was too busy. A seventh person declined before hearing what the study entailed.

sometimes continuing into the early hours of the morning. I began interviews by establishing basic demographic information, then proceeded
to explore five topics through the following questions:

1. How did you become pro-life?
2. How did you come to act on your beliefs?
3. What have you done as an activist?
4. How did you come to do the particular things you did about
    your beliefs? (That is, Why did you chose the particular forms
    of activism you engaged in?)
5. Why do you consider abortion a significant problem and where
    do you see this (intentionally undefined) going in the future?

Interviews tended to flow naturally from topic to topic, often expanding from the first two questions across the other three without my
prompting.[2] I did not interrupt or redirect interviewees when they appeared to digress. They usually brought their discursive excursions back
to their activism, enlarging my understanding of their motivations by
providing me a context for their decisions to sit-in (or stop sitting-in).
In this way they described their activist experiences in the context of
their whole lives, not as discrete phenomena.

I made sure interviewees understood that the purpose of the interviews was to gather data for my research. I explained to them that I was attempting to portray their movement accurately from an anthropological
perspective, with an emphasis on the reasons underlying individuals'
participation in direct action. I assured them that my analysis would not
address the morality of abortion per se. When interviewees asked my
position on abortion, I told them that I had trouble reconciling abortion with my personal values, but neither could I know what another
woman would best do. As I recall, only one activist pushed me to take
a stand on one side or the other of the pro-choice/pro-life divide, but
I did not feel a need to define myself according to that dichotomy. The
other interviewees appeared to accept, or at least tolerate, the neutrality
created by the tension between my beliefs. I do not think interviewees
considered me a potential advocate. Rather, they found the interviews
cathartic, often thanking me for the opportunity to think through their
experiences and to be heard.

---

[2] Several of the first interviewees reported paranormal experiences that reinforced
     their commitment to activism, so I probed this topic with subsequent interviewees,
     but very few described paranormal experiences.

The long-term observations and in-depth interviews incorporated in this book provide a contextualized description of the development of anti-abortion attitudes and allow me to relate individual reasoning to the practice of collective action. Maslow noted long ago that individual motivation and environmental forces (such as situational determinants) "both have their places in the larger structure" that accounts for behavior (1970:29). My approach in analyzing this instance of collective action attempts more to portray these two factors, the individuals' motivations and the complex, multidimensional, "larger structure," than to pursue a particular theoretical perspective. Consequently, I present a history of the pro-life direct action movement centered on the factors that most closely related to individual activists' motivations. (This approach draws on numerous theories in a process termed *open-ended theory construction*.)

The moral and legal status of abortion is not, of course, solely a preoccupation of contemporary America. It has been debated and documented, if inconsistently, over the last 2,000 years, and around the world (Noonan 1970; Rodman, Sarvis, and Bonar 1987). This long history makes the meaning of any one point in this contentious dialogue contingent, and its use as a starting point dubious. Consider the 1973 *Roe v. Wade* decision, which halted a state-by-state revamping of abortion law in favor of a national standard that legalized abortion, with few limiting provisions. Depending on the point in history one choses to hark back to, *Roe* could be considered: 1) the lawful reinstatement of a legal and at least tacitly accepted practice; or 2) the reversal of a long-standing legal position and legitimization of what was previously construed to be a crime. The first perspective privileges history prior to the nineteenth-century physicians' campaign, which was conducted throughout the last half of the 1800s (as part of a larger national trend to centralize and rationalize society; cf. Ginsburg 1989). At the turn of that century, "no jurisdiction in the United States had enacted any statutes whatsoever on the subject of abortion" and "those American women who wished to practice abortion did so" (Mohr 1978:vii). The second perspective focuses on the legal context that the physicians' campaign eventually created. By 1900 the physicians' campaign had brought about laws circumscribing and criminalizing abortion in "virtually every jurisdiction in the United States" (Mohr 1978:vii). Such radical changes in the legal status of abortion indicate equally pervasive changes in popular attitudes toward abortion, and, consequently, in its moral status.

Each seemingly discrete phase, every significant turning point, and each set of opposing arguments and factions is framed by those preceding it and by the larger social context within which it emerges, and is recorded and later remembered or reconstructed. In general, media reports (and even some scholarly work) regarding pro-life direct action present truncated or biased descriptions of this movement, usually emphasizing the brief but highly visible influx of evangelicals that swelled its ranks in the late 1980s and brought about its essential demise in the early 1990s. This was the period dominated by Operation Rescue. Many of the individuals I interviewed were direct activists years before Operation Rescue arose; some tutored its founder, Randall Terry. Understanding their personal experiences, and the movement as a whole, requires a framework that predates Operation Rescue. In Chapter 2, I have drawn an oral history of the movement from activists engaged in its various stages, beginning in the 1970s and lasting through the 1990s.

Chapter 2 begins with the personal experiences and ideology of the movement's founder and describes the strategy that generated activism throughout the continental United States, making forays into Canada, Great Britain, and Eastern and Western Europe. I focus, however, on events in the midwestern metropolitan area of St. Louis, Missouri. This approach allows me to consider the interaction of individual-level microprocesses (such as forming commitment and ascribing meaning), group-level dynamics (such as organizational life cycles), and environmental factors (such as community attitudes, changes in law, and historical contingencies) – all disparate, but important, influences on this movement.

The activists' oral histories illustrate diverse political and social science theories. For example, the movement's organizational infrastructure shaped its life course in interaction with environmental constraints, opportunities, and stimuli. Such factors included inter- and intra-group relationships, and police, court, and community responses to direct action as it arose and as it changed over time. New organizational forms emerged not only in response to such external pressures, but also as a consequence of innovative processes activists undertook. Changing levels of participation in the direct action movement had a powerful effect, not only on practical areas such as its potential for success (in preventing abortions) or punishment (of individuals who sat-in), but also on the social contexts activism offered participants and its consequent attraction to recruits. Sitting-in was personally costly, however, contrary to some political science theory, direct activists did not commonly succumb to "free-riding" (first described in Olson 1971).

That is, they did not tend to back away from participation when sit-ins were large, even though they knew their absence would probably not alter a sit-in's outcome. Yet, over time, shifts in the movement's demography altered its ideology, organization, tactics, and scope.

Rescuers' demographic profile alone suggests that models explaining *conventional* pro-life activism (that is, legal activism) are inadequate to explain participation in pro-life *direct action*. Direct activists were not the socioeconomic marginals some authors suggest. They would not be accurately described as downwardly mobile, disenfranchised, socially isolated, poor, undereducated, underemployed, and so forth. However, their opposition to abortion was radicalized to some extent by their own ideologically derived perceptions of marginalization. That is, many activists perceived themselves to be excluded from the mechanisms through which people control and change society. They spoke of their religious values as making them a targeted, disenfranchised minority vulnerable to the havoc wrought by a dominant "liberal," "humanist" majority.

The various groups comprising the pro-life direct action movement over time each went through a series of developmental stages, as did the movement as a whole (cf. Stewart, Smith, and Denton 1989). Identify-ing these stages helps explain divergent trends in the frequency of vio-lent and nonviolent acts at abortion clinics. However, although helpful, stage theory only provides a partial explanation. A closer look at the way individuals reacted to their political environment illuminates the rise in violence that coincided with decreasing participation in sit-ins (cf. Festinger, Riecken, and Schachter 1956). Such considerations bear implications for future radical opposition to abortion (as discussed in Chapter 2).

Throughout this book I focus on individuals' interpretations of their activism – that is, what they considered their activism to have been, what they hoped to accomplish through it, and how they came to pursue those objectives. This approach draws on the cognitive theory of moti-vation (Maehr 1989). Contextualization is essential to this analysis. The activists' private symbolism, linked to personal quests, played a major role in their own definitions of the costs and benefits of participating in direct action. People flexibly interpreted pre-existing ethics when deciding whether or not to participate in sit-ins. Immediate personal cir-cumstances, as well as social and political environments, influenced such choices by conditioning individuals' experiences. The ideology, rhetoric, group dynamics, and tactics individuals encountered leant meaning to specific actions, and so entered into their decisions to join and to leave direct action.

The activists' narratives richly illustrated these dynamics. In Chapter 3, I follow Bailey's transition from pro-choice to pro-life ideology, tracing her path from conventional to radical activism.[3] I then illustrate the key social and psychological processes embedded in activists' narratives by recounting Rick's, Jan's, and Dylan's experiences of entering and leaving direct activism. Their motivations hinged on such processes as ascribing meaning, assessing costs, and interpreting (and reinterpreting) their own existing ethics. Their stories highlight the roles of such personal experiences as grief and salvation in activism. I use Loren's narrative to explore the nexus of grief and activism in more detail (Chapter 4), then turn to the narratives of women who had aborted prior to sitting-in, to illustrate the powerful role diverse concepts of God and salvation played in this activism, and conversely, the important role activism played in individual psychological processes (Chapter 5). The complexity underlying most activists' motivations could as quickly dissipate the impulse to sit-in as arouse it. This complexity undermined commitment to direct action at the individual level. Consequently, participation was often transient. The narratives in Chapter 5 illustrate the impact of this transience on the direct action movement.

Through these stories I examine the generation and collapse of commitment. Recruitment to even mainstream pro-life activism differed from recruitment to pro-choice activism. Kristin Luker noted that less than 10% of the pro-life activists she interviewed "were recruited in the way the typical pro-choice activist was" (1984:147–8). Although Luker attributed abortion attitudes and activism to individuals' life situations (their socioeconomic status, their peers, the values they learned as children, and especially their participation in paid labor), she noted that anti-abortion activism was often initiated by personal, idiosyncratic motives. She concluded that "almost all" people opposing abortion self-recruited (unlike people supporting legal access to abortion, who generally became politically active through formal activities of the pro-choice movement) (1984:146). Pro-lifers' self-recruitment often stemmed from a "personal experience that 'brought the issue home' to

---

[3] Organization and business (including abortion clinic) names that might identify interviewees have been changed. All names not given in full are pseudonyms, as well.

them" (Luker 1984:146). Faye Ginsburg (1989) also noted a conversion-like experience that precipitated anti-abortion activism. In Chapter 6, I explore such experiences, which direct activists referred to as becoming "convicted to pro-life." Conviction radicalized activism.

I argue that "conviction" was a secular form of conversion, and that conversion is an intense instance of a creative, ongoing, and generally nonpathological process (cf. Cucchiari 1988; Heirich 1977; Stark and Bainbridge 1980). Reflection on one's own life history and identity, critical life events, distressing social changes, and exposure to other pro-life activists and their rhetoric all helped bring about "conviction." These factors were couched within larger social dynamics such as the contest between egalitarian and hierarchical relational strategies (which I describe in Chapter 6), and national trends supporting the legal status of abortion. Conviction established consistent moral, social, and relational strategies, and this uniformity promoted participation in direct action.

When activists described their conviction experiences and the meanings they ascribed to their activism, they illustrated the relationship between their personal experiences, sources of their self-identity such as their regional backgrounds, and the development, interpretation, and application of their personal ethics. This nexus is an underdeveloped area in the study of moral reasoning (Berk 1989).

The literature on moral reasoning recognizes that moral discourse often differs from future behavior and that people may not apply ethics in a logically consistent manner from one situation to another. Direct activists' narratives suggest one explanation for these tendencies. That is, they suggest that adults conduct an ongoing reinterpretation of relatively stable ethics. Personal circumstances and pressing psychological or emotional needs shaped individuals' assessment of the practical implications of their ethics. Here, my findings build upon those of Oliner and Oliner (1988).

The Oliners closely examined the precedents, contexts, and correlatives to moral decisions associated with altruistic behavior (in their case, saving Jews during Nazi occupation). Their study necessarily relied on recall many years after the events under consideration, given their emphasis on early childhood experiences and the social and political attitudes interviewees held at the time they chose to rescue Jews. My study also relies on recall, but examines moral decisions much closer to the time of the act in question. Amid the complex reality underlying moral decisions, the Oliners found a sense of inclusiveness, a "willingness to see different types of people as essentially similar to" oneself that was crucial to altruistic action (1988:178). This attitude is called an "ethic of extensivity," and it was prominent in pro-life direct activists' narratives. Almost all of the activists adopted an extensive attitude toward the "unborn" (fetuses), but several activists developed extensive attitudes toward women contemplating abortion. This disposition guided behavior long before the "helping" act, and afterwards, as well. However, a precipitating event was necessary to lead most people to act upon their moral inclinations. As the Oliners note, "It took a catalyst to translate predisposition into action," but the actions arose not from "objective external events" but rather from "the subjective meanings rescuers conferred on them" (1988:187). I have drawn together extensive excerpts from activists' narratives, so that they might describe, in their own words, the dynamics that converged to bring about extraodinary responses. This approach provides a contextualized consideration of individual moral reasoning (following the example set by Coles and Coles 1978).

The activists' situated interpretation of ethics made their approaches to moral dilemmas appear to spiral between "care" and "justice" orientations – two approaches to moral reasoning first described as a dichotomy (cf. Gilligan 1982). Pro-life activists thus presented a pattern somewhat different from the linear progression embodied in traditional developmental models of moral reasoning, and different still from Gilligan's alternative to the linear model (cf. 1982). Furthermore, and again contrary to a dichotomized model, pro-life activists' impartialist moral orientations appeared to be dependent on, or at least interactive with, particularistic approaches to moral reasoning. (Blum [1993] concisely describes these theories of moral reasoning, and I discuss them more fully as I consider specific activists' narratives throughout this book.) The point to be taken here is that activists' narratives suggest that an individual utilizes a broader range of moral reasoning approaches than either a dichotomized model or a model describing linear development would account for. Moreover, the connections activists' narratives describe between one approach to moral reasoning and another suggest an interdependence between different types of moral reasoning.

The people interviewed for this study clearly undertook important psychological tasks through their activism. (I base the significance of the psychological events activists described on the work of Glick and Zigler [1985] and Harter [1985].) The activists' narratives illustrated the potency of intellectual and emotional convergence (cf. Leahy 1985). They often sought or responded to such consistency through their activism. For example, Loren's story of real, remembered, and imagined death (Chapter 4) illustrates the importance of both thinking and feeling in attaining self-realization (cf. Maslow 1970; cf. Wikan 1990). Again, women who had aborted and later joined the movement addressed the dissonance wrought by various traumatic life events (including their abortions) through their activism. Many activists' stories illustrated a struggle to balance diverse personal needs against the desire to form connections to others (including God). Such struggles varied the force of meaning, ideology, and material circumstances in shaping commitment to direct action.

The success of the pro-life direct action movement, that is, its ability to sustain collective action, depended on negotiating a balance between two potentially conflictive value orientations: instrumental rationality and value rationality (two concepts described by Weber [1978]). Activists whose reasoning was guided by instrumental rationality aimed to achieve immediate practical ends and encourage future political success. Activists who took value-rational approaches were satisfied by the sheer act of participating, even if abortion was neither prevented nor recriminalized. That is, instrumental rationalists sought objective goals external to their own acts, while value rationalists achieved their goals in activism itself. In Chapter 7, I turn from the personal voices of the individual narratives to a quantitative analysis in order to describe the effects of these two types of rationality, and the conviction experience, on levels of participation in direct action.[4] In Chapter 8, I again examine the sample as an aggregate to explore the different themes men and women developed in their narratives and how these themes related to persistent participation in sit-ins.

What shaped the course of this collective action, both from within and from without? The activists' decisions to engage in and withdraw from direct action, and to adopt or reject specific tactics suggest answers to this question. As reflections upon actual lived experiences, (as opposed to hypothetical situations posed by researchers to assess moral reasoning processes) direct activists' narratives illustrate relationships between thought and action over time. They show how people interpreted their personal experiences, what their activism meant to them, how they understood the circumstances of their activism, and how these meanings affected their participation and, so, shaped a social movement. My focus on the activists' stories allows me to explore extrarational

---

[4] This analysis appears in more detail in Maxwell and Jelen 1994.

motivations to collective action while taking account of its environmental contexts.

Defining Direct Action

The range of practices termed "direct action" by interviewees varied over time and differed somewhat from "direct action" practiced by other unconventional activists (such as those opposing war, nuclear power, or clear-cutting timber). Since I wanted to understand why activists chose to do what they did, and to learn what those actions meant to them, I asked them to define "direct action."

Despite the evolving nature of "direct action" in St. Louis, the epitome of pro-life direct action was always "rescuing" – that is, attempting to stop specific, planned abortions from taking place. "Rescuers" directly attempted to stop abortions in three ways: intercepting and dissuading patients, blocking clinic entrances, or causing clinics to close for business. (Some activists stretched the meaning almost to the breaking point when, occasionally, they defined prayer as direct action.) The recurring theme in direct activists' discourse was that the hallmark of rescue was risking arrest (for sitting-in or trespassing). Tactics that did not expose activists to arrest seemed complementary rather than focal.

Direct activists attempted to close clinics by contaminating or damaging doctors' equipment, occupying or contaminating clinic premises, increasing legal regulations so that continued operations would not be profitable, or by dissuading landlords from renewing clinic's leases. By blocking clinic entrances, activists intended to turn pregnant women away with their ruckus, hoping the women would later decide not to abort. Direct activists employed several rhetorical tactics to dissuade the women impeded by their sit-ins. They termed their key rhetorical strategies "sidewalk counseling" and "truth talks."

"Sidewalk counseling," which entailed speaking to "abortion-bound mothers," potentially achieved the same end as sitting-in, and so was often classed as direct action and called "rescuing." In fact, many saw it as the *sine qua non* of rescue. Like sitting-in, sidewalk counseling often entailed "risking arrest" (for trespassing on clinic property in violation of an injunction). "Truth talks" were conducted by two-person teams of activists. In one version, a male-female team entered a clinic waiting area posing as a couple and implying that the man was pressuring the woman to abort. The couple would start to argue and the woman would accuse the man of not caring about her or her baby. She would become angry and leave, "deciding" not to abort. In the other version, two women would pose as mother and daughter. The older woman would ask the younger if she was sure she wanted to "go ahead with this," and the younger woman would respond uncertainly, show her "mother" the pro-life literature she had picked up on her way into the clinic, then turn to the other women in the waiting areas, show them the literature and ask them what they thought. The pair would end their performance by "deciding" against the abortion and leaving the clinic.

Sometimes direct activists entered clinics and either quietly stuffed pro-life leaflets into the clinic's magazines or openly handed out their literature and tried to talk women into leaving with them. Either activity might precede a sit-in, and would be considered an integral part of the direct action event.

The definition of direct action hinged on the private meanings people gave to particular practices. Some people limited the definition of direct action to sitting-in and sidewalk counseling. Other people extended the definition to include picketing outside abortion clinics, either because it contributed to the impression that "something is wrong here" (and so might dissuade incoming patients), or because the actions termed "picketing" by observers were understood differently by participants. For example, some people understood "picket lines" to be powerful, prayerful proclamations of God's authority and injunctions against the "evil" abiding in clinics. Other people explained that "picketing" was showing one's gratitude to God, fulfilling a Biblical enjoinder to "stand at the gates and give warning," or "witnessing" to God's will.

Direct activists closed clinics several times by vandalizing them. In addition to fouling entrance door locks, or padlocking them closed, which was done repeatedly, they employed several tactics that were never repeated despite their effectiveness in preventing clinic operations. For example, several interviewees recalled that in one instance, while occupying a clinic, they slipped a box of frozen fish above the drop ceiling of a procedure room. The fish spoiled quickly and the odor was so powerful that the clinic closed for several days to locate the problem. In another instance, they staged a "car sit-in" by abandoning many cars tightly packed in front of a clinic's doors. In yet another instance, an activist obstructed a clinic entrance with massive cement blocks.

Such contamination and blockading tactics were effective, did not result in arrest, and entailed less emotional strain than the face-to-face confrontation most activists dreaded during sit-ins. This emotional stress was, perhaps, the most salient cost of sitting-in and sidewalk counseling.

Most direct activists said they would rather be arrested for sitting-in than endure the personal confrontation involved in sidewalk counseling, yet they also reported feeling nauseated before each sit-in due to anxiety over the thought of confronting police and clinic personnel. The relative infrequency with which contamination and object blockades were employed indicates the complex motivations behind other, more personally costly tactics such as sitting-in and sidewalk counseling.

RESEARCH ON PRO-LIFE DIRECT ACTION

The contest between pro-life and pro-choice activists is not a microcosm of sentiment felt across the nation. Pro-life direct activists' adamant opposition to abortion (like pro-choicers' staunch support for it) diverges sharply from the nuanced attitudes expressed by the broader American public. General Social Survey data from 1987 through 1991, assessing the general public, show "considerable overlap between characteristics of pro-life and pro-choice citizens"; even people at either pole, that is, those who agree with either pro-life or pro-choice stances, "share many values with their ostensible opponents" (Cook, Jelen, and Wilcox 1992:155–6). Cook, Jelen, and Wilcox found among the broader citizenry "a narrow majority [of] . . . situationalists, who favor legal access to abortion in some circumstances, but not others" (1992:156). Cook, Jelen, and Wilcox note that, while different positions on abortion exist within the general public, and demographic differences do matter, "the image of two opposed camps, each questioning the integrity and morality of the other, does not describe the mass public in the United States" (1992:156). However, they point out that, at the activist level, the debate about abortion "seems concerned with such ultimate values that compromise is difficult to envision" (1992:11).

Abortion sets core American values in conflict, and public opinion on abortion reflects this contest (Cook, Jelen, and Wilcox 1992). Abortion sets Americans' belief in individualism in conflict with a general Judaeo-Christian tradition. These values give rise to more concrete issues: the importance and status of child bearing, gender roles, sexual morality, and the sanctity of human life. Cook, Jelen, and Wilcox found that "most Americans hold values that pull them in both pro-choice and pro-life directions" (1992:156). Balancing these opposite pulls, "a majority of Americans appears to believe that the status of the embryo and the prerogatives of the mother must be weighed and balanced in some fashion" (Cook, Jelen, and Wilcox 1992:11). Accordingly, most Americans (76%)

support legal access to abortion when the mother's health is threatened, the pregnancy results from rape, or the fetus is defective; only 7% oppose abortion in all three traumatic circumstances (Cook, Jelen, and Wilcox 1992:35). However, polls indicate that Americans are divided over abortions undertaken due to social circumstances. Forty-seven percent oppose abortion for reasons of poverty, for unmarried women, and for couples who want no more children; 37% support legal abortion in all three of these social circumstances (Cook, Jelen, and Wilcox 1992:35). The public appears to value both embryonic life and personal choice; valuing both, the general public accords neither "the status of a fundamental right" (Cook, Jelen, and Wilcox 1992:13). This nuanced and compromising attitude was rare among pro-life direct activists, but neither did rescuers mirror the demographic profile of the anti-abortion movement as a whole.

Direct activists differed in important ways from conventional pro-life activists. Their demographics and attitudes differed from those of the anti-abortion movement as a whole. These differences may have been a function of changes in the pro-life movement over time, or the sociogeographic areas studied, but I also think they related to the personal inclinations that lead to disparate types of activism.

Kristin Luker's (1984) seminal work on abortion activists made demographics (such as socioeconomic position, age, gender, and so forth) a prominent consideration in subsequent studies. After concluding that "the abortion debate has become a debate among women," Luker argues that the social position of women on either side of the issue is "dramatically" different, and that social positioning is crucial to activists' attitudes toward abortion, guiding both their ideology and their commitment to activism (1984:194).[5] She (1984:199,200) explains that,

---

[5] Most of the pro-life women she interviewed were housewives; 44% lived in households with annual incomes under $20,000. Only one-seventh lived in households with annual incomes over $50,000, and 63% of the pro-life women in her sample did not work in the paid labor force. Half of the working pro-life women earned under $5,000 annually, and the other half earned between $5,000 and $10,000. Only two of her pro-life interviewees earned over $20,000. Referring to a period beginning in the late 1960s and lasting through the early 1980s, Luker characterized the average pro-life activist as a deeply religious Catholic woman, 44 years of age, married at age 17, having three or more children, some college or perhaps an undergraduate degree, not employed in the paid labor force, but rather, a housewife in a family with an annual household income of $30,000. This profile contrasted strikingly with that of the pro-choicers Luker interviewed. Pro-choice women tended to be well-educated, employed, very highly paid, and nonreligious. They also tended to marry later and have fewer children.

Activists on both sides of the issue are women who have a given set of values about what are the most satisfying and appropriate roles for women, and they have made *life commitments that now limit their capability to change their minds* . . . For most of these activists, therefore, their position on abortion is . . . a shorthand way of supporting and proclaiming not only a complex set of values but a given set of social resources as well. [Italics in the original]

Luker concludes that "the abortion debate is a conflict between two different social worlds and the hopes and beliefs those worlds support" (1984:194). She described that conflict as, ". . . a debate about women's contrasting obligations to themselves and others" (1984:193), adding that it is ". . . a referendum on the place and meaning of motherhood" resting on "the question of whether women's fertility is to be socially recognized as a resource or as a handicap" (1984:193,202).

Luker tied both male and female pro-lifers' abortion ideologies to their socioeconomic positions. She argued that, "pro-life people and pro-life women in particular," because of their low educational and occupational attainments, "see an achievement-based world as harsh, superficial, and ultimately ruthless; they are relatively less well-equipped to operate in that world" (1984:207). Luker explained that acceptance of abortion "strips the veil of sanctity from motherhood" demoting it "from a sacred calling to a job" that receives little respect in our society and is threatened by the liberalized approach to sexuality and relationships that abortion presumably encourages (1984:205). Luker reasons that pro-life women's limited educations and the accompanying lack of access to well-paying jobs, dependence on spousal support, and lifetimes lived within conservative peer groups, made motherhood a resource for them and a more rewarding option than the types of paid labor they were qualified to obtain. By opposing legal abortion, pro-life women were, in effect, lobbying for the naturalness and social value of motherhood.

Other researchers describe similar demographic profiles for pro-lifers. Himmelstein (1986) summarizes these findings. He argues that,

Supporters and opponents of abortion are not polarized in any simple way by social position nor is there any clear connection between the personal situation of women as housewives or breadwinners and their opinions on abortion.

Ginsburg (1989) characterized pro-life and pro-choice ideologies much as Luker did. However, like Himmelstein, Ginsburg did not find the demographic disparities Luker described. She reports that in Fargo, North Dakota, where she undertook her research efforts, grass-roots "pro-choice and pro-life activists do not divide neatly along ethnic, economic, occupational, or even religious lines" (1989:6). Nor were activists clearly divided by education, religiosity, or marital status.[6] Ginsburg found generational differences between pro-life and pro-choice activists to be more marked than their socioeconomic differences (the majority of pro-life activists in her sample being about 10 years younger than the pro-choice activists).

The leveling of demographic differences suggested by Himmelstein's and Ginsburg's studies may represent changes in the pro-life movement over time, or may reflect sociogeographic differences between studies. Ginsburg's findings in particular may be a function of the small town setting she observed and her small sample size.

In the relatively homogeneous context of a small town, Ginsburg found that activists' disparate responses to abortion grew out of the nexus of their particular sociohistorical experiences and their own life-cycle transitions. She argued that their "narratives revolve around transitions in the female life-cycle that were experienced as stressful and incongruous, generating a 'life crisis,'" aggravated by rapid social change that called into question the "social rules for an assumed life trajectory" (1989:13,138). Ginsburg found that through abortion activism, women created "both an interpretation and arena of action" that they used to "reframe in social terms what they had experienced initially as problematic shifts specific to their individual lives" (1989:139). In so doing, "activists create alternative 'life scripts' to what they considered to be a conventional cultural form for a female life trajectory" (1989:144).

Such confluences "often related to reproduction" (Ginsburg 1989:141). In fact, Ginsburg sees women's efforts to define their reproductive roles and experiences as crucial to their abortion activism, concluding that "for almost all of the activists, reproduction is central

---

[6] Ginsburg's (1989) sample consists of 21 pro-life women and 14 pro-choice women; she used the narratives of 7 pro-lifers and 6 pro-choicers in her analysis of women's "procreation stories." Most of the pro-lifers she interviewed worked before having children, left wage labor when they became mothers, and had young children at home during the period they were activists. Seventy-seven percent of these women were born between 1950 and 1964. A few were born in the 1920s. Ginsburg was not explicit about the demographic characteristics of her sample. However, citing Luker (1984) and Granberg (1981), she characterizes them as "primarily white, middle-class, and female" (1989:6).

to these critiques" (1989:143). Cast "as a class of life-cycle events," reproduction forced women to encounter "the inequalities of a gendered social world" (Ginsburg 1989:143–4). In response, they became concerned not only about "the place of procreation in women's lives," but with the ethics and relationships society accepted and promoted. That is, they wanted to influence the way society would structure relationships and shape lives in the future. Through their concern for gender relations and power, Ginsburg situates her informants in our nation's long history of female activism. This concern with "the reproduction of the culture as a whole" (Ginsburg 1989:144) also was evident among Luker's informants and my own, and may be present to some degree among activists in general, regardless of the issues they address.

Ginsburg insists that, in the narratives she collected, "every plot rests on some sense of tension between domesticity and the workplace" (1989:144). Like Luker, Ginsburg argues that women's responsibility "in relation to nurturance is the salient issue and contradiction for women on both sides of the debate" (1989:144). From the pro-life perspective, nurturance is "a source of female moral authority," and it is accepted as a desirable source of identity. From the pro-choice perspective, nurturance is rejected as "a cultural frame that puts women at a disadvantage socially, economically, and politically," confining them "to the culturally and materially devalued tasks of caring for dependent people" (Ginsburg 1989:145). Like Luker, Ginsburg argues that the narratives of activists on both sides of the debate centered on "these two mappings of the 'proper' place of reproduction and nurturance in the female life course," concluding that these perspectives "mark and claim the terrain of the abortion conflict" (1989:145).[7]

The narratives of the direct activists in this study did not suggest so coherent an ideological basis for their activism. While such broad, political issues characterized direct activists' opinions on abortion, they

---

[7] Without impugning Ginsburg's perceptive analysis of the issues involved in the abortion debate, I would suggest that the topics she insured interviews covered directed interviewees to expand on particular aspects of their motivations. Ginsburg ensured informants discussed the role of "gender arrangements, sexuality, and reproduction" in activism (1989:279), asking interviewees to discuss the roles of work and family, and to consider the way their position in society affected their activism. She asked them to critique contemporary life, connect that critique to their activism, and explore the impact of undesirable aspects of contemporary life on themselves. In this way, Ginsburg focused on particular aspects of her informants' motivation. (Luker did not describe her interview questions.)

only partially motivated their activism. Political issues were overshadowed in their narratives by diverse idiosyncratic motives to participate
in activism. Such motives were not described in either Ginsburg's or
Luker's analyses.

Ginsburg does not attempt to account for all abortion activism on
the basis of her study, which she describes as a "fine-grained long-term
research" project done in a small, local, social context (1989:140). She
notes that such studies can "suggest or reveal new understandings but
not necessarily prove broad generalizations" (1989:140), a caveat that
pertains to this study, as well. However, both Luker's and Ginsburg's findings have been broadly generalized by subsequent authors and extended,
at times, to characterize direct activists. The notion that demographics-
equal-psychology has given rise to particularly misguided presumptions
(Faludi 1991; Tribe 1990). I hope to provide an empirically based description of direct activists to expand this perhaps overconfidently accepted
model of pro-life motivation.

While Himmelsein's and Ginsburg's studies describe more complex
relations between activists' demographics and their abortion attitudes
than Luker found, the demographic characteristics of the St. Louis
sample, alone, suggest that the social positioning Luker linked to pro-
lifers' ideology may not apply to direct activists. Direct activists differed
from pro-lifers in general and conventional pro-life activists, as well,
and they differed in important areas. Perhaps the most notable difference is that both Luker's and Ginsburg's samples were so overwhelmingly
female that both authors based their analyses of pro-lifer's worldviews on
women's narratives alone, while 40% of the St. Louis sample was male.
Although men were a minority among direct activists, they were not
tangential to this activism. My sample included a higher percentage of
males than Granberg's (1981) sample of conventional pro-life activists
in Missouri (which, in turn, included a higher percentage of males than
the pro-choice group he used as a basis of comparison).[8] Also of particular interest was the higher rate of employment among direct activists,
as compared to Luker's (1984) conventional activists. Luker found 63%
of the pro-life activists she interviewed to be homemakers, and the

---

[8] The higher rates of female employment and income in St. Louis may also have
related to their lower rate of marriage (79% were married in Luker's sample and
68% in St. Louis). However, women in Luker's sample tended to have fewer
children on average than individuals in the St. Louis sample (two to three children,
compared to three to four children).

remainder to be almost uniformly employed in poorly paying jobs. In contrast, only 25% of female direct activists (and 15% of all direct activists) were homemakers. Perhaps as a consequence of these two factors, direct activists' income was more evenly distributed between low, middle, and high ranges than that of Luker's pro-life sample. Religious affiliation differed dramatically. Although most pro-lifers in both samples professed a religious faith, 80% of Luker's pro-lifers were Catholic, while 29% of the St. Louis sample were Catholic. (The proportion of Catholics was higher in the first group to practice direct action in St. Louis than in the groups that followed over time.)

Higher rates of male involvement, female employment, and greater religious and income diversity may relate as much to generalizable demographic distinctions between conventional and direct activists, as to differences in the timing and sociogeographic settings of these studies.[9] To explore differences between conventional and direct activists I will compare the St. Louis sample to Granberg's sample of anti-abortion activists in Missouri.[10] Table 1.1 illustrates this comparison.

Overall, direct activists' income was substantially higher and more evenly distributed among low, middle, and upper ranges, than the markedly lower and more skewed income of Missouri Citizens for Life (MCL)

[9] Activists of any type tend to differ demographically from nonactivists to some degree, activists tending to be more highly educated and more consistent in their political opinions than other citizens (Cook et al. 1992:135). Cook, Jelen, and Wilcox, analyzing data from General Social Surveys conducted between 1987 and 1991, found that geographic variables were important predictors of abortion attitudes (although education was the most important social variable) (1992:64).

Luker (1984) studied elite activists throughout California, a coastal western state; Ginsburg studied grassroots activists in the small, homogeneous northern plains town of Fargo, North Dakota, and I studied a cross-section of direct activists in a large midwestern metropolitan area. Each of us focused on a different segment of the pro-life movement. Luker focused on elite conventional activists, Ginsburg explored the world of grassroots conventional actors, and I studied grassroots direct activists, several of whom became national figures. All three studies interviewed then-current activists; Luker's and mine included former activists, as well.

[10] Granberg (1981) surveyed dues-paying members of Missouri Citizens for Life (MCL), a statewide, ostensibly secular organization, and the largest anti-abortion group in the state. MCL was affiliated with the National Right to Life Committee, the largest national-level anti-abortion organization. Granberg sent surveys (and letters authorizing his survey from the head of MCL) to 377 MCL members (81% of the organization). The 232 questionnaires he received back constituted a 62% response rate.

Table 1.1 Comparison of Members of Missouri Citizens for Life and Direct Activists in St. Louis*

Characteristics	MCL	Rescuers
Gender/Marital Status		
Women	64%	60%
Married	85	68
Separated/Divorced	1	14
Age		
Under 30	18	9
31–45	46	56
46–64	29	31
Over 65	7	4
Educations		
No High School Degree	5	
High School	23	20
Some College	27	29
College Degree	27	30
Graduate/Professional	18	21
Household Income		
$0–30,000	71	34
$30–50,000	20	34
over $50,000	9	29
Occupation		
Full-time Employment		
% of Sample	43	68
% of Women in Sample	16	50
Part-time Employment		
% of Sample		11
% of Women in Sample		17
Homemakers		
% of Sample	34	15
% of Women in Sample	57	25
Family Size		
Average # Children	3.4	3 per person
Average # Siblings	3.8	4.1
	N = 232	N = 80

*Items in Table 1.1 make generally equivalent comparisons. The 21% figure for Graduate/ Professional education among St. Louis direct activists combines people with some graduate education and people with graduate degrees. The number of children and siblings recorded for direct activists includes adopted and step-children. The 20% figure for high school education in the St. Louis sample combines people who attended all high school levels available to them and people who obtained high school degrees (almost all obtained degrees). Occupation percentages do not add up to 100 because the categories presented do not include retired and temporarily unemployed people. Percentages for income in St. Louis do not add up to 100 because the income data for two people were unscorable.

members. Direct activists evidenced a much higher rate of full-time employment (especially female employment) and included a much lower percentage of homemakers than the MCL sample. (Granberg did not provide part-time employment figures.) In addition, direct activists had somewhat higher educational attainments and represented a narrower age range than conventional activists.[11]

The high rate of employment among female direct activists bears consideration. Looking at a broad cross section of the American public, Cook, Jelen, and Wilcox found that "Women were significantly less supportive of abortion" than men, but that this "relationship is entirely due to less support among housewives" (1992:64). After analyzing many abortion attitude polls, Plutzer (1987) concluded that women and their spouses are inclined to approve of abortion if the women have ever worked outside the home, no matter how briefly. He found women's and wives' experience in the job market to be the most powerful correlate to both men's and women's abortion attitudes. These significant correspondences between homemaking and opposition to abortion corroborate Luker's (1984) findings, lending credence to her arguments. However, the very high proportion of employed female direct activists suggests that dynamics that obtain in a more general pro-life population may not pertain to direct activists. Most direct activists were exposed to the cross-cutting ties that employment forms, and they were not excluded from the wage-labor market. Sixty-five percent of direct activists, a clear majority, received annual incomes that exceeded the national median income. Direct activists' relatively high levels of income, employment, and education make explanations of their ideology and activism based on their assumed exclusion from wage-labor's rewards unsatisfying. The liberalizing effects of employment seem not to obtain among them, suggesting that direct action was motivated by factors other than those underlying conventional activism and abortion attitudes in society at large.

Furthermore, equating homemaking and freedom from constraints trivializes the ongoing and primary responsibility homemakers often feel toward their children and husbands. This equation might include an

---

[11] Such factors may have contributed to direct activists' more evenly distributed income levels. The higher percentage of female direct activists divorced or separated may relate to the much larger percentage of direct activists in the labor force, and the slightly lower average number of children per person, as compared to MCL members.

assumption that housewives are either more replaceable than employees (that is, that their absence during activism and jail time is inconsequential to those who depend on them), or that they are generally unencumbered throughout their days. This approach also sets up a false and abrupt division between women in the workforce and homemakers that does not apply well to the past three decades, during which many women have experienced wage labor and child rearing, either simultaneously or episodically. Both male and female direct activists' stories frequently illustrated the conflict between their urge to join sit-ins and their work and family responsibilities. If conventional activism interfered with pro-lifers' business and family ties, direct action did so doubly. Yet housewives in this sample were neither more nor less likely to persist in direct action than were working women. An analysis of variance found no relationship between individuals' marital status, income, or occupation and the extent to which they participated in sit-ins (Maxwell and Jelen 1994).

Caution should be used when attributing abortion attitudes to activists' demographics. Cook, Jelen, and Wilcox conclude that the "demographic and attitudinal differences between pro-choice and pro-life activists described by Luker and Granberg are mirrored in the general public" (1992:140). However, they also demonstrate that *the importance of demographic variables should not be overstated since they account for only 9% of variation in abortion attitudes* (1992:62). Echoing Himmelstein's (1986) review of survey data in the United States, Clarke's (1987) study of pro-life activists in England also challenges the thesis that abortion attitudes derive from socioeconomic status. He found that pro-life activists "did not express a desire for status advancement or display feelings of status deprivation"; he tentatively concluded that, "participation in the anti-abortion movement can be explained independently of any status considerations" (1987:250). Cook et al. (1992) concluded that the relatively weak explanatory power of demographic variables "suggests the need for additional explanations of abortion attitudes" (1992:62).

Ginsburg points out that in our society, ". . . a critical task for social actors over the life course is to constitute a social identity" (1989:220). Given the paucity of "regular forms of person-defining ascription that characterize other cultures, such as kin group or a caste" system, as well as the "American charter myth of 'starting over,'" Americans often turn to "social forms that focus on making or remaking the self in new terms" through "association with like-minded others" (1989:221). Ginsburg concludes that as abortion activists "redefine themselves through their efforts to reshape society, they are accomplishing a paradigmatically American task" (1989:221). This task was a predominate theme in direct activists' narratives.

Before turning to the individual narratives, I will present an oral history of pro-life direct activism in St. Louis and examine national trends in violence against abortion providers.

CHAPTER TWO

PRO-LIFE DIRECT ACTION
IN ST. LOUIS

"Cultures" do not hold still for their portraits.
— Clifford and Marcus 1986:10

Between early 1978 and late 1991 three distinct pro-life direct action organizations emerged in St. Louis. Fairly distinct cohorts comprised these three groups. Different religious groups predominated in each cohort, and each cohort passed through a series of developmental stages, even as the movement, as a whole, evolved. The changing legal and political circumstances activists encountered influenced their strategic choices, as did the disparate meanings successive cohorts attributed to their activism. Activists' strategies, in turn, affected their environmental circumstances. Consequently, activists simultaneously encountered and helped create a variety of social and political environments. A straightforward description of these conditions, however, would not fully explain individual decisions to join or abandon direct action. Such choices rested on subjectively defined costs individuals associated with participation in direct action, as well.

The history of this activism illustrates the interactions between personal motivations, group dynamics, and environmental contexts, and the impact such interactions have on social movements. The shifting nexus of these factors gave rise to pro-life direct action in St. Louis and shaped its life course. On the one hand, the way direct action was organized shaped the direct action movement's responses to changed environmental conditions. On the other hand, the individuals in this study attributed diverse meanings to their activism; these understandings guided individual participation and, consequently, influenced the course of the movement. This chapter tells the story of local pro-life direct action to provide the social and political contexts surrounding individual decisions to adopt or abandon direct action.

Oral histories, by dint of their origins, benefit from the advantages of insider knowledge, but suffer from the disadvantages of subjective recounting. This oral history describes the experiences and motivations of one side of the current contention over abortion and does not attempt to convey the full impact of that side on other dimensions of the larger phenomenon. The stories that could be told by activists' families, clinic personnel, clients, police, and politicians, would surely expand the tale. The objective, here, is to focus on the factors that drove activists' behavior and on the activists' perceptions.[1]

1978 TO 1983: YOUNG LIBERALS AND MIDDLE-AGED MAINSTREAMERS

Pro-life direct action did not originate in St. Louis (although in 1991 an Operation Rescue member and historian cited that city as its birthplace).[2] Both Catholics and evangelicals recognized the activist I call Kevin as the "father of pro-life direct action." Kevin, a lifelong Catholic and

---

[1] This account is a composite drawn from activists' narratives and my field notes. Activists often disagreed on the character, timing, and even sequencing of events. In order to construct a general history, I have reconciled disparate oral accounts, sometimes by speaking with additional people involved in an unclear aspect of the history, other times by comparing conflicting information with dates recorded in newspaper articles, and so forth. Consequently, many individuals' accounts would not correspond completely with this collective tale. Cross-checking narratives, double-checking facts, and striving to create an atmosphere of honesty during interviews had the added advantage of counter-balancing the subjective nature of personal accounts. To their credit, the activists did not approach their interviews with an aura of bravura or defensiveness; they were amazingly open and ready to explore and critique their own experiences.

[2] The historian was speaking to a massive audience during a rally in Wichita, Kansas during the summer of 1991. Apparently the historian was unaware of the movement's history prior to events in St. Louis. I date the movement's beginnings to the events that actually promoted sustained collective action. In January 1970, university students staged a small sit-in at Planned Parenthood offices in downtown Dallas, Texas and that June five people attempted to occupy George Washington University Hospital in the District of Colombia during an anti-abortion protest (Risen and Thomas 1998:21). These incidents did not generate further activism or alter the strategies and structure of the extant pro-life movement.

experienced antiwar and antinuclear activist, told me that he first contemplated abortion in 1972. At that time he was performing alternative
service as a conscientious objector during the Vietnam War. While serving as an orderly in St. John of God Hospital (Brighton, Massachusettes),
he was prompted to formulate an opinion on abortion after a coworker
and close personal friend spent the last hours of a night shift with him
reflecting upon her abortion. Kevin said he left that evening convinced
abortion had harmed his friend, much as taking a life would harm a
killer. He related these thoughts to his brother's death, recalling that

> The first time I heard he was killed, a really central part of my
> response was overwhelming sorrow for the person that killed him.
> There was some Vietcong soldier that fired a mortar that took
> off my brother's head. Nobody who knew my brother would kill
> my brother... At some point beyond death, they will meet, and
> he killed my brother... Death can be filled with meaning, with
> overwhelming value and preciousness. Killing is meaningless! ...
> Killing tears apart the human person. This is what happened to
> my friend in Boston. Her child was dead and she had participated
> in that. She was badly hurt!

This perception was reinforced later, as Kevin watched his own sister
grieve for years after aborting.

Kevin recalled that, while actively resisting the Vietnam War, "I be-
came convinced abortion was the same thing and I had to resist it, but
I didn't see how." He spent the following summer praying in a New
Mexico monastery and trying to articulate his thoughts on abortion.
There he explicitly linked anti-abortion activism to his antiwar resis-
tance, calling abortion "the war in Vietnam come home."

Kevin initially rejected the modern pro-life movement, then ending its first decade. He explained that he first perceived the pro-life
movement to be peopled by "angry, right-wing, uptight, conservative
Catholics" whom he "didn't want to have anything to do with." A third-
generation Harvard graduate, Kevin strongly identified with his family's
century-long history of intellectualism and Democratic defense of the
working man and the underdog. He approached abortion as a social
activist intent on making society responsible for all its members.

After establishing a support group for pregnant women, Kevin expanded on his earlier reading of Thomas Merton's passivism by exploring the work of Mahatma Gandhi and Martin Luther King, Jr. He
was "deeply influenced" by King's contention that "his most important

service was protecting whites from the hatred in their own hearts." His reading convinced Kevin that in a polarized situation an activist could help people on both sides by responding "in a loving way." He began trying to figure out how to incorporate King's "insights and his methodology" into the pro-life movement. The "sides" Kevin conceptualized in opposition were two individual entities (a woman and her child) rather than two aggregate political opponents (the pro-life and pro-choice movements). He remembered that,

> My idea about it was, in the original thought, if you go into the abortion clinic with your body, you're saying, 'Here I am; I'm with the child. My fate is linked to the fate of that child.' So you've finished that part. You've said that with your body, so your mouth is free. So you can use your mouth to counsel and to offer loving support. 'Say, look, there is an alternative and we will help you, and this isn't what you want, and for God's sake, let's get out of here.' So it seemed to me that sit-ins offered a way to help women and children at the same time. When I saw it was possible to do both at the same time, I thought, that's the thing to do.

Kevin's Catholic heritage provided a model for the activism he proposed. He noted that, "Catholics have a long history of taking their words and putting them into action politically, socially," remarking that Catholics "were deeply involved in the leadership and the rank and file" of the labor, civil rights, peace, and pro-life movements. Kevin argued that Catholic direct activists tended to be religious charismatics (as he was), and that their activism rested on a biblical analogy. He explained that,

> Peter resisted the idea that Jesus was going to have to die ... He struck out in the Garden of Gethsemane ... with violence. Later that night, when he couldn't be violent, the next thing he did was turn his back. Mary is the model for the third way between apathy and violence. She stayed with her son. Now her presence ... didn't protect him from death, but her presence there was an act of solidarity in which she suffered much and it's a model of solidarity for us. It's a way between violence and apathy ... We did what we could to link our fate with the child ... We were conscious that we tried to accept the suffering that came to us ... The results of our action are not ours; [they are] in God's hands. Most of the time we fail overwhelmingly. We do what we can; we act in solidarity with them.

In 1974, having returned to Boston from New Mexico, Kevin began talking to friends throughout the Northeast about using nonviolent direct action to oppose abortion. In this group he addressed an experienced audience of antiwar activists. Kevin left the area, and in his absence, his friends began to organize sit-ins. In August 1975 the first significant pro-life sit-in took place in Maryland near Washington, D.C.; the second followed on July 4, 1976 in Washington, D.C., and a third sit-in occurred early that fall in Cleveland. By then Kevin had returned to join his friends. Together they formed an organization that conducted 1 or 2 sit-ins in each of 25 states throughout 1977 and 1978; sit-ins occurred more frequently in the Washington, D.C. area, St. Louis, and St. Paul, Minnesota during that period.[3]

Kevin explained that the group that organized the first sit-in feared media coverage might confound the meaning of their actions if men participated. Consequently, he recalled, "the women told the men very firmly to stay out" so they would avoid the appearance of "a bunch of men forcing their morality on women." Although women organized and conducted the first sit-in, only allowing men to picket, they let men join subsequent sit-ins and men soon participated equally with women.

These first pro-life direct activists "thought you toss a match and the fire will start; it was an obvious idea." They later concluded that, "That didn't work." Persistence and skilled leadership were required to spread this activism nationwide.

THE PRO-LIFE NONVIOLENT ACTION PROJECT

In 1977, Kevin and some of the people who had organized the second sit-in formed a group called the Pro-Life Nonviolent Action Project (PLNAP) and "worked as systematically as possible on a small budget to promote sit-ins across the country."[4] They networked through existing pro-life organizations (such as the National Right to Life Committee

---

[3] Andrews with Cavanaugh-O'Keefe (1989) and Cowden-Guido (1988), two controversial sources, contradict the first date. Local activists agreed that the Andrews-Cavanaugh-O'Keefe chronology was inaccurate. When I interviewed him in 1990, Kevin confirmed that the first sit-in occurred in 1975.

[4] Kevin recalled that "that group started on the Harvard campus . . . at Elliot House," then "went from Harvard to Yale," and finally to Maryland, as one individual after another took primary responsibility for organizing and promoting the nascent movement. Kevin's sister was instrumental in sustaining the fledgling organization at Harvard and later initiated and coordinated pro-life direct action overseas.

and the National Youth Coalition) to promote their message. These organizers were college-educated liberals who drew on their peers for support. Headquarted first at Harvard University, then Yale University, and finally in Maryland, PLNAP staffed booths at national pro-life conventions. They were well-received; their representatives remained hours after official exhibits closed explaining their philosophy and tactics to keenly interested individuals.

Throughout the remainder of the 1970s they formed a core group that traveled to cities across the country to mentor local activists. These organizers coached, accompanied, and often led new groups in their first sit-ins. Kevin explained that,

> After people decided it was a good idea, then we kept pushing and prodding until people did it. Usually even after people thought it was a good idea, and decided firmly for themselves that they would risk arrest, that they would participate, still, what they're ready to do is to follow and then somebody else would go and lead it.

In this way, Kevin and his colleagues inspired and nurtured a small group of St. Louis's college-aged pro-lifers in 1978. Some of these recruits had been active in earlier antiwar, antinuclear, or prolabor protests; others were new to direct action. Over the succeeding decade, the organizational structure of pro-life direct action changed several times. Eventually, this movement engaged thousands of middle Americans across the nation in their first encounter with political activism, sometimes sensitizing them to other social justice issues, as well.

PEOPLE FROM A TO Z (PAZ)

In the late 1970s, "Allen" drew together the first pro-life direct action group in St. Louis. Allen had come to St. Louis exhausted from his participation in earlier pro-life and peace activism in the Northeast. He intended to escape political involvement by entering a Franciscan order and completing his religious studies at St. Louis University. As Allen's religious commitment developed, he concluded that rather than withdrawing from worldly concerns, his religious commitment obliged him to confront the world's problems. This conviction was encouraged by various priests he encountered at St. Louis University and in the Franciscan House of Studies, which he characterized as having a "tradition of activism."

Organizational newsletters and university newspapers linked activists and recruits. During the two years he withdrew from activism, Allen kept in touch with the nascent direct action movement in other states through the newsletter of an organization he had helped found, the National Youth Pro-Life Coalition (NYPLC). After renewing his commitment to activism, Allen wrote articles and letters to the editor of his own university newspaper questioning abortion. He then contacted people who expressed similar concerns in editorial and comment pages. Their varying philosophies and unequal degrees of commitment converged through frequent group interactions. They often gathered in the dorm room of a co-ed who affectionately dubbed them "the Catholic Ghetto," referring to their unusually intense religiosity, compared to other students in their (Jesuit) university. With the moral support of a few long-time mainstream pro-life movers-and-shakers (all life-long Catholics), these students met to plan St. Louis's first sit-in, which took place in January 1978. The second followed in March of that year. Along the way they adopted a name for public relations purposes; many interviewees remembered PAZ as more a group of people that cooperated than an organization.

This student group presented lectures and movies, and published a newsletter. All of the first activists were Catholic. Most recruits attended local universities, a few were either too young to attend college or were working rather than studying. During the first three years, they held frequent sit-in training sessions incorporating lectures on Gandhian strategic philosophy and the tactics of Martin Luther King, Jr. Their leaders placed great emphasis on communicating their philosophy to arresting officers and sought media coverage of their events to increase the educational impact of their activism. Self-realization figured high in the motivation of these activists, but was accompanied by sincere and intense disapproval of abortion.

The early activists' interviews indicated that empathy, based on an ethic of extensivity (that is, the conviction that others are like oneself) powerfully informed their participation in direct action. One such activist, whom I call "Elliot," explained that such empathy was linked to idealism and "indignation with the system" they perceived to condone "legalized, institutionalized killing . . . [as] a part of the consumer society, and the exploitation of women." Activists' empathy was aroused by their conceptualizations of women as abandoned – abandoned by the men who impregnated them or by the men who employed them without options for maternity – and duped by society into believing their best, or their only option was to abort. Empathy was also directed toward "the unborn" whose lives were forfeit due to the plight of their mothers and the "betrayal" of those who might have helped them. (Throughout this text I will present terms frequently used by activists, such as "the unborn," in quotation marks without attribution.) Allen described these activists as people who were "co-dependent on an imperfect world" and felt the need to be "always trying to fix everything." Their perceptions and inclinations were coupled with a religious faith that demanded that "if you really believe this, you have to sacrifice," as Elliot concluded. Many of the early activists' political convictions were further reinforced by a family background of conventional political involvement.

Rather than the moral imperative later activists assigned to rescue, the early liberals saw abortion opposition as one among many worthy causes to pursue. One early "radical" remembered that, "The issue was important, but I always thought there were plenty of issues around." Several early timers clearly stated that they were looking for a cause, and this one fit. One recounted,

> I was riding my bike to school and I saw Eric fasting with a couple other people on the corner of Women's Health Center. And I had been looking for something radical to get involved in and this seemed like nice people, a great cause.

But the content of their cause was meaningful, as well. The same activist explained that,

> Pro-life brought things to a white heat. If you were going to do it, now was the time to be as radical as you'd ever been because it was such a clear right and wrong issue – it brought out whatever passion you had. There was personal risk involved. I think for most of these people it was the first time they'd been arrested. It was more radical, but the cause brought the radicalism out of them.

The image early direct activists projected attracted peers who wanted to respond "radically" to abortion and were dissatisfied with existing anti-abortion activism. One early college-aged activist explained that,

> They tended to be more left-wing type of people who say, 'I hate abortion but I want to do something different. I want to make a more direct statement and I want to separate myself from more mainstream pro-life.' They very much viewed themselves that way. As breaking away from the mainstream, more left-wing, different.

There was always a perception that there was something a little tacky about mainstream pro-life. They were agreed with mainstream pro-life but they thought they could go one better, and that they definitely didn't see themselves as conservative people. They didn't despise mainstream pro-life but there was something middle class and stodgy about it and they wanted to be different in style from it. One guy went around speaking and intentionally dressed in New Age and hid his religious [Catholic] beliefs.

Disillusionment with the Democratic Party's stand on the issue, and with existing political conditions, reinforced younger activists' "radical" self-identities, increased their sense of mission and, in their minds, vindicated direct action. Many were staunch Democrats and felt betrayed by their party's tolerant position on abortion. As one man put it,

> I feel a deep and abiding sense of resentment at the left for coming out the way it has on abortion. I feel betrayed on a really deep level . . . To pro-lifers [Geraldine] Ferraro's counting the cost of abortion versus the cost of raising a child on welfare was utter treason. That person was not a Democrat. You can't talk that way. That was Barry Goldwater. That's why you find so many bitter, bitter Democrats who were baptized Catholic but conceived Democrat.

Their adherence to what they thought should be shared ideals stood in bold relief to their party's departure from those ideals. This contrast separated direct activists from their larger reference group (liberal Democrats) and left them a community-in-isolation. Isolation, and the homogeneous community-in-agreement it generated, reinforced their sense of righteousness. One activist's words were echoed by other early- and middle-timers. He asserted,

> The people that were left wing sitting-in felt that the left had sold out. Democrats are the ones that support abortion now. They thought that was madness! [whispered with strong emotion] . . . I'm pure; I'm left wing. I have kept the faith. They're wacko, they've gone off the deep end.

They saw abortion as part of "the Establishment." One activist from that period explained that,

> The issue had all the elements that would appeal to the left-wing imagination. It had big business people, which were the abortionists, were making money off deceiving innocent people and

screwing up their lives and abandoning them. We're talking about the abortion industry. They very much tied it into: this is a part of a disease, this is a part of our militarism, this is our industrialism. This is another part of the tip of the iceberg and we're fighting it. They say it's no accident that you have so many nuclear arms near so many abortion clinics. You're fighting the same thing. You sit-in at General Dynamics, it's no different than sitting-in at an abortion clinic. It's the same evil; it's a disregard for human life...Ultimately I think people thought the Barry Goldwaters were pulling a big coup; it was just a way to 'get rid of the niggers.' Ultimately everything else was a big smoke screen...It was just a great triumph on the part of men and businesses that they had deluded women into believing this was in their best interests when really it wasn't in their best interests at all. It was in the employers' interest, it was in the government's interest.

Although many later rescuers were staunch, conservative Republicans, the image of a greedy, immoral, exploitative industry displacing other options to crisis pregnancies and luring women to it alone, in order to pursue a profit motive, remained strong and widespread among pro-life direct activists. Both middle- and late-timers made statements that literally paraphrased the words of an early activist who said,

It was the idea of money being involved more than anything [that] catches the imagination of people. It's a crime that's being perpetrated on the woman and the child for the sake of the money. Creative solutions were possible but the money was too strong of an influence.

Conventional activism's failure to overturn *Roe v. Wade* called into question the effectiveness of existing forms of dissent. Sit-ins, public prayers and fasts, and direct confrontation with abortion clinic staff and clients provided "'concrete, realizable objectives which are of immediate use to the people'" (DeNardo 1985:260). Such provision is necessary to satisfy "the burning impatience for change" characteristic of both revolutionary and reformist movements, and so necessary to sustain them (DeNardo 1985:260).

The student activists were quickly joined by older, mainstream Catholics. Owing to their traditional, religious upbringing, these recruits were lifelong pro-lifers. Many of them had spent the post-Roe years attempting to recriminalize abortion through conventional activism, and some had worked against liberalization of abortion laws prior to *Roe v. Wade*. (Modern conventional pro-life activism was well-organized by the late 1960s, but not widespread; the *Roe v. Wade* decision ignited the cause in 1973. Luker [1984] provides an excellent history and analysis of this period.) In fact, their long years of relatively unsuccessful activism contributed to their enthusiasm for direct action. They had pushed and pushed, but *Roe* had not budged.

Frustrated by their inability to recriminalize abortion, mainstreamers turned to direct action both as an immediate solace for their personal, unfulfilled desire to stop abortion and as an astute political move. Some attended the direct action "training seminars" conducted by the college students during the summer of 1979. Together they sat-in once each month the following September, October, and November. By March of 1980 the group was conducting weekly sit-ins at local abortion clinics. This was the first regular, persistent pro-life direct action in the country. By January 1980 several students from a local Presbyterian seminary and a few non-Catholic individuals had heard about the sit-ins and come out to join them.

In retrospect, these early direct activists described their first sit-ins as a gentle, "civilized" period, guided by a nonviolent political philosophy, characterized by orderly (almost orchestrated) sit-ins, accompanied by singing and guitar strumming. These sit-ins were generally attended by between 100 and 200 picketers who were reported to be "inexpressibly" proud of their "fellow pro-lifers in handcuffs" (Missouri Citizens for Life Newsletter, October 1979). For the most part, the first few sit-ins enjoyed restrained and respectful interactions with the police. No arrests occurred during the first sit-in. The news media attended closely to the early sit-ins and gave them relatively thorough and friendly coverage. Pro-life organizations applauded the new tactics; they carried detailed stories of sit-ins in their newsletters, as well as notices of upcoming direct action events and stories about individual activists. Elliot remembered that even pro-choice college students praised him for doing something "real" about his beliefs, apparently valuing the early activism's novelty and romance. An aura of social acceptability mantled the sit-ins. When the first arrests did not result in convictions, the pace of direct action increased and ever more conservative pro-lifers joined the nascent direct action movement. For almost five years most of their court cases were either won or dropped, and convictions were reversed on appeal.

Toward the end of 1979, when sit-ins became larger and more frequent, they also became more disruptive. The police grew annoyed at having to carry limp adults from clinic premises. Interviewees remembered that impatience was followed by physical violence. (Activists said that police broke one priest's thumb and collar bones in a pain-compliance hold and beat several men with batons.) When police violence subsided in a matter of weeks, the activists concluded that communication between Catholic and police officials constrained the arresting officers, possibly owing to the high percentage of Catholics in local police departments and in the voting population (between 22% and 28% at that time; records in The Official Catholic Directory, 1999, and the U.S. Census Bureau, 1990, vary somewhat).

After this initial trouble was put to rest, the base of support for direct action within St. Louis's Catholic community broadened and the numerical support for direct action soared. By the spring of 1980, weekly sit-ins drew crowds of over 200 supporters and typically entailed 25 to 40 arrests. Activists agreed that St. Louis became "*the* focal point of direct action and the pro-life movement."

At this crucial point, in April of 1980, when even very conservative Catholics were talking about participating in sit-ins, a dramatic move by St. Louis's Archbishop John May disrupted the movement's momentum and dissipated support for direct action. His disapproval probably grew from his fear of lawsuits against the Catholic church, and his lack of prior involvement with abortion activism (cf. Risen and Thomas 1998). May, newly assigned to St. Louis, publicly and unequivocally denounced sit-ins and he privately and secretly forbade priests' participation in them. May pronounced sit-ins "counter-productive and ill-advised," words burned into the memories of those involved at that time and taught to their successors. His dramatic delivery had a powerful impact on many people who remained in direct action. It both shocked and galvanized them.

One activist, astounded by the archbishop's "betrayal," remembered,

I was sick that day and I was home, and Dotty called me and said, 'Turn your TV on.' And here's the archbishop and the abortion mill. And my immediate thought, 'He's rescuing! He came out there to sit-in, because he's standing in front of the doors.' And he's saying these words, and they don't fit with what I believed was happening, so I can't even understand because the words are something about we shouldn't be there. And it doesn't fit. And I'm like horrified. And I'm going, 'No! No! No!' And then I could see because I'd been out there and you get pretty attuned to seeing women that are coming in for abortions. All these pro-life people are gathered around arguing with him. Instead of being there to rescue, he's there as a distraction. And these people are distracted and I could see women going in for abortions. And it was just horrifying. It was just the image of him standing in front of Auschwitz and the Jews are being led in behind him and he's having an argument with the people that are trying to stop it. And it just was mind-boggling. I never in my life encountered anything as mind-boggling as that.

The archbishop's disapproval allowed people conflicted over their participation sufficient reason to opt out and diminished the community appeal the movement had built. May's denouncement called the whole project into question for Catholics contemplating joining the movement. Many refused to set foot on clinic property, even to picket, for fear of disobeying the archbishop. Within Catholic circles, direct action was no longer a socially acceptable, theologically correct activity – it had become rebellion against the archbishop. Some Catholic direct activists felt May's presumptuousness in speaking authoritatively to non-Catholics may have offended the small (but persistent) number of Lutherans and Presbyterians among them and weakened their fragile ecumenical coalition. Non-Catholics contemplating engaging in direct action saw a public conflict where before a growing consensus had been apparent. Through May's few statements, direct action lost its broadly appealing image of "a community in action."

The most risky area of pro-life direct action, the sit-ins themselves, drew participants directly from lower-risk areas such as picket lines and prayer groups. Very few people were initially attracted to the idea of sitting-in; most people first went to abortion clinics simply to picket and support the sitters. Even those who intended to sit-in, usually first went to picket and observe sit-ins before committing themselves to risk arrest. New sit-in recruits either increased the number of people already sitting-in or replaced people who stopped risking arrest. The archbishop's denouncement was followed by an immediate drop in the number of people accompanying sitters. Prior to May's denouncement, sit-ins regularly saw 30 to 40 people arrested; afterwards, between 25 and 30 people sat-in at a time. In sharp contrast, the number of picketers dropped, sometimes, to half the prior turnout. By reducing the number of people actively supporting the sit-ins (that is, the people who came to picket and pray), May not only cut off a major source of growth for the sit-ins, he also increased the impact of attrition on the movement.

May's pointed disavowal of civil disobedience rang hollow to direct activists who persisted. They had expected that his prior involvement in civil rights activism in the South would predispose him to support their efforts. Rather than crediting his criticism of their strategy, they labeled him a hypocrite and so dismissed his opposition as morally unfounded. They had imagined official support from church hierarchy; the demise of this illusion heightened their sense of isolation and self-reliance.

The police and courts became less tolerant of activists after the archbishop's pronouncements against sit-ins, further chilling the environment. Courts soon issued injunctions against trespass at one abortion clinic after another. The injunctions increased the likelihood of activists being convicted and severely sentenced, since breaking an injunction entailed defying a judge's direct orders. Defendants up to that point had been charged with trespass and defense attorneys built their cases on the "necessity defense" which argued for the right to break a lesser law (by trespassing) in seeking a greater good (preventing death). The increased prospect of conviction and sentencing further reduced the number of people participating in direct action.[5]

Injunctions for separate clinics were issued one at a time by different judges. St. Louis had four abortion clinics when pro-life direct action began; after injunctions had been issued against sit-ins at the two most frequently targeted clinics, Meadow Park and Women's Health Center, the activists saw two options. They could continue sitting-in at Meadow Park, their primary site, in spite of the injunction and risk the relatively certain penalties such action would bring, or they could redirect their activism toward a different clinic. After intense debate, they chose to

---

[5] Argument in the first trials centered on defining the act of sitting-in, which in turn entailed defining the fetus, the beginning of life, and so forth. These trials dealt with more negotiable issues than breaking an injunction, which is rather clear cut. Through an injunction a judge mandates that certain people will not do certain things. In this instance, judges mandated that those who had been arrested for sitting-in would not set foot on the property of specified abortion clinics, and no one else would enter such areas for the purpose of obstructing patients. After these injunctions were issued, anyone sitting-in would be guilty of breaking an injunction regardless of the moral or legal status of sit-ins or fetuses, or any decision about the point at which life begins. Risen and Thomas (1998) also note that at about this time the Missouri Court of Appeals ruled that the necessity defense could no longer be used in anti-abortion protest cases in state courts.

do the latter. Despite concerns that they would be seen as "paper tigers," they reasoned that they could do more good while out of jail, sitting-in at other clinics, than they could with the very limited number of sit-ins at Meadow Park that convictions would enforce. This choice was repeated later, when an injunction prohibited sit-ins at a third clinic, leaving only the fourth clinic unprotected by an injunction.

In the early 1980s this activism changed locus three times. The activists also switched the timing of sit-ins from weekends to weekdays and back again as abortionists adjusted their schedules, apparently in response to the pressures of activism. Each change of location or timing reduced the number of people sitting-in. Scheduling conflicts undoubtedly accounted for some reduction in participation; however, many people welcomed changes as an excuse to stop doing something that was personally costly, frightening, and difficult. As one activist put it,

> This stuff is so uncomfortable personally – it's terrifying. We're all scared, especially where people had families and children and jobs in the lurch. I think all of us wanted a way out and the bishop gave it to a lot of people.

By reducing the number of picketers, Archbishop May undercut the movement's ability to replace activists lost to changes in the location and timing of sit-ins.

Nonetheless, when injunctions had deflected activism to the third clinic, 20 or so people enthusiastically persisted. Several men remembered that their intense activism was facilitated by a police officer who handled bookings at the local station. When he heard the names of people arrested at the abortion clinic over the radio, he would pull out their old booking sheets and use them to prepare new ones while police loaded and transported the activists. Because of this rapid processing the activists sometimes sat-in 2 or even 3 times a day, prolonging their impact on the abortion clinic despite their reduced numbers, and encouraging them to persist.

When the third injunction restricted activism to the sole unprotected facility, the 12 to 15 people who persisted doubted they could hold out for long. However, they saw a green light for their activism when the judge who received their cases refused to try them. One man recalled the judge's remarkable words,

> He said, "These people aren't lawbreakers. They're lawabiding citizens. And they're out there to try and keep," I think he said "babies

from being aborted." And he said, "I'm not going to put lawabiding citizens in jail." And he just acquitted us from everything. You couldn't even call it an acquittal because there was no trial. He just up front said, "They haven't done anything wrong."

However, when that clinic reopened after closing for the Christmas holidays of 1980, it no longer performed abortions on Saturdays. The switch to weekdays severely reduced the activists' numbers. Five or six people continued to sit-in for a while. Some moved away, their numbers dwindled. Eventually only one remained.

1984 TO 1986: A MISSION RESUMED

Dylan, the one activist who persisted, sat-in alone throughout most of the early 1980s. This solitude was partially the consequence of two decisions he had made prior to the collapse of PAZ. He had decided not to publicize his sit-ins or actively persuade others to join him. These decisions followed an argument he had with Ella, a key figure in PAZ.

Ella remembered criticizing Dylan's willingness to allow "pregnant women and manic depressives" to sit-in. She had argued that he should choose tactics that would promote "good press" and persuade the public to oppose abortion. This position suited her pragmatic approach to activism intended not only to stop abortions, but to persuade the public to disapprove of abortion. Ella criticized Dylan for using aggressive tactics, such as forcibly invading clinics. She told him such tactics would not only drive away community support and make direct activists all "look like a bunch of crazies," they would also "make women run into the clinics faster to get away from **them!**"

Dylan, guided by purist ideals, defended his tactics. He argued that rescue was an act of conscience, and he could not tell anyone to violate their conscience, regardless of their health conditions. But he took away from the argument a conviction to eschew publicity. After that argument, Dylan stopped calling the press before sit-ins because, he explained, his activism was a "witness" that should compel others to join him. When PAZ's numbers dwindled, Dylan remained alone and silent.

He continued to target the one clinic not covered by an injunction. During those years he sat-in alone at least once a week for a period of seven months. Meanwhile, the rescue movement dwindled throughout the country. (At that point, the nascent movement lacked sufficient depth of leadership to counter the first wave of resistance, such as newly issued court injunctions. Kevin's greatest success had been in St. Louis; when PAZ waned, so did the movement he had worked to initiate [Risen and Thomas 1998].) Other activists agreed with Kevin's assertion that Dylan was the only anti-abortion activist sitting-in during that period. Dylan's project encountered considerable resistance from clinic personnel, observers, and the police. Being alone he was susceptible to physical abuse by arresting officers, abortion clients, their companions, and clinic personnel. Dylan recalled that, "Even the mailman kicked me," one day as he sat blocking the clinic door. Police pain-compliance holds left Dylan's wrists numb or painful for months at a time. Most of all, Dylan contended with the fear and stress that his own aversion to interpersonal confrontation created in those situations.

Why did he persist alone? Dylan had come to view direct action as, ultimately, a strictly individual endeavor. This concept arose from his personal experience of direct action, and was in accord with the perspective adopted by the group that had indoctrinated him. Dylan recalled that,

> It always boiled down to the individual, because I knew that I was the one who was going to sit in jail, and I was the one that was going to be separated from my family. Or I was the one that was going to, at the point of arrest, face whatever would happen by the police officer or whomever else was there. And I also knew that I was there out of my responsibility to the community and to the baby. So it was very personal in that respect. And I would say that when there were people there, as opposed to when I was there by myself, I don't know that my anxiety level was very much less. I think I was just as anxious and scared, and terrified in a lot of respects. So it always stayed real personal. We also got trained through the years by our lawyers to always speak in individual terms. But the bottom line was, you know, that we always rescued alone . . .
>
> I just was aware of what was going on. Part of it was that nobody else was doin' it. And I kept thinkin' that, well, if I do my part, that'll be the best witness I can be. The best witness I can be to other people to do it is for me to do it. Not to talk about it, but to do it. It was kind of like, nobody else is doing it, so I'm going to do it . . .
>
> It was a real strong belief that this is what I needed to do, that this was my responsibility. That it was real personal to me. It was like I just had always been raised that the more helpless people are, the more our responsibility to those people. And then I was

just real, real aware that they were killin' babies. That was one of the keys, focusing on that child. It was like no matter how I tried to rationalize it, everything else I could stack up against it didn't compare to a measly once a week. Didn't feel like a measly when I did it, but it didn't compare to what was going on. It was like this is the least I can do.

And I think probably habit. I had a sense of, if I ever get away from this thing, it's so scary and overwhelming – and it is – that I didn't know when I'd get back to it. And so it was just helpful to stay with it, keep a regular commitment. And I really had a belief that other people would join at some point. But it was just supposed to happen, by my example.

In turn, he applied this individualist ethic to would-be supporters, explaining that, "I just didn't ask anybody; I didn't talk to anybody. I thought, 'They know what's going on. They have the responsibility to get here.'" And so he kept on, until others did join him.

Dylan's lone activism was facilitated by the personal ethics of the judge who received his cases. This was the same judge mentioned above. Dylan recalled the judge stated during a hearing that he deemed Dylan's actions socially responsible and legally justifiable. He shelved Dylan's cases indefinitely. The judge's moral bias allowed Dylan to persist in direct action in spite of a complete lack of support in numbers. The strength of Dylan's activism was not in the extent, but rather in the positioning of his support: One judge made it possible for a lone individual to keep sit-ins going for almost two years.

During that period, in 1982, when injunctions covered three abortion clinics in St. Louis, several pro-lifers in Chicago named September 18 as a National Day of Rescue. These people were friends of the activist I call Eric. Margaret remembered reading a newspaper article in which Eric hinted that St. Louis would defy one of the injunctions to participate in this national effort. She thought it was a misquote; the St. Louis activists had agreed not to break any injunctions. But Eric soon called her, Dylan, and Joan Andrews to "go after the injunctions." They sat-in, and were arrested. Surprised that they were released from jail after this act of defiance, they sat-in week after week at the same clinic until their cases came to trial. Their multiple arrests resulted in sentences ranging from 225 to 314 days in jail (served mostly on work release). These long sentences were the first issued for anti-abortion sit-ins in St. Louis, and they shocked the activists. Almost two years passed before another group coalesced.

Pro-life direct action might have ended in St. Louis, if not the nation, in the early 1980s had a newsman not initiated contact and then written a story for a local newspaper about Dylan's lone sit-ins. The article informed local pro-lifers of Dylan's persistence and inspired several women to come out and support him. To his surprise, they arrived one afternoon to pray and picket at the clinic while he was sitting-in.

According to Dylan, their support came at a crucial time. He had fallen into a mechanical approach to his activism which overrode his emotional resistance to confronting abortion clients and his dread of the physical pain arresting officers inflicted. He had routinized each step that took him from work, along several bus routes, to the clinic, to the clinic door, because he was afraid any deviation would allow him to quit. That day Dylan remembered praying all the way to the clinic that something would prevent him from sitting-in. Perhaps one bus would run late and make him miss the next; perhaps the clinic would be closed – he was grasping at straws. He felt he could no longer face the fear and anxiety sitting-in entailed. The women's supportive presence alleviated Dylan's sense of isolation and strengthened him when he was nearly unable to continue – and they returned week after week so that he was never alone in his activism again.

Dylan eventually emerged from his ordeal the charismatic leader of a second phase of pro-life direct action in St. Louis. His supporters expanded into a small group of dedicated followers commited to direct action, some new to the movement, some returning, all inspired by his solitary "sacrifice." The liberal, college-aged intellectuals did not return to direct action, although several college-aged conservative Catholics returned and even helped found later phases of this movement, including a group calling themselves The Lambs of Christ.[6] (This group is discussed later in this chapter, toward the end of the subsection titled *Family Support Ministries*.)

THE LEAGUE

Dylan began, in 1983, by addressing small audiences. Together with several conservative Catholics who had supported PAZ, he asked listeners to commit to sitting-in if they could bring together 100 people willing to risk arrest. After their first few rallies, they realized their goal was too

---

[6] St. Louis's influence was wide, but little known. For example, "Kurt" remembered inventing tactics he taught to Joseph Scheidler, who later practiced and expounded them widely.

high and recontacted the people who had already signed on; 35 agreed to sit-in. This group soon coalesced into the Direct Action League (DAL, or the League), which held its first sit-in in September, 1984 at the only clinic not protected by an injunction. Like PAZ, this group was dominated by Catholics. DAL was incorporated that fall.

Their first sit-in became an invasion when a police officer, newly arrived on the scene, insisted clinic personnel open the door for her, and most of the 35 activists poured past her into the waiting room. Within a few weeks that clinic, too, was granted an injunction. After discussing the ramifications of further activism in this new legal environment, 15 people agreed to continue sitting-in. In short order, 13 of them received sentences ranging from 5 days to 5 months, with fines up to $500. Although the activists later overturned the judgement on appeal, most of those convicted had already served their sentences – in jail, not on work release. By sending "family people" to jail, the judge outraged a number of conservative pro-lifers, and they rallied to support direct action. Hundreds of worshipers in one evangelical congregation marched directly from their Sunday service through a drenching midwestern downpour to picket the clinic. Instead of squelching direct action, this time, the long jail sentences spurred it.

By late 1984 Dylan had formed a new core of direct activists supported by picketers, lawyers, and babysitters (who cared for fellow activists' children while the parents were participating in an event or serving time in jail). Once he accepted the idea of asking for help, Dylan began to speak regularly at national pro-life events and found he could bring large audiences to their feet, cheering the direct action he advocated.

PAZ had combined people experienced in direct action, but new to pro-life activism with people experienced in pro-life activism, but new to direct action. By contrast, most people forming DAL were new to both the pro-life movement and to direct action. Several PAZ supporters rejoined direct action through DAL. However, the link to other forms of civil disobedience (such as experience with antiwar protest) was lost when the liberals did not return. Most of them "moved on" with their lives, graduating from college, marrying and entering careers that drew them away from direct action, although not necessarily away from politics or the pro-life cause. That they left was not extraordinary; persistence was the exception in all three cohorts. (Subsequent chapters discuss the formation and dissolution of commitment in detail.)

Those who did return to sit-in – mostly conservative Catholics – shared a new attitude toward activism, one that was typical of the new recruits, as well. Many members of this second cohort made profound commitments to activism, far surpassing the involvement typical in PAZ. Their personal motivations to sit-in were not uniform, but their expectations were framed and conditioned by a shared perception of their predicament. They understood that the honeymoon was over. Not only were arrest, conviction, and jail time very real possibilities, but the likelihood of changing abortion law through their court hearings was remote.

The League forged a new kind of activism, combatively resistant to police authority and intent on literally disrupting abortion practice. During the earlier sit-ins activists remained outside clinics and blocked access by sitting or collapsing in front of clinic doors. The second cohort went beyond the sit-in format. For example, they sometimes prevented access to clinics by chaining themselves to cement blocks, furniture, or each other, gluing clinic doors shut, or obstructing clinic entrances with parked cars. They aggressively entered clinics; once inside waiting rooms they sometimes jumped through receptionists' windows, occupied procedure rooms and either damaged or contaminated surgical equipment. Rather than indirectly stopping abortions by informing observers and attempting to prick the consciences of arresting officers in a Gandhian fashion, they took control away from clinic operators and actively stopped abortions.

The increased instrumentality of direct action was reflected in new terminology; "intervention" replaced the older term "sit-in," with its Gandhian connotations of passivity. This change was thought to distinguish pro-life direct action from other "sit-ins" and to more accurately represent what the activists intended. That is, they "intervened to stop abortions from taking place," as opposed to "sitting-in to protest abortion," or, as Kevin put it, to mediate between mother and child. The term sit-in also rankled this new, more conservative cohort because of its connection with the long-haired radicalism of the 1960s. Years later, after the term "rescue" had replaced "intervention," as well, one St. Louisan explained that, "'Sit-in' didn't sound right. People think of a bunch of crazy kids, the wild things. 'Rescue' makes people think."

DAL affilitates' narratives illustrated a growing theme of religious calling and divine purpose that displaced the earlier concern with social justice and political idealism. An activist who bridged these first two phases of pro-life direct action explained,

I do think the Protestant elements that have come in more recently have added a great deal to the rescue movement in terms of the theology of it and an understanding of the Biblical nature of what is rescue . . . The methodology as how do you as a Christian confront a nation that's killing its children?

Another such activist indicated the ideological rift that separated PAZ and DAL. He complained that people in PAZ, "tended to take as a model Gandhi. They kept saying, 'Remember Gandhi!' and things like that, which used to drive me nuts. I'd say, 'Gandhi! Baloney! Remember Christ!'"

After the news article that brought him unexpected support and relief, Dylan decided he had to appeal for help if he wanted to arouse a community response to abortion. DAL built a financial base among the 6,000 people nationwide who came to read its newsletter. The newsletter was free, but it came with an appeal for support. Eventually, Dylan resigned from his counseling position and became a full-time activist, supporting his family through donations from the network of colleagues and supporters he had developed.

In 1984, Dylan and, by extension, the League came to the attention of the national pro-life community through the National Right to Life Committee (NRLC). The NRLC invited him to speak at their annual convention that year and publicized his organization in their newsletter. The NRLC was composed of officers and delegates from their 50 state affiliates, each representing smaller divisions within its state, based on county or parish lines. This structure offered the League broad exposure on many levels of organization. NRLC's attention legitimized the League, introduced Dylan to other direct action leaders (mainly active in organizing pickets in other states), and helped him become a national leader himself.

But the broad-based, national support for direct action that affiliation with the NRLC brought about was not to last. In 1982 the American Life League (ALL) formed in opposition to the NRLC. This division curtailed support for rescue. Although direct action was not the only point of contention between the two organizations, it was a factor in their division. In the mid-1980s ALL endorsed direct action and NRLC disassociated itself from it. Perhaps NRLC officials saw the increasingly aggressive tactics of direct activists as too alien to their own focus (which centered on legal action to curtail abortion practice) or too dangerous. They might also have foreseen the exposure the leaders of such media-rich activities might capture as a challenge to their own positions as spokesmen for the pro-life movement. NRLC reversed its previous policy and position, and expunged all mention of sit-ins from their mass communications, reducing the exposure direct activists received and implying censure. ALL recognized anyone who donated to their organization as a supporter and so had a large "subscription" base, but lacked NRLC's complex grassroots structure. Consequently, ALL did not replace the speaking and networking opportunities formerly available to Dylan through NRLC.

In retrospect, mainstream activism's rejection of direct action is not surprising. When the majority of the population resides somewhere between the extremes of unqualified support and complete rejection of an issue (as it does regarding abortion), it is thought to be susceptible to persuasion. In such a case, pragmatic activists resent any danger raucous tactics pose to base building. Such tactics might anger the public and sway it away from the cause. In a more completely dichotomized environment, the incentive to persuade potential supporters is absent, as is the fear of offending them (DeNardo 1985:83). That is, with one portion of the population clearly unswayable and few "undecideds" to lose, aggressive tactics pose few strategic liabilities and so are more broadly acceptable to activists of varying stripes.

In 1985, shortly after the NRLC purge, Missouri Citizens for Life (MCL), the state affiliate of NRLC and the largest conventional pro-life group in the state, formulated policies to distance itself from direct action. (MCL, although established as a secular entity, was peopled almost exclusively by Catholics, and functioned as a joint parish pro-life organization.) Beginning in 1986, MCL required its officers to pledge not to risk arrest, declined to supply picketers to accompany sit-ins, and denied DAL a booth at its annual convention. These actions were profound policy changes; many of the most ardent direct activists were also MCL officers. In fact, the woman elected president of MCL in 1986 refused to stop sitting-in or to give up the presidency; MCL removed her from office.

Many direct activists bitterly resented MCL's actions. Some MCL members insisted that they not only supported direct action in the past, but felt it was a vital and necessary component of the pro-life movement, which they wanted to see continued. For example, Ella was both the first conventional activist to join PAZ and the woman who initiated MCL's antidirect action policies and would replace the ousted MCL president the following spring. She insisted that "it was important to continue direct action as the cutting edge," but argued that it should be conducted separately from pro-life conventional activism. She depicted direct action as a parallel to Stokely Carmichael's role in the civil rights movement.

MCL members separated themselves from direct activists in reaction to direct activists' increasingly assertive and uncivil conduct. Court injunctions situated local direct action in a context that some activists considered ambiguous. When injunctions covered three clinics, the single remaining clinic was one where doctors saw both abortion and maternity patients. Some of the earliest activists not only worried about sit-ins there distressing maternity patients, they also felt uncomfortable using DAL's assertive tactics with pregnant women who intended to abort. They argued that activism under DAL not only had become distastefully raucous and politically inept, it was also practically ineffective in dissuading women from aborting.

Two incidents cemented MCL members' resolve to force direct activists to develop as a self-sufficient faction within the pro-life movement. Shortly before the 1985 decisions, MCL had planned a silent prayer vigil outside a hospital administrator's home and explicitly told local direct activists not to come unless they intended to participate in a quiet, prayerful manner. DAL supporters arrived with bullhorns and picket signs that enraged the more conservative people in MCL. Someone photographed license plates, then issued lawsuits against individuals without distinguishing between the quiet MCL members and the more contentious direct activists. MCL members' anger turned to outrage when they were "slapped with lawsuits for millions of dollars."

While the lawsuits were still only "in the air," a second incident propelled MCL away from direct action. The (nominally) secular MCL and St. Louis's Archdiocesan Pro-Life Committee (APC) planned a joint event for the day before Mother's Day. The two groups had organized a demonstration that focused on children picketing at Women's Health Center (an abortion-only clinic). Event organizers had assured all the children's parents that no one would sit-in that day. During negotiations Dylan reluctantly agreed to keep his group away from the clinic, then, just before the event, APC organizers learned he intended to stage a sit-in immediately before or after the children's picket. Ella explained, "We couldn't reason with Dylan or any of them. They broke their promise. That was the beginning of the end; that precipitated the separation." Ella vehemently objected to Dylan's and his followers' insistence that they could not violate the dictates of their consciences.

The new MCL policies forced individuals to chose between significant participation in legislative and educational activism (through MCL) and direct action (through DAL), a choice many direct activists insisted was unnecessary on philosophical grounds and politically motivated. The direct activists who supported this separation included both liberals and mainstreamers.

Outright resistance (however slight) and verbal aggression did not fit the agenda of pragmatic, legislation-minded activists, but they were justifiable, if not morally requisite, to those who went to the "abortuary" to stop a "baby from being torn limb from limb." In fact, such activists argued that political utility was a minor, negligible, or even shameful reason to participate in direct action. A common sentiment expressed by direct activists in this cohort was articulated by one woman who explained,

> It's a very little thing to do. It's a very minor thing when you think of the atrocities being committed inside [the clinics]. I think it's laughable, sometimes. How mild a response it is to say, 'Over my limp body'...It's such a nothing thing, and yet it's so much more than I see being done for the children...I don't do it just for strategy...You're holding on for dear life...I feel very close to them spiritually, especially when I'm inside the abortion mill. And I'm with children who are about to be killed and I feel very strongly that they know that somebody loved them; they know that we were there for them.

These differences over tactical strategy represented a serious cleavage between conventional and direct activists. The growing distance between these two factions within the pro-life movement was expressed in the same woman's lament that,

> The world has gone mad, just for me to have to explain this to people gives me the eerie feeling that I have to explain to them that because babies are being killed that I'm going over there sitting in front of the door to stop the mother from going in, or I'm going to plead with her and beg her not to kill her baby. That I have to explain that, why I would do that, just gives me the creeps.

The severance of ties with local conventional activists reinforced a we-they distinction that augmented direct activists' conviction that what they did required "a little more grace," that they were on a mission, fulfilling a "higher calling" through their strategy of direct intervention.

As the hope that thousands would join them waned and expired, the conviction grew that direct action demonstrated the truth to onlookers, and thereby inculpated such immediate observers for their inaction.

THE PRO-LIFE ACTION NETWORK
AND OPERATION RESCUE

Early on, acceptance by the National Right to Life Committee had drawn direct activists into an overarching organization that encompassed people pursuing diverse strategies. Later, excision from NRLC released direct activists from cross-cutting social constraints. In the mid-1980s independent direct action organizations around the nation, no longer even putatively connected to mainstream activism, formed tentative links to one another. Those in contact were a group of roughly 30 men and women, all seasoned direct activists. (The affiliation was informal and shifting, and so, difficult to enumerate.) Repeated interactions among these leaders and their groups eventually solidified into the Pro-Life Action Network (or PLAN), a loose association of rescue groups representing most regions of the nation. A history of collaborative sit-ins linked cooperating groups through friendship. But their leaders all balked at the prospect of creating a board and holding regular meetings, since activism in their own regions taxed their time heavily enough. Margaret, one of the founding officers, explained that PLAN served mainly to keep members in touch with one another. PLAN did, however, put on annual "working conventions," which inadvertantly changed the face of pro-life direct action by introducing nascent leaders to direct action and to one another.

The first annual PLAN convention assembled in Appleton, Wisconsin, in 1985; St. Louis hosted the second in 1986. Such conventions centered on training and indoctrinating new activists, and culminated in massive sit-ins that initiated novices and gave them practical experience, while providing seasoned activists the chance to sit-in with a large group of peers.[7]

---

[7] PLAN held its first annual convention in Appleton, Wisconsin in 1985 and the third in Atlanta, Georgia in 1987. Subsequent conventions, held in New York and then again in Atlanta, were co-opted by Operation Rescue. Several of PLAN's founding officers and other activists involved in its inception, described PLAN as a loose affiliation of regional leaders that mostly served to keep members in touch with one another. Their characterization contrasts with the image of guiding, dominating personalities depicted by Risen and Thomas (1998).

One of the 1986 neophytes was Randall Terry, the future founder of the first national direct action organization, Operation Rescue (OR). This particular event was the largest pro-life sit-in in the country up to that point, and purportedly Randall Terry's first. (Four interviewees remembered Terry saying at the time that this was his first sit-in, and an Operation Rescue member, designated as that group's historian, reported it as such in his 1991 address to OR followers in Wichita, Kansas. Risen and Thomas [1998] report it as Terry's first experience with direct action away from his hometown. Terry's [1988] own description of his first sit-ins differs somewhat from both versions, but confirms his first sit-in occured in 1986.) That evening, in jail, Terry announced to his fellow inmates that he was going to bring "evangelicals" into pro-life direct action. (He was referring to Protestant evangelicals, a connection uniformly made by the activists interviewed for this study. For simplicity's sake, I will employ their convention throughout this book.)

Prior to the meeting, Terry had submitted a cassette recording of a song he wrote, requesting time to sing during the convention. The activist I call Kurt, a prominent member of the St. Louis direct action community at that time, said he took pity on Terry, whom he described as a "squeaky little fellow" mouthing the same ambition to instigate mass activism they had all voiced, yet failed to achieve. Kurt told his fellow activists to "let the little guy sing his song." In spite of his personal distaste for Terry, Kurt, one of the few Protestant evangelicals in DAL, said he supported Terry's request because "he was the only other Christian there" – meaning non-Catholic. (This distinction is discussed more fully in the next section of this chapter.)

In founding Operation Rescue, Terry's subsequent leadership fulfilled one of the early activists' longtime hopes, but did not produce the anticipated benefits. Both PAZ and DAL were dominated by Catholics. After losing both the Catholic community's official and broadbased practical support, the perception grew among rescuers that their success depended on "bringing the evangelicals in" to join their cause, which Terry did with amazing success. Several activists concluded that Terry had succeeded where others had failed because he spent two years organizing his first mass sit-in (which took place in 1988).[8] They respected Terry's vision, diligence, and organizational skills, but concluded that his success could be attributed mainly to the time he spent preparing prior to

---

[8] The term "rescue" originated among the early Pennsylvania direct activists but was popularized by Terry.

acting. During those two years, Terry established the organization he eventually dubbed "Operation Rescue"; it was the first single nation-wide pro-life direct action organization. Previously, the largest sit-ins had seen slightly over 100 people arrested, but no one had planned and organized, tested the waters, and then initiated "the big one." In 1988 Terry brought hundreds and then thousands of people to Pennsylvania, New York, and finally, Atlanta – a high proportion of evangelicals among them.

Operation Rescue's newcomers institutionalized a religious zeal ab-sent in prior pro-life direct action. The early direct activists, as individ-uals, often understood their activism to be spiritually meaningful; some evidenced extreme, enveloping, and ongoing personal commitment to their cause. In contrast, OR defined activism as a religious activity, and demanded only moderate personal involvement from affiliates.[9] In this way, OR drew large numbers of people into short-term or occasional participation. OR's agenda included squelching legalized abortion, but, as one Protestant member explained, "Operation Rescue was never in-tended to be an organization; it's a movement . . . It's a prophetic vision, or a prophetic exhortation to the church to be the church."

Through its involvement with PLAN, the Direct Action League in-advertently promoted the changes Operation Rescue brought to the organizational structure and demographic composition of the direct ac-tion movement. These changes would undermine DAL, later, when a power vacuum developed.

1987 TO 1991: FISSION, EXPANSION, AND DISSIPATION

Catholics dominated both PAZ and DAL. DAL had a 60% Catholic majority, but included 13% denominational Protestants and 27%

---

[9] Many oldtimers considered the newcomers to have lost sight of the purpose of rescue and ridiculed them through anecdotes. One woman at a large OR event in New York saw people approaching policeofficers beside the clinic and lining up to be arrested without even having attempted to sit-in. Another woman told of a group of OR newcomers who returned to their home city and went out to "rescue." They alerted the police, then went to the clinic. Although they arrived before the police, they made no attempt to block the doors or dissuade women entering the clinic. Instead, they waited until the police arrived, then knelt on the road and attempted to crawl to the clinic doors past the waiting police. She commented wryly, "Now, somewhere along the line, somebody forgot to tell them that you're going there to block the door and stop the abortions."

nondenominational (Protestant) evangelicals. Regardless of the formal relationships of these proportions, many Protestants felt isolated among, and dominated by, their Catholic companions (cf. Jelen 1993). Their particularism was evident in the language they used in retrospective accounts. Protestants, and particularly evangelicals, used the term "Christian" in a specific manner. When used to distinguish among a group of direct activists, "Christian" meant non-Catholic. For example, evangelical activists would occasionally remark, "I was the only Christian there," indicating that all other activists present were Catholic. Several evangelicals remarked that through their activism they had met some Catholics who were "real Christians," even though they "didn't know it," illustrating the division between evangelicals and Catholicism. This sense of differentiation was overridden by their shared purpose until a shock (unrelated to religious affiliation) opened the latent fissure along denominational lines (cf. Cook et al. 1992:144). Before relating that incident, I will describe the social context that made it so potent.

For three years Dylan led DAL by 1) developing a support network that supplied adequate resources, 2) providing staunch moral leadership that served to legitimize direct action for otherwise conservative, law-abiding folks, and by 3) organizing frequent personal interactions – impromptu pizza parties, birthday parties, costume parties – that promoted strong emotional bonds between activists.

Direct action groups tended to be small, "resting, in Lenin's words, upon 'personal friendship or an instinctive confidence for which no reason was given'" (quoted in DeNardo 1985:22). Like PAZ, DAL was an association of loosely affiliated individuals, bound together not only by common goals, but by shared, emotionally charged experiences. The instant intimacy of jail experiences helped create an almost anonymous friendship, calling forth feelings of fraternity and acceptance. One activist voiced a common sentiment when she remembered that the relationships she formed in jail were some of the closest she had ever experienced. She added, "We were very intimate in that short period of time," and explained that the closeness arose because she "knew these were committed people, they were honest, they loved the important things of life that I loved." She felt she could "trust these people because of their values." Her husband added, "There's a bonding that takes place; it's the Holy Ghost . . . You may have only seen them once or twice – there's a bond, there's just a bond." Over and over local activists told me that they felt they could count on their fellow activists to help them in personal crises, even when they were not sure of the other activists' surnames and had little or no knowledge of their personal backgrounds or circumstances. Some activists encumbered their homes to post bonds for near-strangers from out-of-town, assuming that anyone who would sit-in could be trusted. Apparently, the shared moral commitment that their activism implied was sufficient to convey a sense of interpersonal acceptance and anticipated trustworthiness.

Dylan's moral uprightness was essential to his credibility as a leader. His conservative followers argued that the "wrongness" of abortion obliged them to stop it actively, but they also insisted that lawfulness was "right." Dylan blended his followers' respect for doing right with their objections to abortion and modeled a righteous negotiation of social conventions and moral demands. Even Dylan's detractors respectfully remembered the time police beat him in the stomach with their batons while he was on his hands and knees, calling out "God bless you" after each blow. His followers' admiration of Dylan's response reinforced his moral qualifications for leading righteous fellows. This circumstance made a betrayal of trust among their ranks all the more difficult for members to bear, and thus more divisive.

Dylan had married shortly before forming DAL and for six years he and his wife had tried unsuccessfully to have a child. DAL supporters sympathized with the couple's yearning and rejoiced when Dylan's wife conceived. However, some friends noted at the time that Dylan took almost no interest in the coming child. Dylan's wife was distressed by his complete absorption in activism; she complained that he paid little attention to her. One friend remembered that, "She confessed to me, 'I don't know what to do – he's obsessed. I don't know whether I'm standing in the way of a saint or if he's crazy.'" Several friends observed considerable tension between Dylan and his wife in the years preceding this pregnancy and faulted his wife for haranguing him about his activism while visiting him in jail.

Shortly after his child's birth, Dylan's followers learned he was having an affair with one of their fellow activists. The shock they felt would be difficult to exaggerate. Instead of modeling uprightness and reconciling the conflicting demands direct action placed on their conservative morality, Dylan had abrogated the most basic premises of their movement: the innate desire and inherent responsibility to love and care for one's mate and offspring. His successor explained, "I watched him yell to boyfriends, 'You're going to abandon your baby!' He did the same thing to his. He can't yell that anymore; he lost the mantle." Dylan's affair violated the purity that justified direct action and called into question the close, upright relationships that bound the group of activists in moral communion.

The League had previously coped with disagreement by allowing all individuals to voice their opinions, then voting democratically and abiding by the majority's will. When Dylan's moral conduct became an issue the normal practice of relying on open discussion to resolve conflicts was displaced by rumor and gossip that amplified Dylan's "sins," aggravated the emotional response of League members, and did not bring about a solution. Dylan said he tried to explain his behavior to the activists he considered his closest friends, but their antagonistic reactions shocked him. He gave up trying to reconcile himself to his friends. The sparse organizational structure their hostile political environment encouraged was inadequate to cope with the intense emotion direct activism evoked.

For seven months an interim committee led DAL. During that time contention over the direction the League should take heightened, spurred on by divergent reactions to Dylan's unfolding scandal. A few key DAL supporters persistently tried to reinstate Dylan as leader, or at least convince others to let him act as a consultant. This was anethema to others.

Divisions opened in DAL along pre-existing lines of tension. Contention over Dylan's moral status gave vent to personality clashes, opened up divisions between denominations, and allowed dissension over tactical strategy and organizational design to surface. While attitudes toward Dylan did not divide neatly along denominational lines, he received generally harsh criticism from evangelicals, and strong support from a few Catholics. Denominational cleavage did not grow so much from an attitude toward Dylan; rather, *the scandal over Dylan created an atmosphere of dissension and upset that allowed denominational factions to coalesce.*

In April of 1988 DAL held an election that replaced Dylan with Duncan, an evangelical, and a relative newcomer who aspired to leadership. But rather than reinstituting leadership, this election served to further divide the League. When Dylan's supporters refused to acknowledge Duncan as their leader, DAL's ambiguous, minimal official organization and lack of established operating procedures eased the way for this ambitious individual to first redefine the organization and, later, draw off disgruntled followers.

Dylan's scandal foregrounded two divergent concepts of "rescue" held by DAL affiliates. Were direct action groups religious people undertaking a secular project or were they religious people involved in a holy activity?

One faction argued that pro-life direct action existed apart from the private morality of its practitioners. Referring to Dylan, one woman voiced their contention that,

> It doesn't matter what he did in his personal life; he can still rescue and he can still be a leader. This is not a Christian group – a church group – so we can't hold to this kind of standards.

The other faction argued that pro-life direct action was a religious activity that obligated activists to live in accordance with "high moral" standards. One man explained that, "This has got to be a Christian group. You can't do that. It has to be centered on Christ."

Dylan's supporters claimed that Duncan was unqualified to lead them. They particularly resented his minor role in rescue up to that point and his attempts to reorganize DAL along rational organizational lines. They argued that Duncan failed to realize that DAL only survived financially through divine providence; it's leaders had to act on faith, not write budgets. Margaret, Dylan's staunchest supporter, argued that Dylan succeeded in fundraising because of his charismatic national profile and insisted that no one could supplant him just by being elected. She feared that DAL would fail without its national connections and the spiritual leadership Dylan had provided, and argued that Duncan lacked the personal charisma to maintain such support.

Duncan later euphemized this period of contention by saying he "led DAL for seven months on a committee basis" with Dylan. Duncan recalled that previously, "The director's position had been all powerful." In an attempt to "provide accountability" Duncan said he "rewrote the rules," forming an "executive committee" of seven that could override any of Duncan's decisions by a simple majority. However, Duncan remembered that,

> It just got to be that every decision I made, somebody didn't like it, and so they'd go lobby the rest of the committee to overturn it. We were just infighting so badly. There was a real dissension as to what our direction should be.

Duncan explained that the struggle to define DAL as either a religious or a secular organization was "a big point of contention among our committee . . . we couldn't reach a consensus on that and it was one of the big things" that led him to start a new group.

Ironically, the drama of Dylan's "lone ranger" activism conditioned the social relationships that facilitated this disintegration. Dylan had reinforced and extended the ties of friendship within the League, but he was the central figure that united those relationships. When he lost the aura of moral leadership that had accrued to him, the relationships that had revolved around him unraveled and the trust that people needed to feel in order to follow him to jail was dispelled. At this critical time Dylan underwent a severe depression. Feeling personally empty and unable to cope with the (unanticipated) antagonistic reactions of his friends, he left his wife, withdrew from activism, went into seclusion, and so left the group rudderless in their emotional storm.

In the fall of 1988 Duncan ate lunch with Randall Terry in an Atlanta jail. Both men had been arrested during a massive, long-term "siege" against an abortion clinic. As the two men ate, they discussed the League's problems. Duncan recalled that during that conversation Terry advised him to start a new group. Duncan also explained that several "Christian" friends in St. Louis, whom he "really respected," including one of the League's lawyers, offered the same advice. In this way Duncan explained that he broke away from DAL, not in rebellion, but in accord with others' best judgement. He argued that, "If everybody says, 'Start a new group,' I'm going to start a new group. And I did." After establishing a "consensus" to support his actions, Duncan left the League with a mainly Protestant faction and formed Family Support Ministries.[10]

FAMILY SUPPORT MINISTRIES

Duncan anticipated that his new organization, Family Support Ministries (FSM), would address interrelated social problems by providing support services to the women direct activists diverted from abortion clinics. Through "shepherding homes" activists incorporated pregnant women into their households indefinitely. FSM also provided material relief such as food, clothing, and transportation to other women. The unrealized portion of their plan included providing these women personal counseling, continuing education, job and parenting skills training, and so forth. (They conceptualized women contemplating abortion as needy and to some extent incompetent or problematic.) Through this strategy Duncan intended both to satisfy the "needs of women in crisis pregnancies" and to strengthen his organization by diversifying and, so, expanding support for it. He argued that direct action groups could "strengthen [them]selves by being well-rounded." In contrast,

---

[10] Several activists' narratives place this division in the spring of 1988.

DAL pursued a single-issue approach and drew on other existing organizations to support women considering abortion. This strategic distinction between the two groups did not extend to personal conduct. Individuals in both groups reported that they and their fellow activists helped neighbors on a one-to-one basis, or assisted their communities through other organized efforts.[11] As one DAL affiliate commented,

> I have a problem with people standing out here and saying, 'Don't kill your babies' and if they went to [a shelter] they'd see a lot of single mothers homeless there. And if we're down here and not down there doing something, too, then we're hypocrites.

As FSM began to flourish, evangelical involvement in direct action received a boost from a former PAZ supporter, Joan Andrews. Kevin called Joan Andrews's,

> ... sacrifice the principle event in the pro-life movement in the last decade for sure, and maybe since Roe versus Wade ... The key for our movement.

Andrews received national media coverage while serving two-and-a-half years in a Florida prison for having illegally entered an abortion clinic and broken the wiring of a suction aspirator. The judge who convicted Andrews in 1986, sentenced her to five years in jail; the same day, the same judge also sentenced two murder accomplices to shorter sentences than that of Andrews. Upon arrival at a minimum security prison, Andrews protested her sentence by refusing to cooperate with anything it entailed. For example, she refused to fill out required paperwork. Because of her non-cooperation, she was sent to a maximum security prison where her noncooperative behaviors (such as going limp during transportation or hanging on to her clothing during strip searches) were punished by 30-day stints in disciplinary (solitary) confinement. At the end of each 30-day period, prison officials asked Andrews if she would fill out her paperwork, she refused, and they assigned her another stint in disciplinary confinement before she left the cell.

---

[11] DAL supporters were instrumental in founding a home for pregnant homeless women; they were well-represented in the group that rehabilitated a dilapidated city building to house this project, and many of them later staffed it. People in both groups donated food and household goods on an individual basis to mothers they had dissuaded from aborting, and actively supported community assistance projects run by other organizations.

Andrews's protest was not against the length of her sentence. It was against the idea that she should be punished for "saving lives" and that by incarcerating her, the "government" would repress rescue by frightening off potential direct activists (Andrews and Cavanaugh-O'Keefe 1989: 189–90). Andrews said she hoped to "identify with the helpless babies" while confronting the "corrupt system" that punished people for trying to "save lives" and pressuring that system to "release large numbers of rescuers"; failing that, Andrews was content to "suffer lovingly for the babies" (Andrews and Cavanaugh-O'Keefe 1989:191,192,194). Above all, she aimed to act as she thought Jesus would have acted in the same circumstances (Andrews and Cavanaugh-O'Keefe 1989:191).

The perceived harshness of her treatment, her long sentencing, and the apparent contrast between her crime and that of the two murder accomplices, resonated to make her a martyr for direct action. Many of Andrews's friends and relatives sought to bring her plight to the attention of public officials, religious leaders, and various news media.

By the end of her first year in almost constant solitary confinement, Peter Lennox, who corresponded daily with Andrews, had brought her story of personal sacrifice and apparent victimization to the knowledge of well-known Christian radio personalities. Kevin, who met Andrews during the early rescues in St. Louis, marveled that,

> The story was so outrageous. This judge on the same day, he sent the pro-lifer in for 5 years, then 2 murder accomplices, they got 4 years. Same judge, same courtroom, same day. It was just a powerful story . . . Peter Lennox went to them and said, the people who did murder are already out; Joan's still in there. This is crazy; You've got to do something about this . . . In 10 years of recruiting I think I reached 2,000 people . . . When the televangelists heard the story of Joan, within a matter of months tens of millions of people were hearing the story. And they were being pushed to think about rescues. It was a quantum leap.

As Andrews completed her second year in jail, Lennox's persistent efforts to bring her story to the public bore fruit. The Christian media were actively disseminating the tale of her personal sacrifice and, among other awards, she was named "Christian of the Year" in 1988 by Pax Christi, a Catholic peace group.

This influx of publicity prepared the soil for Randall Terry's cultivation. Through Andrews's story, radio personalities and their audiences learned what rescue was and why it was done, just as Randall Terry began to campaign for his 1988 Atlanta event. Using the same, mainly Protestant, Christian media, Terry capitalized on the attention Andrews brought to abortion and to direct action. Terry called listeners to action with phenomenal success, according to both pro-life and pro-choice observers. Direct action advocates congregated infrequently to show support for Andrews. Such gatherings were rare; Terry used them rather opportunistically to promote his plans (Risen and Thomas 1998). Kevin reflected on the rise of Operation Rescue and concluded, as did other direct activists, that Andrews personally absorbed the "start-up" costs of initiating large-scale, nationally based collective action. Terry bene-fitted from the attention, distress, and commitment her imprisonment generated.

This analysis accords with political science theory regarding the gen-eration of activism. In the beginning, collective action arises in response to, or as a consequence of large sacrifices of time, effort, or personal in-vestment on the part of a few individuals.

From the Protestant evangelicals' perspective, Terry had initiated a new movement. Like Allen and Dylan, he articulated and justified a moral basis for direct action and defined and defended its tactics. Un-like either Allen or Dylan, Terry set long-term, large-scale organizational horizons for direct action and apparently possessed sufficient expertise to attain them. During the August 1985 PLAN convention, 61 peo-ple were arrested; the 1986 PLAN convention in St. Louis saw 107 people arrested at one sit-in, the most pro-life direct activists arrested anywhere up to that time. Terry's November 1987 Cherry Hill, New Jersey sit-in, strongly supported by the people he had met in PLAN, saw 210 people arrested. Then, in 1988 Terry co-opted what had begun as a joint sit-in with PLAN in New York, and counted 1,647 arrests over four days that May. A three-day July 4th sit-in in Pennsylvania resulted in 600 arrests, and 3,000 people were arrested in various cities over several weeks when Operation Rescue gained national attention in Atlanta, Georgia during the summer and fall of 1988. By January 1989 OR wielded sufficient numbers to have 900 arrested in one day in New York.

The 1988 "Atlanta Rescues" persisted long enough to draw intense, sustained national coverage that helped recruit people who had not pre-viously considered sitting-in. This sudden influx of new activists changed the movement both nationally and locally. Such changes were suggested by new terminology, adopted by all pro-life direct action groups, new and old, Catholic and evangelical. Activists abandoned the terms "sit-in" and "intervention," with their rational, instrumental, and civil-liberties connotations, and adopted the term "rescue," based on a Biblical injunction, thus heightening the emotive character of their call to fulfill a duty to come to others' aid. (This term was first used in Pennsylvania by a group of activists affiliated with PLAN.)

From the movement's beginnings very few people joined direct action upon hearing about it; most people came to participate at least in part through some association with those who were already active in it. The nationwide publicity surrounding the "Atlanta Rescue" altered this pattern of recruitment. The first step many new recruits took to become active was to call the central OR office which directed callers to Operation Rescue affiliates in their home locales.

In this way Operation Rescue not only grew after the Atlanta event, it influenced the growth of other, older direct action organizations. The Atlanta event brought a windfall of new recruits to local direct action organizations across the nation, but DAL was not able to capitalize on that event. In St. Louis the OR affiliate was not DAL, but rather Family Support Ministries.

The influx of evangelicals, directed to FSM and not to DAL, furthered the original tendency for the two groups to be characterized by different denominations and caused considerable bitterness among DAL members. Duncan framed FSM in terms familiar to evangelicals, who consequently considered FSM to be based on a more spiritually correct foundation than the League. This amplified evangelicals' preconceptions of Catholics and aided their departure from the League. Years later, this bitterness continued to reinforce the antagonisms that accompanied the group's fissioning.

The remainder of 1989 was marred for activists by rumors of police brutality and sexual abuse of female activists by jailors. Incidents involving sexual abuse were all placed in northeastern cities or in southern California; no local activists personally experienced such abuse, although several reported being beaten or physically abused by arresting officers. The year ended with Terry's conviction and incarceration. Rumors circulated that his conduct was less than heroic; he was depicted as fretful and whinning. In conjunction with his absence, these rumors helped dampen his movement throughout 1990.

In 1991 Operation Rescue rebounded under a new name, new leaders, and a new organizational structure; it was called Operation Rescue-National (OR-N). OR-N drew thousands to Wichita, Kansas that summer where 46 days of direct action resulted in 2,657 arrests of more than 1,700 people. Oldtimers from PLAN were a strong presence in all these events, although outnumbered and overshadowed by newcomers.

OR's sporadic, but high-profile events presented the image of a nationwide movement, but unity was more an impression than a reality. "Judah" (Father Weslin), leader of "the Lambs of Christ" (a group discussed later in this chapter), depicted a situation fraught by ideological disagreement and fragmentation. In a 1991 letter Judah wrote:

> In recent years, there have been many attempts to coordinate the activities of local rescue groups around the country. These efforts have failed mainly because of the wide differences in focus and philosophies between the different organizations.

OR brought a huge influx of recruits to the movement, but it did so in a way that resulted in philosophical inconsistency and created a loose organizational structure that eventually retarded the movement. As the 1980s progressed, activists held fewer training sessions than their predecessors and so failed to produce a uniform ideology in the various affiliated groups. Individual activists had considerable autonomy and latitude in their behavior during sit-ins. With three distinct groups demonstrating at abortion clinics (DAL, FSM, and the small but persistent group of independent demonstrators) activists often resented the actions of others, whom they considered to be unmannerly, obnoxious, unbiblical, and consequently, inappropriate or counterproductive. But no one had the authority to counsel or discipline "unruly" demonstrators. Consequently, individuals and, at times, whole congregations withdrew from direct action to avoid being associated with behavior they did not condone.

The history, relationships, and organization of DAL (and other PLAN members) and that of FSM (and other OR affiliates) differed. PLAN came into being to serve the needs of existing local rescue groups, whereas Terry created OR and worked to inspire a pool of recruits to feed it. Prominent individuals emerged from their own direct action groups to play leadership roles in PLAN; Terry constructed a pyramid of administrative authority headed by a close group of lieutenants, followed by regional and local directors in a top-down management fashion.

Dissension continued to color relationships between DAL and FSM; many activists believed this unresolved tension suppressed direct action in St. Louis (and limited the effect of St. Louis's activists on the national movement). Interviewees' descriptions of the division that formed FSM generally consisted of emotion-wrought attempts by each faction to negotiate reality. These accounts were characterized by territorialism and particularism (that is, the belief that only one's own group is correct), arising from interdenominational and personal antagonisms. They were contradictory enough to be reminiscent of the proverbial Five Blind Men examining an elephant and reporting incomplete, yet accurate images.[12] (The activists' divergent interpretations of reality provided a "thick" and nuanced description of events. Consequently, I found interviewing a full range of activists crucial to reconstructing a history of their movement.) Nonetheless, without dampening their antagonism, the two groups collaborated at sit-ins through early 1990.

While bolstered by an expanding evangelical presence FSM conducted large, well-organized sit-ins, often augmented by DAL. FSM "field marshalls" officiously scouted the proceedings, directing activists and "dealing with" disorderly picketers. Their headsets, beltloop transmitters, and identifying arm bands gave field marshalls an authoritative appearance. FSM often conducted "Minute Man Rescues," during which the marshalls dispatched rescuers in pairs to sit-in, rather than approaching clinic doors en masse. Pairs of sitters and pairs of sidewalk counselors were forewarned that they would be the next to leave the picket line. Then, when a woman was spotted on the parking lot, marshalls dispatched the sitters to "buy time" for the counselors to intercept and dissuade the woman. (Perhaps the military tenor of these events foreshadowed Duncan's future role as pastor to a local militia.)

Such large sit-ins usually generated a tense emotional atmosphere. Knowing friends were in imminent danger of being arrested and manhandled, seeing them handcuffed and (at times) dragged like sacks of potatoes, or lifted in a pain-inducing manner, generated much emotion regardless of the number of friends involved. But large sit-ins seemed to amplify both anticipatory and reactive emotions, apparently with good reason. Police appeared to approach large events more aggressively than small events. At times, during large events, I saw police arrest picketers who had no intention of sitting-in, who either had not actually stepped on forbidden territory or had done so inadvertently. At small events, police appeared calm, even indulgent; they often warned sitters in a quiet manner, repeatedly, before arresting them. I never saw police handle activists in a rough manner during small events. During large events

[12] In this story five blind men examined different parts of an elephant (the trunk, ear, tail, side, and leg), then proudly announced their discoveries. Their perceptions were accurate as far as they went, but being incomplete, they led to erroneous conclusions – that an elephant is like a snake, fan, rope, wall, or tree.

arrests of obvious violators sometimes entailed unnecessary roughness. For example, one time I watched as police tossed a handcuffed septuagenarian priest head over heels in a cartwheel despite his obvious frailty; a young female activist recounted being lifted painfully by her long hair. Many activists recalled the times police beat nonresistant male activists.

In addition to apprehension over possible police violence and the inevitable personal confrontation sit-ins entailed, the diversity of faiths present at joint FSM-DAL rescues created a confusing hubbub of sound and activity. Some people would pray loudly in tongues while others prayed the rosary or sang. Individuals might call loudly or offensively to arresting officers, pro-choice escorts, or women entering the clinic. Affiliates of one rescue group often dreaded the behavior of the other group and this anticipation further aggravated the atmosphere.

Despite evangelicals' energetic foray into direct action, FSM did not thrive. After several years of growth, FSM suffered a crisis of leadership. Duncan proved to be willful and his followers either lost confidence in his ethical qualifications or his ability to lead. Some people claimed he was dishonest and hurtful. Others declared he was a good and sincere person, but not competent to lead. Several people resented his unwillingness to include them in decision making; others accused him of leaving the local group leaderless in difficult times while glory seeking in other parts of the country. As one supporter put it, "I couldn't organize my way out of a paper bag! But Duncan isn't an organizer either. I'm twice the organizer he is – and I'm no good!" One woman commented that, "He just did stupid things, because he really wasn't a leader . . . It was more that he just wanted to take control."

During the summer of 1989, Duncan convinced almost all the pastors and many members of a large evangelical church to join FSM in a rescue in nearby Granite City without forewarning them that, following the preceding sit-in, the local judge had threatened to severely punish any further direct action. All of the men in the church's leadership positions (except one pastor who was out of town at the time) wound up in jail for most of a week. The next morning all those qualified to lead the Sunday services for a congregation of over 2,000 were in jail. Activists involved in that sit-in criticized Duncan for not forewarning participants and for not adequately preparing followers to choose among their legal options in the threatening situation that particular sit-in created. Supporters began to withdraw from participation in FSM, failed to respond to Duncan's calls to rescue, and began to openly criticize him as a leader. Several followers suggested solutions, but Duncan apparently would not respond to their concerns, and the group continued to dwindle. FSM had burgeoned when local evangelical churches ventured into direct action, much as PAZ had benefitted from an enthusiastic Catholic community. FSM subsided when the evangelical churches withdrew. This coincided with the general disenchantment with Duncan's leadership.

In 1990 Terry, who had been serving a sentence for his activism in Atlanta, accepted "anonymous" payment of his bond and was released from prison. He emerged a defeated man in the eyes of many local activists, who had served jail and prison sentences without complaint or the benefit of an anonymous rescue. Activists indicated that, although they understood his difficulties, Terry had not "risen to the occasion" by using his jail experience to demonstrate his strength as a leader. This image of a defeated weakling dampened the ardor of new recruits and followers alike.

Terry's faltering leadership weakened the momentum OR had lent local affiliates. Terry's disappointing performance as leader might not have undermined a dynamic local group, but FSM was already disin-tegrating. Keith Tucci and Joseph Foreman took the reins from Terry, later separating to form their own organizations.[13] At the time of Terry's withdrawal from leadership, both Tucci and Foreman were respected in St. Louis, but little known. A charismatic national leader might have strengthened FSM, but the relatively unknown replacements provided no local dynamism.

Local and national pro-life direct action went into a lull for most of 1990. Arrests at abortion clinics in the United States dropped from over 12,358 in 1989 to around 1,363 in 1990 (according to the Na-tional Abortion Federation's Oct. 14, 1993 quarterly report on clinic violence). Euthanasia, the Persian Gulf War, and other social justice issues distracted St. Louis's activists.[14] Several annual national pro-life

[13] Tucci and the group of lieutenants dubbed "Terry's Little Buddies" headed Oper-ation Rescue-National. Foreman headed The Missionaries to the Pre-Born and Rescue International. Foreman and Tucci continued to collaborate periodically; both were major figures in the leadership of "Summer of Mercy '91" in Wichita, Kansas.

[14] In 1990 the Nancy Cruzan case determined the legality of withholding food and water from patients thought to be in persistent vegetative states. One long-time activist remarked that all of the people she saw on the television news, sitting-in to protest the Cruzan case, were either active or past rescuers. In 1991 many local activists found their patriotism and desire to promote national unity to be in conflict with the horror they felt over the loss of Iraqi life during the Persian Gulf War.

events were canceled or reduced in size because of the war. No national events were sufficiently salient to pull relative newcomers like
Tucci and Foreman into the limelight and create the sense of mission
and leadership that might have saved FSM. In 1991 observers and even
sympathetic members pronounced FSM defunct.

As FSM waned, DAL persisted in small-scale weekly rescues and
awaited a return of lost supporters to rekindle its activism. A few people leaving FSM joined DAL, but most FSM supporters just stopped
sitting-in. Consequently, the division between the two groups effectively channeled the evangelical influx into FSM, then dissipated that
growth when FSM collapsed.

As DAL shrank throughout the late 1980s, those who persisted increasingly emphasized a single goal: "to save that baby" (a frequently iterated objective). Although strategic philosophy did not correlate with
persistence in activism for the sample as a whole, it appeared to play an
important role among those few who remained active during this period.
They counted the closing of three of St. Louis's four abortion clinics as
their victories. Although activists might have celebrated such closures
as a measure of success, they rarely mentioned them, appearing, rather,
to refer to them to counter a sense of failure, or to justify their former
efforts, than to incite further activism. Perhaps they sensed that business pressures may have played a larger role in the closures than did their
activism.

From the mid-1980s onward, DAL almost routinized their activism,
sustaining a small but regular presence at local abortion clinics and participating in numerous out-of-state sit-ins. In the late 1980s and early
1990s, while Operation Rescue captured headlines with massive sustained demonstrations, the other reality of pro-life direct action was
small-scale, persistent, personal participation that generally went un-
noticed by all but those whose lives it touched. As one of the nation's
earliest direct activists remarked, "We in St. Louis are known for our
faithfulness more than our numbers."

The most common local rescues occurred weekly. These tended to be
quiet, slow-paced afternoons that ended near the close of the clinic's day,
usually resulting in two to five arrests. These rescues had a personal quality; the acts that led to arrests were familiar patterns of behavior rather
than strategized or mass activities. Throughout the rescue day, people
who came intending to risk arrest individually approached women entering the clinic to dissuade them from aborting. Some days officers
immediately arrested activists, other days the police simply escorted

activists off clinic property a time or two, then told them not to return. At the end of such a day the remaining rescuers typically looked at each other and, like Margaret one evening, asked, "Well, are we going to do it"? Then they went out one or two at a time to talk to the last women approaching the clinic in front of police officers who had already clearly stated that further trespass would result in arrest. Although television cameramen occasionally recorded these very small-scale events, the footage generally did not appear on the news. Picket groups ranged from approximately 3 to 20 people.

In 1991 DAL held several large sit-ins that were clearly preplanned group activities. The activists incorporated flamboyant tactics such as invading clinic premises, padlocking themselves to furniture, or doing "lock and block" (in which two activists inside a clinic closed a "Kryptonite" bicycle lock around both their necks). That year they performed "citizens' arrests" during which they tried to indict a local abortionist for operating without a license. These events received substantial news coverage.

DAL supporters explained that they persisted in order to accomplish their highest aims: stopping imminent abortions, living up to their own moral standards, and responding to their best understanding of God's will. They also harbored an almost wistful intent to recriminalize abortion by then (1991).

DAL's sheer persistence, together with the changing public response to its cause, helped alter its political environment. Far from invoking concessions, by the early 1990s their activism, largely ignored by the press and deriving little support from sympathizers, often brought down heavy penal censure. Local direct action leaders spent months in jail. The low level of participation meant that both sit-ins and jail time lacked the uplifting and fulfilling group dynamic of earlier activism.

In 1991 court cases dating as far back as 1985 were "suddenly resurrected and redocked"; DAL's newsletter reported that, "As many as 200 cases are now being prepared for trial in the 'Mega' court system" and two of the most persistent activists "if convicted on all charges against them, could each receive a total of 20 years in prison" (DAL Newsletter, October 1991). The alarming possibility of extraordinary sentences did not materialize. Judges offered convicted activists 1 or 2 years' probation, which most accepted. St. Louis's "hard core" of about 10 direct activists initially refused to accept probation. Eventually judges gave them 1-day sentences with probation that stipulated they would not sit-in in unincorporated areas – that is, areas not incorporated into townships.

Since the only clinic in an unincorporated area had closed down earlier the year of their sentencing, activists readily agreed to that condition. Probation, and the onerous threats the megacourt had posed, brought about inactivity.

Inactivity created inertia, encouraged by individuals' dread of either confrontation, time-consuming trials, or sentencing. The satisfaction these former activists took in living "normal" lives, free from the self-instigated threat of confrontation and arrest, reinforced this inertia. Years earlier Dylan had adhered to a habitual regime to perpetuate his lone activism; similarly the habit of activism appears to have helped his successors persist. Pro-life direct action halted in St. Louis in the following years (from 1992 onward), and activists turned to picketing, public speaking, and "life chains" (long, stationary picket lines stretching for miles – ideally, from one side of a city to another.) As of this writing, direct action had not resumed, although a few local activists spoke of participating in sit-ins outside the United States.

Throughout its history, pro-life direct action teetered between the twin dangers Rosa Luxemburg warned the socialist movement must negotiate (Waters 1970:129):

> One is the loss of its mass character, the other the abandonment of its goal. One is the danger of sinking back to the condition of a sect, the other the danger of becoming a movement of bourgeois social reform

or in the pro-life case, mainstream conventional activism. In the end, this dilemma eliminated direct action in St. Louis. Most interviewees either abandoned direct action and left the political arena altogether, or turned exclusively to conventional activism. Only a few entrenched their commitment by joining the Lambs of Christ. This group, usually referred to as "The Lambs," played a provocative role in the direct action movement.

Those few who left St. Louis to become "Lambs" joined a small, emerging national-level organization that brought pro-life direct action closer to its logical extreme. The movement had been plagued from the late 1970s onward by a persistent flaw in the fit between their ideology and their practice. Periodically, activists became stymied over contradictions they perceived between what they thought they were doing, what that understanding implied they should be doing, and how they actually went about their activism. This conflict arose from the following line of reasoning, voiced by activists in all three cohorts: If activists were sitting-in because they believed that real people were going to be killed in a hideous manner if somebody did not stop abortions, then why were they not acting with a greater sense of urgency and more proactively? Why were they only sitting in front of the doors, and why were they only doing that a few days a month, at best? In the late 1980s, some activists responded to this perception of discrepancy between belief and practice by forming the Lambs of Christ, which was the direct action component within a Catholic organization called Victim Souls of the Unborn Christ Child. "Missionaries to the Pre-Born" arose later as a Protestant alternative to the Lambs.

The Lambs drew together people who dedicated themselves to full-time activism. Recruits sold their property or assigned it to relatives, gave away or stored belongings, left jobs and family, divested themselves of worldly obligations and committed themselves to go wherever the "need seemed greatest" and remain there until "called elsewhere." As occurred early on with the change in terminology from "sit-in" to "intervention," and then from "intervention" to "rescue," the Lambs' combative, resolute attitude was reflected once again in new terminology. In his 1997 newsletters, Father Weslin, perhaps the Lamb's foremost leader, referred to sit-ins not as "rescues," but as "sieges."

Along with this complete personal immersion in activism, the Lambs were distinctive in that they regularly initiated continuous, long-term sieges and sustained a mass approach to noncooperation with legal authorities.[15] A further credo of the Lambs was that they would not leave one of their fellows behind, "stuffed in the cracks" (that is, left to fend for themselves in jail or court).

The Lambs' tactical strategy overcame weaknesses that undermined previous pro-life direct action groups. Long jail sentences dissuaded most of the early activists, whose strategic philosophy centered on their actions at abortion clinics and in courtrooms and was only weakly developed regarding subsequent penalties. The Lambs' strategy encompassed their conduct in jail. Their postarrest tactics created a sense of victory among imprisoned activists and eroded the penal systems' capacity to punish them. Although they practiced much more aggressive activism than other pro-life direct activists and incurred long jail sentences, they effectively retained supporters.

---

[15] The Lambs' noncooperation consisted mainly of refusing to give their real names to authorities (each Lamb had a code name), refusing to move voluntarily (except to satisfy their own bodily needs or to worship), and refusing to pay money into "the evil system that kills Jesus' babies."

The Lambs' intensified the confrontational attitude that the activists of the mid-1980s brought to rescue. Earlier activists hoped to persuade their opponents to play by an alternative, but established, set of rules; loosely speaking, the Lambs made their own rules and defied those who opposed them. People in PAZ, DAL, and the Lambs alike, believed their actions were justified because they conformed to God's law. Religious belief was central to the Lambs' philosophy and intimately connected to their strategy. Their activism was, in their own understanding, composed of unambiguous acts of worship. In this way, the Lambs followed the trend toward sanctifying rescue while divorcing it from its Gandhian heritage.

Trends in Violent and Nonviolent Activism

The widespread character of pro-life direct action prior to the advent of Operation Rescue is evident in the National Abortion Federation's (NAF) statistics on clinic violence. NAF found that 92% of abortion clinics had reported harassment by the end of 1985 (Forrest and Henshaw 1987).[16] However, a sharp increase in arrests followed Operation Rescue's national debut in 1988.[17] NAF (2001) reports that, while only 290 arrests were made for blockading clinics in 1987, 11,732 blockading arrests occurred in 1988, 12,358 in 1989, 1,363 in 1990, 3,885 in 1991, 2,580 in 1992, and 1,236 in 1993.[18] Ginsburg (1993) notes that prior to October 1988 arrests had taken place in 32 cities, 19 states, and Canada. She then points out that 6 months later sit-ins had been held in 64 cities, "bringing the total number of arrests to 20,000 in less than a year" (1993:567). Ginsburg (1993) estimates that by fall of 1991 between forty and fifty thousand individuals had participated in Operation Rescue sit-ins.[19] (Discrepancies in the number of sit-in participants

---

[16] This assessment includes acts ranging from pickets to bombings and kidnapping.
[17] The scope of Operation Rescue events is ambiguous. For example, activism in Wichita during the summer of 1991 included many non-OR activists, and was, to some extent, the product of years of effort by a local non-OR hardcore.
[18] *The Wichita Eagle* (December 29, 1991) reports that more than two-thirds of the 1991 figure was attributable to arrests made in Wichita, Kansas that summer.
[19] Ginsburg's estimate is based on pro- and anti-abortion newsletters and newspaper articles (1993). The NAF figures total 33,242 arrests for blockading between 1987 and 1993. Neither source includes arrests prior to 1987. The NAF data represents incidents that affiliated providers reported to them, but not all providers are associated with NAF. Consequently, these numbers represent a minimum record of activity.

and the number of arrests may be due to inclusion of picketers support-ing sit-in events, or the sources researchers used.) Although the number of sit-ins began to decline in the early 1990s, the level of participation in sit-ins remained immensely higher than the pre-1988 levels through 1993. At that point the movement's collapse did not seem imminent.

In the early 1990s many direct activists argued that their movement was just beginning and would likely last for decades. They fit their agenda into a progressive framework, arguing that it extended rights to a previ-ously unprotected group. These activists insisted that time would bring the "destined" victory. In 1991 Kevin likened pro-life direct action to the antislavery movement which he described as beginning in the 1600s and culminating in the Civil War, 200 years later. Through this analogy he argued that pro-life direct action was in its very beginning stages and growing at a phenomenal rate. He reasoned that,

> If in 1986 it's one person [Joan Andrews] and in 1990 it's 200 people [the Lambs], that's 4 years to grow by a factor of 200. That's not so bad! [laughs] Just give it some time . . . I don't know if it will take 20 years or 200.

Jerome, a prominent activist in St. Louis, also saw anti-abortion ac-tivism from a long-term perspective. He, too, considered direct action a necessary forerunner of political and social change. Jerome explained,

> I have a sense that the law follows, and historically has followed, activism more than theory. I think this was true in the anti-slavery, and I think it was true in the Civil Rights issues of the 50s and 60s. By activism . . . I mean putting one's money where one's mouth is as far as ethics is concerned. Activism has always preceded and been a necessary precedent to change in the law. That's why I think that this is a cutting edge. I frankly do not foresee a change in the law regarding abortion in the United States in the *Roe versus Wade* just from the theoretical or legal or legislative standpoint. I think it will come about, at least accompanied by, and probably because of activism.

Like many other direct activists, Jerome compared his activism to that of abolitionists, and argued that only material intervention would bring about ideological change. Sharp variations in the intensity of their sit-ins only increased the parallel between pro-life activism and abolition. Jerome continued, saying,

I'm convinced that the parallels between this and slavery and the way that the underground railroad – which was the civil disobedience of the Northerners that were Abolitionists – the way that played such a significant part in the shaping of ideas and the conflict really that lead to the Civil War and ultimately the freedom of slaves. I do think that there is a historical precedent for saying that that will happen again. I don't know if there is adequate force at the present time . . . But, again, historically, if you look at opposition to slavery, it waxed and waned. Opposition to slavery prior to the Civil War lasted for about 60 years. If you read what the Abolitionists wrote in the 1820s, 1830s . . . It looked like it was insolvable. It took a long time. And I think that we tend not to look at history enough to see how ethical and moral battles like this have had to be waged in the past, and how much time they took, and how difficult those battles were.

This long-range perspective was voiced by many individuals in the sample. They anticipated their successful beginning would have consequences far into the future, despite temporary setbacks.

Stewart, Smith, and Denton (1989) argue against the likelihood of such outcomes. The rhetoric, environment, opportunities, and activities that rouse support do not sustain it. Enthusiasm soon fades. The rapid decrease in arrests for nonviolent direct activism suggests that broad-based enthusiasm for rescue did fade in the early 1990s. This change in attitude appears to have been reinforced in May 1994 when President Clinton signed the Freedom of Access to Clinic Entrances Act. Stewart and his colleagues (1989) argue that in the life course of a social movement, the transformation from an enthusiastic mobilization to the maintenance stage is crucial. During this shift, movements either drift toward oblivion (Rosa Luxemburg might have said "sect") or return to moderate tactics aimed at gradual change through existing institutions (as bourgeois social reform movements). In other words, to become sustainable, a mainstream pragmatic strategy must displace purist pursuits. Those direct activists who stopped sitting-in and redirected their energy into picketing or other conventional activities appeared to have made such a transition. Alternatively, with time, the Lambs' more consuming, aggressive, controlling tactics might form the core of a new "enthusiastic mobilization" (cf. Stewart et al. 1989), sustaining direct action of one sort or another, as most direct activists predicted.

Developments during the 1990s suggest that the middle ground pro-vided by sit-ins (which allowed assertive personal action, tempered by a commitment to nonviolence) diminished, and the opposing extremes persisted. That is, sit-ins drastically diminished while picketing flour-ished, acts of extreme violence arose, and terrorist tactics increased. The National Abortion Federation's 1997 analysis of trends in anti-abortion violence found that broad-based conventional activism reached record levels – 54% of clinics in the United States and Canada were picketed at least once a week, if not daily – while blockading only returned to its relatively low 1994 levels (25 blockades resulting in 29 arrests in 1997). In January, 2001 NAF reported only two, three, and four blockades per year between 1998 and 2000, resulting in 16, 5, and 0 arrests, respec-tively; picketing reached extraordinary levels at the turn of the century with between 7,500 and almost 8,800 pickets recorded annually between 1997 and 2000. The 1997 NAF report concluded that "violence and dis-ruption against abortion providers in most categories" were increasing; "sophistication of arsons and bombings" had also increased such that "violence and the threat of violence remains a constant source of anxi-ety for abortion providers" (1, 3). (The escalating violent and disruptive acts they referred to included arsons, bombings, vandalism, stalking, hate mail, harassing calls, and bomb threats.) This combination has had a powerful interactive effect on the provision of abortion services (see discussion that follows). How did this shift to extremes come about?

When rescue flourished, a momentum was established that fed on itself. The stigma attached to a "politically incorrect" position receded during large rescue events. During little sit-ins, with few participants, individuals said they tended to "feel very small and humble" and had a "sense of helplessness, of personal sacrifice against overwhelming odds, of a whole society that's gone berserk." They spoke of "feeling like you are fighting the world." Large ongoing sit-ins created vital social contexts characterized by an intense sense of community, entailing excitement, camaraderie, elation, satisfaction, and relief. During large sit-ins, one man recalled that "the psychology of the thing did shift a little bit." He described the atmosphere I observed during large events when he said:

There was a little bit more of the sense that, 'Hey, we're not any kind of weirdos, in fact, you're the weirdos, you're the ones killing children. When are you going to wake up to what's going on?'

Such social factors provided a powerful incentive to join, multiplying the size of events once organizers established a core of participants.

Peers' praise and respect encouraged individuals to entrench their involvement in direct action. Ella recalled that:

In the beginning people were constantly telling us everything was favorable, even the media. They thought it echoed the anti-war. People were complimented all the time, 'Oh, you're saints, you're going to go straight to heaven.'

Activists spoke of the relief, often giddiness or elation they felt after sitting-in, as well as the sense of community, power, and accomplishment they experienced among other activists. Corrine commented that,

It was a really good feeling to be there. I can see how people could get hooked on rescuing – singing the songs and being there together. It really makes you feel good to be sitting there knowing that no one is going to go in while you are there.

Ella remembered,

The excitement of having a policeman walk up and slap handcuffs on you. Oh, look at the martyr to the cause. That kind of thing can go to your head. You have to watch it.

Sometimes the conclusion that they were "actually saving lives" dominated activists' perspectives, so that the moral demand to sit-in outweighed activism's costs entirely. Some interviewees remembered becoming absorbed in their activism, haunted by their inability to stop "babies" from being killed, angry with friends who would not join them, dreaming of their encounters with angry, mocking women at abortion clinics, constantly reliving the experiences that had become the center of their lives. At least temporarily, these individuals valued their participation so highly as to trivialize its costs. Duncan cautioned,

Don't think getting together once a month and then going out and rescuing the next morning is enough. There are children being killed every day. Don't think, 'I've rescued 3 or 4 times, isn't that enough?' I've rescued 70 times, is that enough? There are children being killed tomorrow. Can I quit?

This perspective, so heavily weighting the value of direct action, oblivious to its costs, drew some activists into continual, intense participation. Ella argued that,

This kind of activity is so intense, I think people become addicted to it, obsessed to the point a lot of people fall out of it. The cause is so great they let other things, even their families, go by the wayside. I've seen that happen. It happened to me. It was like I had to have my fix, be out there every Saturday. Pride is behind it and a messiah complex, I think. I've seen people go from clear thinking to cloudy thinking. Pride and self-righteousness are the biggest things we have to deal with in this movement. I've been both ways. I used to not understand how people couldn't do this!

Pro-life rhetoric offered reinforcement for such obsession. Aside from the continual portrayal of abortion as demanding action and personal sacrifice, some speakers overtly called for extreme dedication. For example, during one local rally, a speaker who apparently thought he had identified a relatively unencumbered, untapped source of support, asked, "When are the childless unmarrieds going to spend their year in jail"? Such calls-to-action evoked responses not only among the "childless unmarrieds"; one family in St. Louis arranged its affairs in order to "pack up and go on the road full-time." Ella knew of "a bunch of almost nomad bums that travel around; whole families living hand to mouth!" She suggested the important role affective commitment to direct action played in obsessive behavior, musing,

> I don't know if you can control people in this kind of situation. It's so emotional. It's the height of electric. It can be very damaging to individuals. This whole thing worries me; it's like David Koresh. It gets awfully close to cult.

She pointed out the chicken and egg conundrum posed by such obsession, concluding, "I don't know if the activism creates the problems or if people with problems are attracted to the movement."

Festinger and colleagues' study of failed prophecy (Festinger, Riecken, and Schachter 1956) suggests an explanation of the dynamics entailed in the drift toward cult status. They found that people who cling to a crumbling ideology intensify their commitment all the more when reality contradicts their beliefs. The isolation of such a hard core is increased as the majority of people relinquish the failed ideology and realign their beliefs with mainstream perceptions. This dynamic may help account for the intensification of some activists' commitment as direct action waned.

From this perspective, PAZ created igniting events in an accommodating environment that brought the whole movement into being. Their activism entailed self-affirming social interactions and was broadly perceived to have a realistic potential for success. As the environment became increasingly hostile, activism was reduced to a core of true believers – the Direct Action League. The outpouring of evangelical support through Operation Rescue and its affiliates, such as Family Support Ministries, reflected widespread frustration with conventional attempts at institutional change and expanded the movement's base of support. The evangelical influx represented what Stewart et al. call an "enthusiastic mobilization," full of optimism, and convinced that theirs was the only way to affect needed change.

In this scenario, Catholics recognized an urgent problem and called attention to it. Early activists such as Joan Andrews and Dylan paid the start-up costs necessary to draw in followers. Evangelicals were the audience Catholics addressed through their activism. Their response was hearty, but brief. Evangelicals' sporadic activism, tied as much to the concept of activism-as-religious-enactment and a struggle for social control as to "saving lives" by stopping abortion per se, was quickly redirected. But the Lambs, and those few DAL members who persisted in the early 1990s, were a hard core who chose to deepen their commitment and entrench their involvement rather than face the failure of their movement and abandon the worldview from which it derived.

Most activists did not foresee the violent turn taken March 10, 1993 when Michael Griffin shot and killed Dr. David Gunn, an abortion provider, in front of a clinic in Pensacola, Florida. Just as the prospects of legislative and judicial support for access to abortion increased (Segers and Byrnes 1995), so did the use of violence and personal harassment. Political marginalization coupled with the social isolation most violent activists experienced may have amplified the effect Festinger et al. (1956) observed.

Blanchard and Prewitt (1993) demonstrated that anti-abortion activists who turn to violence are uniformly socially isolated. Griffin is a good example. I spoke with people who knew him from childhood, and they noted that prior to shooting Dr. Gunn, Griffin had become increasingly withdrawn, even from his wife and children, and absorbed in the vehement anti-abortion discourse of his pastor, John Burt. Following Griffin's act, most conventional activists boycotted direct action events, and the majority of direct activists denounced violence, further isolating a small contingent contemplating lethal force (Maxwell 1995).

While individual, lone-wolf acts of violence may not have been part of the movement's strategy, violence altered the political environment direct activists attempted to control, and so, influenced their strategic choices.

Prior to the mid-1990s, levels of nonviolent and violent acts committed by pro-lifers varied inversely. The 2001 NAF report shows a tremendous increase in blockades during 1988 and 1989, just when clinics experienced a dramatic drop in more violent assaults.[20] As the rate of violent acts increased by 50%, 300%, and 500% in the early 1990s, arrests for blockading dropped to one fourth, then one sixth, and finally one twelfth their 1988–9 level.[21] During the same period the NAF reported sharp increases in hate mail, harassing calls, and pickets.[22]

The trend in this activism was away from sit-ins – a sort of middle road between violence and civility – and toward more violent and intrusive opposition – including stalking, vandalism, and murder (as well as increased picketing).[23] Such violent actions constituted more personalized threats and more assertive attempts to control specific individuals than had sit-ins. Attempting murder may have been a "logical" extension of this emphasis on targeting and controlling individual abortion providers. In general, the trend toward violent acts suggests a shift on the part of a minority away from relatively passive attempts to "save babies" toward more aggressive attempts to control others' behavior, tragically

---

[20] According to NAF (2001), violent acts averaged 138 incidents a year between 1984 and 1986, then dropped to an average of 67 incidents per year between 1987 and 1990; they only increased to 95 incidents in 1991. But in 1992 they jumped to 194, and then to 437 in 1993.

[21] Arrests for blockading reached highs of around 12,000 in 1988 and 1989, then fell first to around 3,000, then 2,000, and finally 1,000; arrests dropped to 217 in 1994, and remained well below 75 annually between 1995 and 2000 (NAF 2001).

[22] Harassing mail and phone calls averaged 24 per year from 1977 through 1990, then jumped to 142 in 1991, 469 in 1992, and 628 in 1993. Pickets averaged 99 per year between 1977 and 1990, then increased to 292 in 1991, 2,898 in 1992, and 2,279 in 1993. Computerized reporting begun in mid-1991 may have contributed to the apparent rise of some types of incidents. However, not all activities were reported to have increased from 1991 onward.

[23] That people who consider themselves to be pro-life should engage in violence implies no special contradiction. Rose (1969:39) cites numerous scholars who conclude that humanity, love, serenity, blessedness, and reason "have always provided justification for violence." The prevalence of violence in political action is rather well masked by the myth that change in American society is accomplished by peaceful, orderly, political means. Hook argues "that violence has been 'an invariable concomitant of all mass movements of social reform'" (quoted in Rose 1969:43).

culminating in the ultimate measure of stopping providers by killing them. Tellingly, prior to conviction in court, Griffin argued that he was justified in killing Gunn because Gunn was on his way into a clinic to kill "children."

Aggression and militancy were not foreign to Operation Rescue's leadership, despite their protests in public to the contrary. Input from early pro-life direct activists tempered the original exuberance Operation Rescue's founder Randall Terry expressed, and directed his activism along established nonviolent lines. One DAL leader recalled that,

> Randy was a little wild when he first came up with the idea [to organize massive sit-ins]. When we were down in Florida at the end of '86 and everybody kind of got up and [he] started talking about, 'Well, we're going to take over the building and we'll hold hostages and we'll throw machines out the window. And everybody's standing there with their mouth open looking at each other and saying, 'What's going on here?' Then they all kind of sat down and talked to Randy for a while and got things back on a level keel.

(Risen and Thomas [1998] tell the story differently, but make the same point.)

Years before, in the late 1970s, a few activists had concluded that the most logical response to abortion was to kill abortionists, but they had no intention of acting on that conclusion. Their law-abiding, middle-class, cultural heritage and philosophical commitments to peace and justice precluded murder. They also held frequent meetings to cope with the anger and frustration they felt after sitting-in. These meetings reaffirmed the ascendent value of nonviolence.

The demographic changes that occurred in the direct action population during the 1980s altered the logic driving their small but persistent movement and eroded the ideological commitment to nonviolence and the training that had instilled it. Expansion produced a loosely organized nationwide movement that provided followers little contact with leaders and peers. Newcomers were swept into a sense of belonging and commitment but lacked the interpersonal interactions early activists found so necessary to cope with the emotional impact of direct activism. Eventually, the Gandhian ethic was abandoned so completely that a major rescuers' magazine carried an article that argued, "The Biblical evidence used to support nonviolent civil disobedience also logically supports violent civil disobedience" (Hill 1993).

Later activists retained the rhetoric of nonviolence, but it was a "survival" – that is, a characteristic that remains although the cultural context from which it originally arose has been replaced by another that would not necessarily have given rise to it. Nonviolence, then, was a tactic initiated by their predecessors but sustained without a coherent, logical basis in their own worldview. While later activists' ideology promoted community and responsibility, it did not eschew violence. Many of these activists qualified the injunction "Thou shalt not kill" with a "right" and "duty" to use violence when necessary to defend their own families and their "neighbors" from imminent harm. Pro-life rhetoric linked this ethic to activism by emphasizing listeners' kinship with the unborn, and their duty to defend helpless "brothers and sisters."

Throughout the 1980s many direct activists had openly criticized pro-lifers for not joining their sit-ins and a few had privately criticized moderates within their movement for not supporting violent acts (such as bombing and arson). In 1991, occasionally, direct activists in St. Louis and elsewhere asked whether one killing was justified to prevent another, but found this quandary irresolvable and simply "tabled it." After Gunn's murder in 1993, most activists were stymied when confronted by arguments such as, "He [Dr. Gunn] was going in there to kill 12 people – that justified killing him to prevent his crime" (personal communications, April 1991 and April 1993). When 10 years of sit-ins had failed to recriminalize abortion, a call for violence surfaced. Speakers at one prominent direct action convention blamed the pro-life movement for censorious attitudes toward bombing and arson that dissuaded those who "might have taken out an abortion clinic" (Ohlhausen and Ramey 1993). An increasingly isolated minority promoted this reasoning. This was a like-minded group, addressing itself, decreasingly challenged in their own forum as dissenters abandoned them (Maxwell 1995).

The blatant advocacy of violence following Gunn's death apparent in *Life Advocate*, the most prominent direct action publication at that time, was a qualitative change in direct activists' public voice. In 1993, Paul Hill published an article in that magazine titled "Who Killed the Innocent – Michael Griffin or Dr. David Gunn?" That was almost a year before Hill murdered Dr. Britton and his volunteer bodyguard as they prepared to enter an abortion clinic in Pensacola, Florida (on July 29, 1994). (Dr. Gunn was murdered at this clinic in 1993.) After citing many incidents in which Biblical characters did "*whatever was necessary* to protect innocent life," Hill argued that the zealous and deadly act of an individual can "turn God's wrath away from the people" and that a person who kills guilty individuals will spare the people as a whole from "destruction" (emphasis in the original, 1993:41). Hill went on to praise civil disobedients (who sit-in), then suggested that they "should also consider the justice of taking all action necessary to protect innocent life" (Hill 1993:42). He brought his point home by explicitly enjoining readers to "take all just actions necessary (including deadly force) to protect the lives of the unborn." Griffin's action opened discussion of such measures; *Life Advocate* began a series of articles on the morality of deadly force immediately following Gunn's death.

In the atmosphere of alarm and apprehension that followed Gunn's murder, Operation Rescue initiated "rescue seminars" that resembled guerrilla training camps focused on teaching activists to stalk, harass, and hamper abortion providers and their clients. Such tactics received wide media coverage in the wake of Gunn's death. Later that same year, on August 19, 1993, Rachelle "Shelley" Shannon attempted to kill Dr. George Tiller, a prominent abortion provider, outside his clinic in Wichita, Kansas.[24] In all, 7 abortion providers were murdered during the 1990s, and 17 more were shot but not killed.

This escalation of violence followed the trend away from sit-ins and toward acts that personally threatened abortion providers. Rather than being aberrant acts, these threatening actions fit into a pattern of escalating, targeted violence. But did they represent the culmination of a long-standing flirtation with the notion that one should "take out an abortionist," or did they set a new precedent to be followed in the future? Whether the pattern of periodic murders continues or not, these extreme acts have played a powerful role in the contention over abortion.

---

[24] Shannon's unlikely trek from Oregon to Kansas to attack Tiller might have stemmed from Tiller's prominent reputation among direct activists as "Tiller the Killer" – said, by them, to be the only late-term abortion provider in the midwest. Shannon admitted shooting Dr. George Tiller in Wichita, Kansas on August 19, 1993. Her role in the direct action movement differed from Griffin's and posed an ominous precedent. She had a history of activism with both Operation Rescue and Advocates for Life Ministries, one of its predecessors (Burnett 1993). Shannon acted in concert; Griffin and subsequent pro-life murderers acted alone. Furthermore, Shannon was a member of the direct action movement, and not a outsider like Griffin, literally all convicted clinic arsonists and bombers, and John Salvi, who later murdered two abortion clinic workers in Brookline, Massachusetts (on December 30, 1994). Militancy has tended to increase among pro-lifers faced with a discouraging political situation and this dynamic may have influenced Shannon's experience in Oregon, famed among direct activists for harsh treatment of pro-lifers who sit-in and punishing sentences for those arrested.

One effect of the killings, the evangelizing call-to-arms, and other aggressive tactics that arose in the early 1990s was to reduce the availability of abortion by discouraging physicians, hospitals, and mixed-service clinics from performing them (Berger 1998; Davis 1998; Goldstein 1995; Heilig and Wilson 1999; MSFC 1999; Rosenthal 1995; Thomas 1996). Jeff Builta, Director of Analytic Studies at the Office of International Criminal Justice, concluded that, "though the number of violent extremists is small, their impact has been disproportionately large" (NAF 1997:2). Although the drop seen in abortion rates in the United States during the 1980s and 1990s may be partially attributed to increased use of contraceptives, increased acceptance of unwed parenting, a decline in the number of women in the peak child-bearing years (that is, under age 25), or changes in the way data on abortion rates are gathered, the number of hospitals, clinics, and doctor's offices providing abortions fell more rapidly, nationally than these other factors would account for (AGI 1997, 1998; Goldstein 1995; Henshaw 1998).

In 1973, when *Roe v. Wade* legalized abortion, services were provided by a grateful cohort of doctors. This cohort had been sensitized to the need for safe, legal abortions by having witnessed the often extreme agony botched or inexpert abortions wrought on their patients (Heilig and Wilson 1999). That cohort is now retiring, and they are not being replaced by an adequate number of new doctors. Not infrequently, abortion clinics in several states depend on a single provider who travels a circuit; Gunn's death eliminated one such provider. In the ensuing years, newspaper articles carried stories citing physicians in Florida, Virginia, New York, Kansas, the District of Columbia, and elsewhere who decided to stop providing services out of concern for their safety. Some had received personal threats, others resigned in reaction to violence against their colleagues. This pattern continued throughout the 1990s (Heilig and Wilson 1999; Henshaw 1998; Sanchez 1999). The National Abortion Federation report, "Anti-Abortion Violence and Harassment, 1997: An Analysis of Trends," based on data gathered over a 20-year period (1977 to 1997), states that "it is impossible to quantify the emotional toll this reign of terror has taken on clinic personnel, their families" and clinic clients (1). The apprehension and fear providers experience was evident in testimonies given at the Senate hearing on "Violence Impeding Access to Health Care" (Senate Subcommittee on Labor, HHS and Education-Related Agencies, May 11, 1995).

The percentage of physicians learning to perform abortions fell sharply in the years preceding Gunn's murder and has continued to fall since then (Heilig and Wilson 1999; Kolata 1990). In fact, preliminary data indicate "that the decline in numbers may even be accelerating" (Heilig and Wilson 1999:486). This decline has several sources. Like the general populace, medical faculty and students are divided over the ethical status of abortion. To make matters worse, common usage stigmatizes physicians who provide abortions as "abortionists," and abortion providers often do not find sufficient collegial support within their own medical communities. Such concerns make avoidance an attractive solution.

But the decline also, and perhaps primarily, stems from fear aroused by anti-abortion violence, and may accelerate if aggressive, personalized harrassment continues. On May 12, 1993 Dr. Pablo Rodriguez, Medical Director of Planned Parenthood in Rhode Island, and himself a victim of anti-abortion violence and intimidation, testified before a congressional committee. Dr. Rodriguez concluded that, "The results of this intimidation campaign are plain to see. Abortion may remain a legal option in this country, but there will be so few providers that access will become limited and in some cases unavailable." In 1999, Heilig and Wilson confirmed this trend, warning that "lack of access can mean lack of choice" (486). In January 2000, Dr. Seymour Romney, Chairman of Physicians for Reproductive Choice and Health, stated that the "continuing decline in the number of New York abortion providers is the result of the climate of fear and violence" anti-abortion activists have fomented (Seymour January 14, 2000).

If access to abortion continues to decrease, abortion's legal status will vie in importance with its availability. *The Wall Street Journal* reported that "medical schools have been cutting back sharply on abortion training, and medical students appear increasingly unwilling to take such courses" (March 12, 1993). In 1975, 93% of "U.S. medical schools offered training in abortion to obstetrics residents," and 26% required it (Goldstein 1995). In 1985 23% of residency programs offered first- and second-trimester abortion training; in 1992, 12% offered first-trimester instruction and only 7% trained residents to do second-trimester abortions (MacKay and MacKay 1995; *The Wall Street Journal* March 12, 1993. This article cites the most current, complete source of these statistics, *The Abortion Fact Book* published in 1992 by the Alan Guttmacher Institute). Heilig and Wilson and Medical Students For Choice cite the same percentages in 1999. A 1995 survey of 244 family medicine residency programs showed that only 5% of "residents stated they certainly or probably would provide abortions, while 65% of residents stated they certainly would not provide abortions" (Steinauer et al. 1997). As the decade progressed and hospitals that formerly provided elective abortions ceased to do so, they also ceased training residents in the procedure (Rosenthal 1995). The chairman of the New York State division of the American College of Obstetricians and Gynecologists, Dr. John W. Choate, summed up the situation, saying that, "The bottom line is that we're facing an impending shortage of physicians who are adequately trained and willing to do the procedures" (Berger 1998).

These shortages materialized throughout the 1990s. In 1993 Medical Students for Choice (MSFC) formed out of concern for the shortage of abortion providers, "lack of abortion education in medical schools, and the escalating violence against providers" (MSFC 1999). MSFC urged their profession's oversight organization to ensure the availability of comprehensive reproductive health training. In 1995, concern over diminished availability of instruction in abortion procedures led the Accreditation Council for Graduate Medical Education to require programs that trained obstetricians to teach abortion skills (Davis 1998). (This policy was "watered down" in 1996 by Congress; Heilig and Wilson 1999:486.) Yet, in 1998, following the murder of Dr. Barnett Slepian, an abortion provider in Buffalo, New York, Junda Woo, a member of Medical Students for Choice, commented, "if more physicians knew how and were willing to perform [abortions], terrorist attacks like this one would be pointless" (Davis 1998). Dr. Choate also connected the shortage of providers to the impact of violence, stating that, "Only with more physicians able and willing to offer this health care to women can we ensure that acts of intimidation against physicians do not prevail" (Davis 1998). In 1999, Heilig and Wilson still argued that, "continued assaults on abortion providers" and the declining number of providers make the provision of safe and legal abortions "an important medical, public health, and ethical concern"; they concluded that "efforts to counter such trends and disincentives are more crucial than ever" (488).

The combined effect of a large, persistent pro-life movement and a limited number of acts of anti-abortion violence commited by a minority of abortion opponents may encourage fear and a concomitant reluctance to perform abortions despite support for legal abortion in the current political climate.[25] Rose argues that, "The threat of potential violence can

---

[25] Pro-choice candidates received strong support in 1993 elections, President Clinton removed restrictions on abortion, the Democratic majority in Congress passed the Freedom of Access to Clinic Entrances Act, and the Supreme Court shifted toward a liberal stance on abortion.

be effective before it actually erupts"; very occasional acts of violence give credibility to the threat of violence, "thereby gaining efficacy for the threat as an instrument of social and political change. The two aspects, demonstration and threat, cannot be separated" (1969:29). Nicki Nichols Gamble's congressional testimony on May 15, 1997, illustrated this principle. She stated that, following Salvi's lethal shooting spree in Brookline, Massachusetts, on December 30, 1994, "the foundation of our sense of security cracked, and the degree to which each and every one of us who provides reproductive health care services acknowledged our personal vulnerability escalated to a ten on the Richter scale." In 1999, when NAF reported one of the lowest levels of anti-abortion violence for the decade, implied threats such as the website "Baby Butchers," which lists "several hundred abortion providers with a line through the names of murdered doctors," and personalized "wanted poster" campaigns, effectively intimidated physicians (Sanchez 1999). The small number of violent acts that have already occurred, coupled with the implied threat posed by persistent, aggressive, personalized activism may reduce the availability of abortion, thus curtailing abortion practice and achieving one of the pro-life movement's goals.

Violent and extremely aggressive acts appear to have discredited direct action, alienated the majority of potential recruits, and exacerbated divisions within the pro-life movement. This may weaken the movement, making it less effective overall. Murdering doctors and clinic personnel not only created martyrs for the pro-choice movement, but drew legislative attention and support to their cause. In either case, the power, or danger, of pro-life direct action, either to itself or to its opposition, may lie in the behavior of the individual outlier, the person who acts on intense and vivid beliefs about the threat abortion poses to "babies," society, or the individual personally (cf. Blanchard and Prewitt 1993).

Over time, pro-choice response to pro-life direct action increased in St. Louis – but at a glacial rate. In the late 1970s, clinic personnel treated the first group of pro-life sitters tolerantly. As direct action became less civil throughout the 1980s, a minority of clinic personnel exhibited antagonistic behavior toward sitters, and pro-choicers formed a volunteer support group to act as "clinic escorts." "Escorts" stationed themselves at clinic entrances and in surrounding parking areas and guided clients and their companions into clinics, shielding clients from the verbal and physical onslaught of demonstrators. Pro-life activists who had joined sit-ins in Washington, D.C., told tales of violently aggressive pro-choice counterdemonstrators, but such were not evident in St. Louis. After direct activists began invading clinics, escorts sometimes stood in a row blocking clinic entrances. The escorts' presence, in general, increased the personal confrontation pro-lifers would face if they chose to sit-in, which was one of the main inhibiting factors interviewees mentioned. However, interviewees noted that the escorts' presence also helped ob-struct clinic entrances and added to the appearance of disorder that direct activists hoped would dissuade women from entering clinics.

For years, St. Louis's clinics relied mainly on police and courts to enforce their right to operate. In the late 1980s, even the widely adver-tised Operation Rescue event I first observed was only met by a small contingent of escorts and police. Later, in the mid-1990s, after self-identified pro-lifers had begun to murder clinic personnel, pro-choicers formed a protective wall of picketers when a notorious group of "res-cuers" came to town. This show of support effectively prevented even a single pro-lifer from approaching the clinic doors, and it was brought about by intensive efforts on the part of clinic personnel to arouse the pro-choice community in its defense. Anti-abortion violence appears to have undermined popular support for pro-life direct action in St. Louis and increased conventional support for the pro-choice cause during the mid- to late 1990s.

The structural organization of abortion services facilitates direct ac-tivists' strategies consciously intended to intimidate and dissuade clinic personnel (Gulden 1994). In 1991, 83% of abortions were performed in clinics, 60% of which provided abortion services exclusively (Ginsburg 1991). As the 1990s progressed, many full-service hospitals ceased pro-viding abortions; such policy decisions were driven "in part by economics and in part by fear" (Rosenthal 1995). For example, hundreds of "private hospitals nationwide" stopped providing abortions when they merged with Catholic hospitals for financial reasons and were obliged to accept the Catholic hospitals' policy of not providing abortions (Davis 1998). Allan Rosenfield, dean of the School of Public Health at Columbia-Presbyterian, added that the change also came about because "of the po-litical issues and harassment related to abortion" (Rosenthal 1995). By 1995, Rosenthal reported that "in some states there are now no hospitals that will perform abortions." While hospital officials cite the efficiency and economy abortion clinics afford, Alexander Sanger, president of Planned Parenthood of New York City, argued, "When picketing and violence first began, hospitals gradually began cutting back their abor-tion services and training, and that accelerated as the violence acceler-ated" (Rosenthal 1995). In 1998, Davis reported that 89% of abortions in the nation were being performed in clinics. This concentration of services facilitated direct activists' attempts to restrict abortion practice by providing clearly identifiable, relatively unambiguous targets. This situation would facilitate violent acts in the future, as well.

The formulation of the abortion debate may also contribute to anti-abortion violence. Rather than resolving antithetical arguments, each side continually attempts to exert power over the other (Condit 1990). This polarized dialogue has resulted in a solid political victory for the pro-choice side – that is, the legal status of abortion, and some (unevenly enforced) legislation protecting access to clinics. Perversely, this dichotomy itself may restrict abortion by excluding its opponents and encouraging drastic, damaging responses on the part of fringe activists (cf. Vanderford 1989).

Theorists have found that violence erupts when conflict is repressed or suppressed rather than regulated (Nice 1988; Rose 1969). While pro-choicers may point out that legal abortion does not force anyone to choose to abort, most pro-lifers interviewed considered abortion a life or death issue. From their perspective, a pro-choice legal context permits "murder" and so is a complete refutation of the pro-life stance. Pro-lifers described the subjective impact of Roe v. Wade as a repressive blow to the life ways and ideals they cherished. It cut off discussion and regional compromise (Cook et al. 1992). Had the decision not been made, and had state legislatures continued to construct their various resolutions to the abortion question, the direction of the pro-life movement may have been quite different, according to Rose's theory that a sustained dissensus promotes a low level of conflict and helps prevent unstructured, violent eruptions.

In sum, political circumstances that favored legal abortion tended to reduce the number of people supporting pro-life direct action, but they also galvanized those who remained active. This occurred when activists began routinely serving jail sentences for sitting-in. In such circumstances, direct activists' rhetoric frequently entailed ideas and images that may have encouraged the outlier, the fringe supporter to take violent action. When other avenues of political redress and opportunity close, such acts may be construed as warranted personal sacrifice. Griffin's decision to shoot Gunn apparently illustrated this dynamic (personal communications with Griffin's associates, April 1993). In what is for pro-lifers an adverse political environment, some direct activists' deep personal commitments to the worldview underlying their attempts to stop abortion may intensify (Festinger et al. 1956; Nice 1988; Rose 1969).

Future actions will define, retrospectively, the nature of these 14 years of direct action. Were they the prelude to escalated violence, a self-contained episode in abortion activism, or the beginning of cyclical waves of nonviolent but direct opposition to abortion? For the present, I will explore the activists' narratives in more detail in order to describe the motivation that underlay this activism from the perspective of those who engaged in it between the late 1970s and the early 1990s.

CHAPTER THREE

VARIATIONS IN THE SOURCES

OF COMMITMENT[1]

...processes of action which seem to an observer to be the same or similar may fit into exceedingly various complexes of motive in the case of the actual actor. — Weber 1978:10

I will turn now to individual narratives to illustrate the dynamics underlying direct activists' decisions to risk arrest. Two salient themes emerged when individuals related their direct action experiences. On the one hand, they generally described a linear process beginning with abortion disapproval and at some point reaching the conclusion that the most appropriate response to legal abortion was direct action. These accounts were punctuated by understandings and attitudes generally shared by the activists' companions. Through these accounts interviewees told *how* they came to sit-in, or "rescue." On the other hand, each individual's activism usually had a very specific, personal meaning. These particular subjective understandings played a crucial role in radicalizing activism, that is, in moving it away from conventional forms of political action and toward illegal and more deeply symbolic actions. This symbolic aspect allowed direct action to play an important role in reconfiguring the self-identities of the people introduced in this chapter.

Self-identities are complex and dynamic. Individuals' self-concepts change throughout their life spans as new information about themselves and others is gained, and as experience and cognitive development

---

[1] This analysis was developed from a chapter published in *Abortion Politics in the United States and Canada: Studies in Public Opinion*, edited by Ted G. Jelen and Marthe A. Chandler, Praeger Publishers, 1994.

provide new ways to process these data (Hart and Damon 1985; Kegan 1985). Change does not occur in a thoroughgoing, across-the-board manner. As the individual is inclined and equipped to deal with the various domains of life differently, so the individual's self-definition tends to vary from one domain to another, and within each domain over time (Hart and Damon 1985; Leahy 1985).

The relationships between three domains appeared crucial to individuals' participation in this activism. These three domains were: 1) the indiviudals' ideology regarding abortion, 2) their material circumstances, and 3) their emotional and psychological needs. Shifts in the relationships between these domains formed the contexts that helped define the meaning of direct action for individuals and so, the objectives they pursued through activism. These personal meanings were prominent in those portions of activists' narratives that explained *why* they first decided to sit-in and, later, decided to stop sitting-in.

Rescue organizers attempted to produce large, protracted sit-ins by bringing together a sufficient number of inspired, willing people and promoting supportive legal, community, and media responses. When they brought these elements all in line, organizers spoke of having created "windows of opportunity." However, individuals considering direct action also needed "windows of opportunity" that aligned their own material circumstances, intellectual orientations to the abortion issue, and certain psychological and emotional needs. People sat-in when the relationship between these three spheres of influence provided a reason to rescue, made direct action practical, and promoted a desire to sit-in that was strong enough to overcome their resistance to the risks direct action entailed.

One evening during Operation Rescue's "Summer of Mercy '91," Joseph Foreman entreated an audience of over 500 men and women to take advantage of the "window of opportunity" then open in Wichita, to "count the costs" and join him in rescue. His speech had been long and well recieved. In a wave of emotion, prefaced by the comment that he "hadn't intended to get into this," he asked, "If you can't set your house in order now, the things that hold us hostage, your debts, your children, your houses, your jobs, when can you? Because the time is getting short!" Foreman climaxed his appeal by asking, "Will all those who'll walk across a street to save a child stand up now?" The atmosphere was electric, qualitatively different from other prerescue rallies I had observed in the preceding two years. I expected the entire assembly to stand, leaving me the only one seated. But it didn't happen.

Only a handful – perhaps three or four people – stood while the great mass of the audience remained seated.[2]

Leading up to Foreman's entreaty, the evening's speakers had constructed links between rescuing and "rightness" based on patriotism, Biblical example, religious ardor and responsibility, and social acceptance. They linked direct action to heroic examples of currently acclaimed civil disobedience (such as popular resistance to the 1991 coup in the Soviet Union) and Biblical "civil disobedience" (such as that of Shadrack, Meshack, and Abednego, who defied their king's command to worship him). Speakers had likened rescuers to Jesus (persecuted by people who manipulated the law) and defined rescue as simple obedience to God. Speakers reassured the audience that friends would support – and opponents would respect – their decision to sit-in. They warned that the "spiritual narcotic" of euphoric emotion the audience was experiencing was insufficient to meet their obligations to God and only real action and personal suffering would suffice (however pale that sacrifice would be, compared to Jesus'). Finally, speakers assured listeners that even opponents unknowingly or unadmittedly held to pro-life values and objectives.

Despite the audience's tremendously supportive response to these points, those assembled did not stand up en masse. This rhetorical appeal coupled listeners' fervent religious devotion with their disapproval of abortion, supported by metaphoric validations and implied peer approval. But it was insufficient to inspire direct action. Although religiosity was a crucial element in many individuals' direct action, something more idiosyncratically relevant was needed to bring one to stand. Furthermore, the same arguments that were sufficient to trigger a commitment to direct action in a particular person at one time, would be insufficient another time.

Foreman's appeal failed because his rhetoric was not sufficient, or even necessarily appropriate, to align the different spheres of influence on each individual so that the urge to join direct action would outweigh the risks rescue entailed. Many of the people who came to Wichita's "Summer of Mercy" did so intending to sit-in. Most who planned to risk arrest had also decided in advance of their involvement approximately how many times and which days they would do so.

---

[2] Forman's friends (and coactivists) later told me that he had made similar spontaneous appeals at numerous previous rallies (in other cities) that met the same uncompliant response.

These decisions were private and individual, not a mass response to incendiary rhetoric.

Rhetoric usually was not the principal impetus for involvement in direct action but, rather, a catalyst or facilitator of complex processes that were contingent on many aspects of individuals' life circumstances and self-identities. Activists' narratives mirrored the findings of Oliner and Oliner (1988:222), indicating that people employed familiar patterns of "moral sensibility," normally used to confer meaning on daily events, in these significant moral decisions. However, at the moment of choice, interlaced idiosyncratic factors came to bear, and gave the various choices regarding activism their meanings.

How People Came to Sit-In

Opposition to abortion in general, of course, was crucial to direct action, but direct activists' guiding purpose was to stop specific, imminent abortions or, as they said, "abortions in progress." Before they engaged in direct action, their general ideological objection to abortion became a personal, practical mission. Sitting-in was a physically active, confrontational form of self-expression.

I will use the narrative of the woman I call Bailey to illustrate the development of "conviction to pro-life" direct action (a concept discussed in detail in Chapter 5). I have chosen Bailey's narrative because she began from a pro-choice stance; consequently, her story illustrates a more complete ideological transition than those of activists who were "always pro-life." Her experiences illustrate cognitive and emotional transitions present in other activists' narratives.

Bailey participated in sit-ins throughout the 1980s. She grew up in a comfortably well-to-do southern family, married, and later obtained a Master's degree, which laid the foundation for her professional life. Bailey was in her late 30s, divorced, and a homeowner raising two children on a modest income when I interviewed her.

BAILEY

Conversion to direct action often involved a precipitating event that connected the individual's life history to direct action in a "natural" progression. A pro-life film or speaker sometimes served as a catalyst for this transition. Bailey's conviction was triggered in this way. However, her response to the catalyst was the culmination of a long process. Bailey's regional history and her own childhood experiences forged the basis of her morality. These early ethics remained constant, but, as with most people, her later life experiences reshaped their practical meanings for her. She described her conviction to direct action as one in a series of significant events that expanded the meaning and, so, extended the practical implications of her early ethics.

Bailey was five years old when her mother died. She was raised by maids, cooks, and a stepmother who "just didn't care for stepchildren" and was "real up front about it." Bailey also spent much time with her grandmothers. When she was seven or eight one grandmother told her a story that allowed Bailey to connect her own loss with those of others. This connection inspired a strong sense of empathy in Bailey and eventually led her to develop an ethic of care and responsibility (cf. Gilligan 1982) that figured powerfully in her direct action. This connection taught Bailey that empathy alone was inadequate; one must act on one's understanding of right. Her grandmother's story instilled an action ethic in Bailey that was reinforced by later life experiences.

This is the story Bailey's grandmother told her:

My grandmother said that her grandmother told her that the earliest memory she had in life was of being three years old . . . and that this is her very first memory. She stepped out on the front porch of their home in Tennessee . . . It was out near Gallatin, Tennessee. And, you know, there's a beautiful, sunny summer morning. And she stood out there barefoot, felt the sun on her feet, and was listening to the birds. And that she heard a sound and at first, you know it was real far away. She couldn't identify it, what it was. And then she realized that it was children. And they were crying for their mothers. And just, you know it was a number of children crying for their mothers. And her . . . [stutters] . . . it just so upset her . . . and y'n'her mother came out, and took her in the house.

And what it was – they were, children [hesitates]. Their house was set back almost a mile from the McGavit which was the big road in those [days], this was like 1835, maybe 1840 . . . And they were driving slaves on the McGavit pike and those were slave children who'd been separated from their parents. And a mile from their house she could hear the children crying for their mothers.

And, you know, that just really touched me because, I think, because my mother died when I was little and I used to walk around looking for her. And more because I was five, and I could remember getting up month after month, and I would forget at night, and I would walk around calling my mother and looking for her. And so, my grandmother told me that story.

Well, what did her mother do?! [spoken in mock child's voice] About these poor children who were walking down the road calling their mothers. I mean this was so sad to imagine! You know these little children walking down the road, calling! Uuh!

And my grandmother said, well, uhm, her mother took her in the house and they closed the doors, and they closed the windows so they couldn't hear them any more. And you know, that made a real impression on me.

What do you do when there is a terrible evil in your country? And this same grandmother who was the child on the porch, at the time of the Civil War wound up in Chattanooga, Tennessee. They had their home on Missionary Ridge, her husband was a banker and they had a very large home and it was demolished for the battlefield. Missionary Ridge was, you know, one of the big battles there. And so they wound up being ordered out of the house in the snow and they walked from Chattanooga to Nashville in the winter! . . . They started out with eight children and three of them died on the road. And she was deaf after that because of illness during the war.

And I just, firmly believe that the Civil War, this is not a popular theory in the South, of course, but the Civil War was God's judgement on the South for the evils of slavery. I mean it really was, it was such an evil, evil institution.

And [I believe] that God judges nations, and that God will judge America for the murder of little children. I just really believe that. That the Civil War was a judgment on our nation, and I think that her mother thought she was protecting her child by bringing her in the house, and we just close the doors and close the windows and all of that. I think that you have to act! Or else, you see what happened. Here this, this little pampered child wound up as an adult, on the road in the winter burying three children on the side of the road.

As a 14-year old, Bailey was introduced to an elderly Jewish couple, a portrait artist and his wife, that had been victimized in Nazi Germany. This exposure crystallized her sense of responsibility to respond to the needs of others. During her childhood Bailey developed an extensive and inclusive sense of community, a sense of attachment to and responsibility for others, and a capacity for empathy. By age 14, these resulted in the conviction that she, personally, would not be a mute witness to injustice. When Bailey learned that the portrait artist had returned home one day to find "SS troopers" burning all of his canvases in the street outside his studio, she recalled:

> Well, I thought, they're killing them! Well, what did your neighbors do? Well they, went in their house and closed their doors! [spoken in mock child's voice] What did you think they did? And I just stood there and thought, no, no, if that had happened, I wouldn't have done that . . . When I would hear that story about them, I would say to them, if I'd been there, I wouldn't have done that! [whispered with force]

The lessons Bailey learned from her own life became a lens through which she read the collective history of her people (this history, in turn, underlay her own experiences). The moral lessons she derived from this reading and the ethical demands they placed upon her ongoing present, made her natal region's collective history personally relevant to her.

However, such ethics did not necessarily lead to disapproval of abortion or participation in direct action. Bailey was, in fact, quite consciously pro-choice until her mid-20s. Bailey remembered that around that time she could hardly attend a social gathering without hearing a troubling story whispered about the damaging effects abortion had had on one or another of the young women she had grown up with. Over time, she became increasingly convinced that many of her friends had been harmed by their abortions. Not long after Bailey began to think of abortion as something detrimental to women, her best friend was emotionally devastated when she acquiesced to family pressure and had an abortion she deeply regretted. Bailey's conviction that abortion solved everyone's problems at the expense of the pregnant woman, reinforced by an ethic of justice, led her to participate in *conventional* pro-life activism. To test her new perspective, she read every book she could find both pro- and anti-abortion, in her graduate institution's library.

She marshalled aspects of her own life story to counter pro-choice arguments and to support a sanctity of life ethic. This ethic was based on the assumption that each human life is inherently valuable regardless of its attributes or circumstances. Bailey argued that women who intended to abort, then bear children from later pregnancies, were operating on the assumption that people were interchangeable. Her mother's death convinced Bailey that individuals were not interchangeable and that motherhood was valuable. She remembered her mother as a "real sweet . . . nice, warm, loving person." Bailey thought of herself as an emotionally healthy person and credited her soundness to the care she received from her mother during the first five years of her life. She contrasted this period with the "really sad childhood" she experienced after her mother's death and concluded that children "can raise themselves" so that poor prospects did not warrant denying them the chance to do so.

Bailey explained that as a child, after her father remarried, she was unwanted by her stepmother. Years later, she once again found herself vulnerable and unwanted. At that point, Bailey was married, the mother of a small child, and pregnant a second time. Upon learning of the pregnancy, her husband threatened to divorce her if she did not abort – a threat he carried out. Having perceived herself to be "unwanted" as a child and again as a vulnerable adult, Bailey pondered the sources of an individual's value and the depredations unwantedness could wreck on a life. This contemplation sensitized her to the effects of particular legal contexts on real lives; she concluded that "a person has value" regardless of who "wants" them. She reflected:

> The whole thing about 'kill unwanted people' . . . I've been an unwanted child and an unwanted wife . . . and you know what they do to unwanted wives in India – they burn them. Over 6,000 a year! I'm really glad I wasn't born in India. I would be killed. So that perspective, the whole idea of 'unwanted' that really offends me, because no matter who wants you, a person has value on their own.

Bailey's understanding of her own life history was an important factor in the development of her extensive orientation toward others. She felt attachment to others and responsibility for their welfare. (Oliner and Oliner [1988:183] describe this link between contemplation of one's own history and the development of an extensive orientation toward others.)

But none of these connections were sufficient to lead Bailey to practice direct action. They laid the groundwork but did not prompt the transformation of perspective that would lead a law-abiding, southern gentlewoman to "make a scene." Bailey recalled that the birth of her own child taught her that abortion "kills babies" but she "wasn't moved to do a thing about it." Her first direct encounter with a friend haunted by an abortion taught her "that an abortion was a baby, and even in the mind of someone that had an abortion, she kept up with the age of her child. She understood it as a baby." (That is, years after the abortion, her friend mourned the date her second pregnancy would have come to term as the birthday of a deceased child.) Bailey's response was to engage in conventional activism; she became a volunteer worker supporting the campaign efforts of pro-life political candidates.

An expansion of Bailey's ability to conceptualize another's point of view precipitated the cognitive conflict (termed cognitive disequilibrium; cf. Berk 1989) that dramatically altered her practical response to abortion. Bailey read an account of the *The Silent Scream*. This video presentation incorporated an ultrasound recording of an actual abortion; pro-lifers argued that the video illustrated the agony fetuses endure during such procedures. Bailey explained that it impressed her by,

> Describing the effect of the abortion on this unborn baby. And when I read that, well, I hadn't thought about abortion very much from the perspective of the unborn babies before . . . At that point, I realized that if what they were saying in the film was true, then this warranted some action.

This alteration in Bailey's perspective taking was instrumental in stimulating her direct action.[3] Upon conceiving of fetuses as real people like herself, she concluded that abortions were real deaths. From Bailey's new perspective, conventional activism was no longer a sufficient response to abortion. She explained that in conventional activism,

> You have a meeting and they say, well, let's write letters. I thought, no, if I were being killed, I would not want a letter written. I really wouldn't. If you were really thinkin' about what would I want if I were being taken into a place to literally have my arms and legs ripped off my body, would I want some lady to write a letter to the editor? No, I really wouldn't. I mean, I would want somebody to be there and speak for me . . . I went to one [local conventional action] meeting [where she heard about direct action] and went

---

[3] Perspective-taking, or the ability to conceptualize another's point of view, is one facet of moral development (Berk 1989). Bailey's ability to conceptualize experience from the fetus' point of view, and particularly the fetus' view of activists' attitudes, expanded her repertoire of perspectives.

right to direct action . . . I hadn't heard of it before, but it made sense to me. It just all fit.

Bailey's new perspective altered her ethical balance. Up to that point, she had concluded that abortion was a moral violation because it harmed people (especially women) and violated individual rights. But she had been raised to behave circumspectly, abiding by social conventions. So far, social conventions had restrained her response to this "moral violation." This restraint ceased when Bailey's sense of propriety was overweighed by her ethics of justice, care, extensivity, and action. This shift in the balance between conventions and ethics occurred when Bailey developed a sense of empathy for fetuses intended to be aborted. From this new perspective, her existing morality demanded a more radical form of activism than it had previously required. She explained her response and illustrated her extensive sense of community by saying that,

These are our people, this is a human being . . . Just the fact that I accept them as members of the human family. Not that they are anything special. They're not above women, or old people, that's just the way you treat human beings. They're people. They have all the rights of any human being. I accept the humanity of the unborn babies and I think that if you realize that people are being killed in your community then it is just your obligation to do something about it. And to act and not write a letter about it.

Bailey experienced other people as part of herself (Oliner and Oliner [1988:249] explain that such perceptions define an extensive orientation). Although such extensivity may be held as a theological or philosophical ideal by many, Bailey incorporated it into her experience of life; she not only knew it, she felt it. Injury or injustice to others threatened her own world with chaos. She reasoned, "I was that small, I was that helpless, at one time. If I live long enough I'll get to be helpless and dependent again!"

Like her great-great-grandmother standing on the porch, Bailey felt herself exposed to an injustice and an evil, and she feared the consequences of not responding appropriately. She said:

And so, you know I was living three miles from where there were probably 40,000 babies killed three miles from my house. Then it just seemed to me, well, what was I going to do, just wait until they started killing Jews? You know, then I'll do something! . . . It was just the most terrible injustice being done, which demands action.

You can't just say, well, yeah, abortion's wrong, and it's too bad about that, but I'm just going to raise my little family over here and not have anything to do with it. You know what I mean? I'm just saying that when judgment falls on the nation, it falls on, my children – you know, it will fall on my children, my grandchildren. And so the appropriate action is to do, is to take action now, even if it is at personal cost. And that there is an obligation.

Bailey's progression from pro-choice to pro-life, and then from conventional to radical activism followed the development of perceptions and attitudes other interviewees described. While commitment to a generalized cause (such as recriminalizing abortion) might inspire sustained activism, conceptualization of "threatened children," adoption of "the children's" perspective, and creation of a sense of personal responsibility for those fellow beings inspired radical action. These developments generally characterized the conviction process. The crucial role such empathy played may explain many direct activists' tendency to emphasize fetuses to the near exclusion of the women who carried them.[4] A small minority of these activists described conviction experiences that centered on the development of empathy for women contemplating abortion or traumatized by it, and the details of such individuals' activism and discourse reflected that particular focus.

Bailey's story illustrates the dynamics most commonly entailed in decisions to adopt direct action. Over the course of her life, Bailey developed a set of values that grew largely from her own experiences. Although her ethics appeared to be established at an early age, her life experiences continued to reshape the practical meanings and implications of her ethics. Her ethics became a lens through which she read the collective history with which she identified. She derived moral lessons from that retrospective reading that made ethical demands on her in the present. Bailey's pro-life conviction was an extension of a long-established, yet continually adapting moral perspective.

The precipitating event that brought about Bailey's direct activism came after a long process that prepared the way for "pro-life conviction." Bailey marshalled ethics of intrinsicalism (that recognizes all lives as

---

[4] Throughout the 1980s, when mentioned, "mothers" were usually figured as innocent, ignorant, or deluded victims of abortion and society. While most activists first sat-in to "save babies," those who persisted often developed empathy for, and a sense of fraternity with, women considering abortion. However, the anguish over threatened "babies" did not diminish with time. In the 1990s, some direct activists came to characterize "mothers" as murder accomplices (Maxwell 1995).

inherently valuable, regardless of their attributes or who wants them) and extensivity (that recognizes others as being human, or like oneself). Her action ethic came into play when she conceived of fetuses as real people, and so construed abortions to be real deaths. From this new perspective her pre-existing morality demanded radical activism. Bailey then redefined the distinction between moral demands and social conventions. Through this redefinition, previously accepted norms of propriety and lawfulness became social conventions. As social conventions, they had to be subordinated to her newfound moral responsibility toward endangered fetuses.

Like most direct activists, Bailey immediately joined a rescue group that helped sustain her commitment to direct action. This group reinforced her concept of fetuses and their "mothers" as potential victims, and provided Bailey with a community that shared her values. This factor was of no small consequence, since Bailey's previous friends and peers eventually rejected her, at least in part because of her activism.

FUNDAMENTAL OBLIGATION OR
BEST CHOICE?

Early on in my fieldwork I noticed distinct attitudes toward direct action that appeared to correlate with persistence in it. On the one hand, some people pursued direct action as a personal mission and, in their view, the only ethical response to legal abortion. When these people coupled this approach with an understanding of direct action as saving lives, they tended to persist in it. Over time, they became less willing to compromise their principles by cooperating with authorities or passively allowing abortions to occur. They tended to become more and more radical in their activism, which often took on increasing symbolic value. On the other hand, many individuals were drawn into direct action because it seemed the best choice, but not the only good way, to respond to legal abortion. These people were readily dissuaded from direct action. They either reframed direct action as less effective than they had anticipated, or they reframed other responses as equally valuable, or more appropriate, or as their own particular "calling." Rather surprisingly, when such interviewees also understood their activism to be a response to a call from God – making it a sacred activity – they tended to participate in very few sit-ins. This was because they not only saw multiple "right" or "good" ways to oppose abortion, they also recognized many ways to respond to God. As one man concluded,

> It's what God calls you to do. If the Lord really lays it on your heart to rescue, then you should do it. A person should do what they're called to do . . . I really don't think God has called everybody to rescue, but He has called some to rescue. The thing of it is we all have our ministry.

This attitude formed a crucial distinction between those who considered direct action a moral obligation all should accept, and those who saw it as one specific calling among many.

These two approaches were not entirely discrete; many activists vacillated between calling direct action the only adequate response, and arguing that all pro-life work was equally important. More commonly, over time activists reconsidered their moral obligation to participate in direct action or recognized other obligations that counterbalanced it. Some people argued for years that every citizen was under a moral obligation to sit-in, then, in response to diverse pressures and changes in their circumstances, redefined direct action as one good tactic among many valuable activities aimed at curtailing abortion.

Why People Sat-In

People joined direct action when the relationships between many aspects of their lives both impelled and accommodated participation. Nonactivists and conventional activists may subscribe to many of the values, feelings, experiences, beliefs, and so forth, that made up the rescuers' stories of conviction, yet not engage in direct activism. Crucial though they were, these major components of pro-life conviction in and of themselves were not sufficient to explain individuals' decisions to join direct action. Rather, their convergence in particular configurations prompted individuals to sit-in.

To gain a more complete understanding of the dynamics that underlay those decisions, I will illustrate the social, psychological, ideological, ethical, and circumstantial underpinnings of three individuals' decisions first to adopt, and then to reject direct action. The interplay of these factors created the contexts that first allowed conviction themes to catch fire, leading initially to activism, then later dampened the force of conviction themes or redirected their impulse into other activities.

Common threads run through the narratives of the activists I call Rick and Jan, as well as that of Dylan (introduced previously as founder of the Direct Action League). Different configurations of ideology, material circumstances, and personal needs preceded their entrance into and exit from direct action. Initially, these factors provided a reason to sit-in, made participation in direct action feasible, and created a desire to sit-in that was strong enough to outweigh each individual's aversion to the costs direct action entailed. Yet each of these three domains was dynamic, and the relationships between domains altered over time. These three activists' narratives illustrate the crucial roles such spheres of influence played in first impelling and later discouraging their activism.

Jan, Rick, and Dylan were active in local direct action groups in the same city; however, their experiences were not concurrent. Dylan joined pro-life direct action shortly after its local inception in 1978; in 1984 he founded the Direct Action League, which Jan joined later that year. Jan stopped sitting-in shortly before Dylan withdrew from direct action in 1987. At that time, Jan had been arrested around 10 times and Dylan had more than 400 arrests. Both were lifelong Catholics. Two years later, in 1989, Rick sat-in for his first and only time. He did so with his fellow nondenominational congregants, led by the local Operation Rescue affiliate, Family Support Ministries.

The historical roles and social characteristics of these three individuals differed substantially, but they were not atypical within the sample as a whole. Compared to their companions, these three people earned moderate incomes and had attained typical educational levels. Like more than half of the sample, they all were married and had children. Several other people in the sample had more arrests than Dylan and many were only arrested once like Rick. Most long-term direct activists were arrested around 10 times like Jan. Some in the sample founded larger organizations than Dylan's. Most of the history considered in this study occurred between the beginning of Dylan's activism and the end of Rick's. As was true for other activists, the interplay of personal interpretations, ideology, ethics, and individual circumstances moved Rick, Jan, and Dylan first to adopt, and later to reject, direct action.

RICK

Rick described his direct action experience as pivotal in resolving a 17-year-long struggle between his resistance to God-as-an-authority and his desire to feel connected to God. In this way Rick described his activism as an extension of his previous religious rebirth. According to Rick, the alchemy worked by his decision to sit-in not only reshaped his relationship to God, it also changed his perspective on other people, and the way he related to them. Pro-life rhetoric harmonized with the purposes Rick addressed and so helped propel him into activism. Rick's narrative illustrates: 1) the way people subjectively and variably assessed the costs of participation, 2) the salient role ascribed meanings played in determining costs, and 3) the link between religious meaning, activism based on a desire for group bonding, and low levels of participation.

As a teenager Rick left college and traveled west from St. Louis to California in search of a religion, discipline, or philosophy that would resolve the discontent that troubled him. He studied briefly under an eastern guru, whom he respected, but returned to the Midwest, unsatisfied. Rick did not return to college at that point, but immersed himself in the drug culture then thriving on the fringes of the University of Missouri, Columbia.

During that period, Rick railed against the model of God "with a big stick," ever ready to punish His own creatures for breaking His rules – rules God had made that were impossible to follow. Rick had decided that "God wasn't too smart if He made a bunch of rules that people couldn't follow ... and He's pretty stupid because He didn't create us properly." Although this paradigm struck Rick as illogical and unbelievable, feeling disconnected from God frustrated and pained him. At times Rick attacked and literally "beat up" Christians because, "It seemed too easy to say, 'I got a relationship with God,' when I had spent a lot of time trying to find what that relationship was."

After six or seven years of fruitlessly looking "for what I thought God should be," Rick received a letter from a friend that answered his objections to Christianity. His friend argued that, "God existed ... and that man wasn't capable of living the life he was created to do." These were both beliefs Rick already held. But the friend continued, arguing that God knew about "man's fallen nature ... and God didn't expect us to live the rules." This made sense to Rick, but what "clicked" was the possibility of a rapprochement between himself and God. He remembered,

The link between the two was salvation through Jesus Christ. That's what clicked. And that God was concerned about me enough. He knew I couldn't keep the rules but He would make a way for me anyway, whether I could follow the rules or not. I'd been trying to link myself to God whether it was through drugs or whatever we were doin'.

This concept resolved Rick's intellectual need for a God who made sense, and his emotional need for a God who cared about him and would make a personal relationship with Him possible. Rick said he "finally just surrendered to God. Just saying, 'OK God, I accept this for me, if this is what you want. I'll do whatever you want me to do. Just give me my life.'"

Years earlier, while still in college, Rick had adopted an intellectual opposition to abortion after viewing Frances Schaefer's film series, "What Ever Happened to the Human Race?" However, this was no more than a dispassionate opinion that prompted no action on Rick's part. Several years after his acceptance of God, Rick had completed college, married, and secured a position as head nurse in a hospital. Some time later, the hospital imposed changes in terminology related to abortion. The term "abortion" was discouraged and replaced with a series of alternative terms (such as "termination" or "interruption" of a pregnancy and removal of "the products of conception"). At one point, Rick recalled that the hospital "had a really big meeting and standing up ... and being real emphatic about [the new terminology] and people were disciplined if they didn't write it that way." He remembered, "that's when I started thinking this is really not good." Rick increased his resistance to this imposition of authority. He refused to help set up operating rooms or relieve nurses involved in abortion procedures. He concluded that, "If they're in there workin', that's their problem. They're goin' to have to take the consequences."

Once he had taken "a stand" Rick's opposition to abortion increased and his need to respond grew. When he and his wife heard about St. Louis's annual pro-life picket, he told her, "I think we need to do something about it and we need to take a stand, we need to say something." After that first picket, his activism fed on itself. He explained,

I think God was in there sayin', 'You as a Christian, have a responsibility to step in and do something.' It seemed like something that I *could* get involved with and I did want to do it also. Somebody has to take a stand. It seemed like the more I picketed, the more I said things, the more I wanted to do it more.

When Rick linked his anti-abortion stance to his religiosity, his activism took on an important element of social communion. This element grew until it dominated his pro-life activities and, eventually, reconfigured his worldview. Rick's decision to sit-in was crucial to this transformation. He and his wife joined a large nondenominational church highly involved in local anti-abortion activism. There they read books on abortion, participated regularly in pro-life activities, and met like-minded people. Rick recalled that they "teamed up" with people in the church who "felt real strong about it" and sensed "a likeness of hearts." Then his brother was arrested for sitting-in. Rick searched the scriptures for a rebuke. Instead, Rick recalled that, to his surprise, he found support for being arrested as a consequence of carrying out one's Christian duties, and in particular, for proclaiming the gospel.

One evening Rick's church invited Duncan (leader of the local Operation Rescue affiliate, Family Support Ministries) to show anti-abortion videos. Rick recalled that these graphic images of both healthy fetuses in utero and the tangled remains of aborted fetuses, heightened his awareness of fetuses' concreteness and stimulated his sense of responsibility toward them. When his scriptural search authorized radical actions, Rick began to take his Christianity as an injunction to act. Direct action became, in his mind, an appropriate response to God's demands and a necessary response to the needs of others.

Rick described his decision to join direct action as a significant shift from a state of conflict, tension, and need, to a sense of security, calm, and achievement. He explained that,

> You always see these pictures of airplanes that try to break the sound barrier, you know, it kind of builds up the tension, at the point, and then when it breaks through, there's a big sonic boom, and then it goes real clearly. And all of a sudden the turbulence is gone and it's free to fly faster. And I think the rescue movement was what God used in my life to kind of break that barrier.

In Rick's rescue decision, God completely lost his "big stick" and Rick stood free-willed and autonomous. God merely proffered a question without threatening to punish Rick for failure, or commanding him to follow a rule. Rick explained that God asked him,

> Would you be willing to be inconvenienced for one person even if you never knew that one person for the rest of your life? Would

you be willing to be inconvenienced to the point of going to jail
for 30 *years?*!

By agreeing, Rick explained that his relationship to God was re-
established on a basis of freely given obedience rather than compli-
ance. This new perspective provided a way to accommodate both Rick's
desire for autonomy and his wish to be connected to his diety.

In this second watershed experience, Rick came to understand himself
as empowered through caring and self-sacrifice. He recalled that he chose
to accept a sense of inherent connection to others and reconceived those
others as valuable. He described this as choosing to care as he felt God
cared. Rick explained that,

> Because I did say yes and go ahead with it, I've had a deeper un-
> derstanding of God in my life and a deeper understanding of what
> He requires of me and a deeper understanding of what His concept
> of the world is. Because *now*, because of the one time, and that
> one point, when God asked me that one question, and I responded
> "Yes" to it . . . it's almost like, I see God's heart a little clearer now.
> And that people are really precious and life is really precious to
> Him. And that He is willing to sacrifice for just one person.

Rick's enhanced sense of the inherent value of others reworked his
experience of interpersonal relations. Like Bailey, he adopted ethics of
extensivity, care, and action. Rick explained,

> I think before, I honestly say, I didn't view people's lives as impor-
> tant as I do now because of the abortion [activism] and because
> I was willing to put my life on the line, not knowing what was
> going to happen, jeopardizing my job, jeopardizing everything in
> all honesty . . . And it's a lot easier for me to talk to other people,
> to do other things for other people, because it's kinda like I took
> that step. I took that step and God responded to that step . . . It's
> easier for me to go to work and do something I don't really want to
> do, because I'm doing it for my children [more] than I did before.
> It's easier for me to take the time to do something with someone
> else because I see their worth now, that they have worth, because
> God sees the fact that they have worth.

Despite the interpretation observers might apply to his actions, Rick
described his rescue as an altruistic act that subsequently increased his

sense of connection to people in general. From his perspective, this was a healing event. These feelings sharply contrasted with the attitudes that arose from his earlier anti-abortion stance.

In effect, Rick's youthful rebellion had ended with the conversion that returned him to mainstream society and planted him in an evangelical Christian community. He returned to college, became a professional, married, and began raising a family. These changes impinged on his autonomy. Through direct action, he found a way to remain within that community, revive his former independent self, and stand once again in rebellion against an externally imposed authority (civil law). His rebelliousness was authorized by God, and so legitimated. He recalled, "It kinda clicked that this is something that in my heart I really felt God wanted me to do and get involved with."

Rick sat-in once, agreeing to accept what he saw as God's challenge and be inconvenienced for an unknown Other. But that one sit-in landed almost all of his church's leaders in jail for most of a week and caused considerable contention within the congregation over the appropriateness of direct action. Rick feared direct action would blacklist him in his profession and ruin him financially. Unemployment would have threatened important aspects of his self-identity, such as his roles of husband, father, and sole provider. He never sat-in again.

Rick retained his commitment to be "inconvenienced" by joining conventional anti-abortion activism, which he considered to be, literally, proclamation of the gospel. By proclaiming God's will, Rick's activism aligned him with God in an ultimately dominant position. This gave him security and a sense of righteous power or, in his own words, "arrogance." This legal but very public activism provided Rick a leadership position in his congregation.

In sum, through direct action Rick found a way to be obedient that integrated conflicting personal needs. This new standard of cooperative obedience to God balanced Rick's desire for fellowship against his need for a sense of independence. He explained that, as a youth, he protested the Vietnam War to prove the war was wrong and to impose his own will. His first (conventional) anti-abortion activism was based on his opposition to abortion and his general resistance to authority. Rick's rebellion against hospital authority and refusal to assist during abortions employed impartialist, justice-oriented reasoning. That is, he employed impartial, universal, abstract principles in his reasoning. In these early experiences, his own will was central. Later, Rick concluded that both the choice to sit-in and the choice to stop sitting-in could be made in obedience to God and independent of others' universalistic arguments in favor of direct action. These evaluations rested on a particularized view of himself and other people; his decision rested on affective responses to specific situations, perspectives, and needs (cf. Blum 1993; Gilligan 1982). Rick understood himself to be setting his fears aside to do something for other people, and he did this because he thought that someone else (that is, God) wanted him to. The morality of this action lay in the responsiveness and connection to others that it represented.

Rick's activism began as resistance to authority and willingness to alienate himself from others, justified by an abstract principle. His activism later became a way to assume authority in unity with God and his peers, and to experience his connectedness to other people. Rescue decentered his will and reduced the primacy of abstract principles in his approach to morality. Rick described rescue as a turning point in his maturity. Through direct action, he integrated concurrent urges to dominate and to be in communion, and tailored them to his new paradigm of partnership with God.

The distress Rick initially addressed through his activism outweighed the costs of participation at that time. When that distress was relieved, continued activism threatened the serenity, vigor, and satisfaction he had attained – amplifying the costs of participation. Rick then rejected direct action, but retained his anti-abortion ideology, moderated by a new collaborative understanding of God that enriched his personal relationships, enlarged his self-concept, and removed the jarring conflicts direct action had introduced into his life.

JAN

Like Rick, Jan sat-in to integrate a conflict within her self-identity. Unlike Rick, Jan approached direct action with a well-developed sense of connection to other people and a desire to conform to "God's standards" as she understood them. In fact, Jan's dismay at her own failure to conform to pro-life standards, rather than a need to overcome resistance to authority, motivated her activism. Through direct action, she struggled to reconcile her tendency toward violence with the standards she set for personal interactions. Her religiosity provided the moral context that made being pro-life the antidote for her violent proclivities.

Jan's interest in activism was triggered by her church's call to become involved in a social issue. Proximity to a newly opened abortion clinic drew her attention to the pro-life cause, which eventually exposed her to both committee work and direct action. She found chairing a com-mittee unsatisfying, frustrating, and distasteful (because she preferred to do whatever seemed necessary herself, rather than delegating work or soliciting help). Picketing showed Jan the potential satisfaction greater personal involvement and risk taking offered. She was tantalized by the potential for confrontation with police during pickets, and excited by strident confrontations she had with the abortionist as he left his clinic.

Just when Jan found herself unsatisfied with conventional activism, Dylan began to organize sit-ins near her home. He provided the organi-zational structure that made Jan's direct action possible, but the impetus to join arose from her personal needs. In fact, Jan explained her in-volvement in direct action through two distinct accounts. She began by recounting external influences that prompted her to engage in activism, steered her toward sit-ins, then away from them. Then she explained how she had personally needed to sit-in because of what participation meant to her.

Woven through Jan's narrative was a tale of conflicting demands on an ethic of care and response (cf. Gilligan 1982). Jan explained that she joined direct action in response to the needs of "the babies." She remembered thinking that,

> If you had anything at all to do with saving the baby and later you saw the baby, and you were holding the baby! What a miracle that is to know that if you hadn't been there that very day and placed yourself between this person and that, this baby wouldn't be there.

However, when relating *why* she became involved in direct action and what it *meant* to her, Jan explained that she sat-in to solace a personal need that had less to do with "the babies" than with her own self-identity. Jan joined direct action to redeem what she described as a "deficiency" in herself. She reflected,

> I was talking to you about how people have disrespect for life, and people. And I'm talking about myself! See? [laughs, stammers] Our family, we grew up thinking the way to solve problems was to have fights, physical fights, fist fights. I'm really prone to hitting people. It's terrible to say! . . . I thought to myself, I see a deficiency in myself, and I think, "This is awful! Why am I like this?" And so I wanted to do something positive to counteract that . . . That's one of the primary reasons I got involved in it . . . I'm a certain kind of person and I see how I am and I want to change that. And

I got involved in pro-life because I want to change it, yet I got involved in direct action because I'm that kind of person and that kind of confrontation just doesn't bother me . . . If I go to one of these things and some clinic personnel threatens me, that's not going to scare me! I take advantage of that. I think I'm the kind of person that should be there because it doesn't bother me. I kind of feed on it . . . I'm trying to make something good out of something to me that's really a deficiency on my part. It's hard.

The disparity between her real self-image (that is, her current view of herself) and her ideal self-image (the ideal person she would like to be) impelled her to "improve" herself, and direct action provided a means to reconcile these two aspects of her self-understanding. (Real and ideal self-images are concepts described by Glick and Zigler 1985:1,2,36.) Jan explained that she turned her deficiency into an asset. That is, her *proclivity* for violence allowed her to *face* violence in order to stop abortion, which she considered to *be* violence.

After several years' involvement and the birth of three additional children, Jan's "little support system" broke down. Her husband left his teaching position and took on a variety of jobs. His hours became erratic and she could no longer rely on him to care for their six children while she was in jail. Other babysitting arrangements proved short-lived. When one of Jan's arrests was televised on the evening news, her mother-in-law disowned Jan's family and refused to accept phone calls from her own son, Jan's husband. Jan described her struggle to reconcile conflicting feelings of connectedness and urges to respond.

That's real hard to measure, too, when you should pull back and when you should work. Because you're talking about lives of babies . . . So it's really hard. You think, "I've gotta be there, I've gotta, I might save a baby!" But then, is your family falling apart back here, too? It's really a hard decision to make.

As participation in sit-ins became increasingly impractical for Jan, one stressful event precipitated her withdrawal from direct action. She reminisced,

I'll tell you I did have one really bad experience when I was in jail when I was nursing my baby . . . I was in real pain . . . I remember trying to express my milk into this dirty sink and I was sick, I was just sick thinking, "I gotta get outta here! I gotta get outta here!

You don't understand!"... At the time I was getting a lot of breast infections and they can really hit ya, really get ya down. And I said to myself I just can't do this when I'm nursing anymore.

Jan did not describe this new attitude as a decision not to sit-in or a rejection of direct action. She assessed each call to rescue in light of her other responsibilities and concluded that she would have to defer until the next call came. As she found herself consistently "unable" to sit-in, she began babysitting other direct activists' children. Finally, Jan became critical of these women for going to jail and leaving their children in her care for weeks at a time, and determined that her own family responsibilities precluded babysitting. These decisions effectively extricated her from active involvement with sit-ins without ending her ideological commitment to direct action.

When Jan's activism had apparently served its purpose, and her method of atoning had become destructive to her, she reassessed the moral value of conflicting claims on her time and commitment. She was then able to relinquish rescue as a responsibility while retaining the ethic of care and response (and the quest for a nonviolent self) that had underlain her activism. She described this shift in the language of self-sacrifice and obligation-to-family. The new mediating ethic was "balance," which required nurturance but allowed self-preservation. Jan reasoned,

You've got to have a balance in your life... if you let even a good issue get in the way of living a normal life, that's not right either... You've got to take care of yourself, you've got to take care of your family or you're not going to be much good to anyone, anyway, in the long run.

Jan's rescue experience is suggestive of Carol Gilligan's model of care-oriented moral development. Jan's exposure to pro-life rhetoric and activism convinced her that fetuses were people, killed by abortion. Her personal ethics demanded a response to the needs of others, especially to prevent violence to others, although this response entailed self-sacrifice. (Such responses are characteristic of the second stage of Gilligan's model.) Read in this manner, Jan's withdrawal from direct action reaffirmed her moral commitment to care and respond, and illustrated a maturing of her ethical reasoning. This maturing alleviated the need for self-sacrificing – and self-destructive – behavior by recognizing an ethical responsibility to balance other's needs against one's own well-being. (Such thinking characterizes the third and final stage of Gilligan's model.) However, Jan's explanation of the personal significance of rescue suggests that self-inclusion was a constant factor in her activism, not an innovation in response to stress and maturation. The two themes in Jan's discourse suggest her underlying psychology was more complex than the (linear) care model.

Contrary to this linear progression embodied in theories of moral development, Jan's narrative suggests an ongoing reassessment and reinterpretation of accumulated moral values in light of changing circumstances. Jan's life was integrated into diverse contexts, and her self-identity altered as those contexts changed (cf. Ginsburg and Tsing 1990). The conflicts that arose from changes in her circumstances caused her to redefine the implications of her values and to adjust her behavior accordingly. This reworking balanced shifting definitions of: 1) practical, external circumstances; 2) internal, personal needs; and 3) persistent, but interpretable, ethics. Jan's desire to embody a principle of nonviolence and her strong feelings about family, motherhood, and the need to care, initially motivated her to address her proclivity for violence by sitting-in. Later, these same values made her involvement seem damaging. Jan sat-in to bring about consistency between her values, her self-concept, and her behavior, and she left direct action for the same purpose.

Jan was conscious of this self-healing project, but her actions were expressed to others in the language of self-sacrifice. That is, she sat-in to "save the babies"; she left direct action to attend to the needs of her family. The need to provide such socially acceptable explanations for her actions was externally reinforced, which may explain Jan's narrative tendency to separate the two accounts of her activism. When Jan hinted to her pro-life friends about the violent side of her nature, she said they quieted her with, "Oh, little Janny, you wouldn't do that! Oh, little Janny, you're not like that!" Jan gave up trying to introduce her "dark side" to her friends. Direct action allowed it to emerge in what was, for Jan, a self-affirming manner. But her friends would not admit that part of her, so it remained private and unacknowledged (cf. Brown and Gilligan 1992).

Jan's religiosity encouraged her self-criticism and her desire to live a morally consistent life, that is, to address that aspect of her identity that made her "not as pro-life as I should be." Religion underlay her activism in that it constructed the moral context within which she employed her own style of moral reasoning and made her own choices.

Like Rick, Jan discounted considerable material costs while addressing the distress her conflicted self-identity caused. As long as her personal distress remained unresolved, Jan's purist approach and her focus on saving babies demanded intense involvment in direct action. When this distress was relieved, changes in her circumstances made participation increasingly difficult. To explain why she stopped sitting-in, Jan cited specific material costs she had accepted for years, saying they were sufficient reason to forego direct action. These costs gained force when the impetus created by Jan's personal needs decreased, that is, when she no longer needed rescue to obtain a highly desired goal.

Through direct activism Jan expiated that part of herself she saw as contradicting her pro-life ideals; she transformed her "deficiency" into an ability to be at the core of something she believed in. By enabling Jan to attain her own goal (of being more pro-life), direct action helped restore the self-esteem her proclivity for violence damaged (cf. Harter 1985). Jan addressed a universal principle that she revered – the primacy of life – but she did so by defining its implications within the particularities of her own circumstances and the specific needs of people around her (such as the needs of companions who were afraid to sit-in, her children's needs, and so forth). When participation threatened the peace she had obtained through it, Jan withdrew from direct action to pursue "balance" in her life and returned to her preferred role as mother and homemaker.

DYLAN

Direct action played diverse roles in activists' lives. It deepened Rick's human attachments and redefined his relationship to God; Jan used it to redefine a troublesome aspect of her self-identity. In contrast, activism played a damaging role in Dylan's life. For him, direct action began as a vehicle for self-expression, a way to establish the identity he thought he should attain. But this pursuit became a trap that he had to escape.

Dylan sat-in because he wanted to live out his ideals – to conform his identity to a set of ideals – and he continued to sit-in because he knew no escape from this purism. Rather than responding to rhetoric, Dylan generated it. Where no organization existed, he created it. Unwilling to deviate from an ideal strategy in response to "the babies," Dylan actively chose to suppress the costs of participation until they mounted up and virtually forced him out of activism altogether. Dylan, like Jan, was a purist who viewed sit-ins as secular activity. This combination of strategic preference (purism) and perception of direct action (as a secular activity) tended to promote persistent involvement in direct action.

Dylan remembered evenings in his parents' home dominated by his father's dinner-table lectures on social justice. As a child, Dylan longed to join the civil rights marchers in the South; as a young man, he followed his father into conventional anti-abortion politics. Dylan, the silent shadow, learned as he watched the older man perform publicly. When his father died, Dylan was "left with the legacy of living out his idealism." He recalled that, "It was like the throne was vacated and I sort of slipped right in there." While his father's translation of ideals into activism was tempered by family responsibilities, Dylan was relatively unencumbered when he began sitting-in.

Dylan first sat-in shortly after his father died, and he continued to sit-in "at least once a week for just under eight years." Dylan's activism became an unmoderated implementation of his ideals, modeled more on what he had heard his father say than on what he had seen his father do. The anti-abortion ideology Dylan embraced dominated his decisions and overrode his other personal needs. He explained,

> I think it was because I never had modeled for me how you live in the real world with ideals. And then I was left with, 'Well, you just do 'em!' And the consequences start filtering down later and it's like, 'Oh, my gosh, now what do I do?' And you just keep doin' it some more.

Dylan had already studied pro-life literature and felt inundated by "the gory details about abortion." This extensive indoctrination instilled in him a vivid concept of "babies threatened by abortion" that convinced him of "the humanity of the unborn child" and his duty to "do something" about it. He remembered reading about people who found "body parts in trash" and said he

> wasn't even thinking about it, but one day, when I went there [to a clinic], there were these trash bags sitting right there outside their door. And I took a deep breath and threw them in the trunk of my car, and went over to Elaine's house.

Together they carefully opened the gauze bags and probed the contents. They took the identifiable fetal parts to a pathologist at a nearby children's hospital who photographed the remains. Dylan remembered that, "In pictures it was just incredible. You could see all the bones and the bone structure." The pathologist "identified it as a 9 1/2 week old child [fetus]". This direct exposure solidified Dylan's concept of abortion as a means of death. He recalled,

> I was shocked, even though I knew it up here [intellectually], seeing it and knowing that was a baby who was alive that day, when I was at that mill, who had died that day at that mill was just devastating. And yet it was like, don't anybody ever try and tell me, if they ever tried before, don't ever try and tell me that's not a baby.

His fortified perception evoked an emotional response that strengthened his sense of personal obligation to stop imminent abortions and heightened the guilt he felt for failing to do so. He recalled that, "Things like that really emphasized the commitment."

Dylan accepted a logical need and a moral obligation to sit-in, but the whole project terrified him. He described the dichotomy between his intellectual and emotional responses by saying, "I was scared to death . . . but my drive and my belief system was in a way almost apart from that . . . It flowed from the Catholic and the anti-abortion." Driven by his ideology and the demands of his position in the direct action movement, Dylan neglected important aspects of his own needs. He remembered that,

> As the years went on . . . I became more and more aware of the emptiness inside. I'd be saying these things; I'd believe 'em. I'm doing them. Where's the land of happy? How come inside I'm empty?

For eight years Dylan-the-person was increasingly displaced by Dylan-the-activist-and-leader. Most of his close personal relationships revolved around direct action, but in rescue Dylan lived out a role based on an ideal model of what to do and say that, he recalled, denied his actual feelings. His real self-image (the way he knew himself to be) languished in the shadow of his ideal self-image (the person he thought he should be). Dylan recalled that, because he presented himself to others through an assumed role, he needed to distance himself safely from them by clinging to his position "on a pedestal."

Dylan became absorbed in his leadership role and was willing to abandon important aspects of his self-identity in favor of the characteristics embedded in that role. In essence, he adopted a radically impartialist moral orientation that defined high ideals for him to adhere to, but denied the morality of attending to his own particular needs. His inclination was not unique. Referring to social movement leaders, Eric Hoffer describes similar dynamics. Hoffer (1951:58) argues that,

> The revulsion from an unwanted self, and the impulse to forget it, mask it, slough it off, and lose it produce both a readiness to sacrifice the self and a willingness to dissolve it by losing one's individual distinctness in a compact collective whole.

While Hoffer describes an urge to escape one's self and seek refuge in a group bond, Dylan explained that he sought to develop an identity he lacked, but felt he *should* have. While the identity he formed was only possible within a group context, it entailed a solitary sense of self and experience.

Dylan's radical activism was impelled by a juridical concept of God (cf. Kass et al. 1991) as "somebody up there kinda lookin' at me and goin', 'Well, you didn't do too hot today!' Makin' check marks on a list." He understood God to have prescribed right and wrong, but, as he put it, all he had were the rules. And they put him in continual conflict with his own inclination to avoid confrontation.

Eventually the conflict between his ideology, the lived experience it generated, and his own emotional needs led Dylan into a severe depression. He recalled, "I was personally empty; there was nothing there. I had to rebuild from square one . . . I was naked with nothing . . . and I had to put my life back together piece by piece." At that point, Dylan acknowledged that the self he had constructed was unrewarding and he recognized the need to turn away from the objective that had come to define his identity. Dylan's actions just prior to the depression (that is, his affair with a fellow activist) caused his followers to reject him both as a leader and as a person. Many refused even to speak to him. His marriage fell apart and he left his wife and newborn daughter.

These actions were a distinct breach of the divine rules that had guided his activism. They made his moral status ambiguous (if not villainous) and severely disrupted his social ties. In essence, Dylan created a crisis in the two areas he had neglected. He acted on his own needs in a way that abrogated his ideals and radically restructured his material circumstances. This crisis forced him out of direct action and toward self-healing.

Dylan retreated to an isolated cabin in the countryside where he reconstructed his understanding of himself and his relationships on a model of connectedness and balance. He adopted a particularistic moral orientation (that considers the self and others from their own personal points of view). To do this he elevated the importance of his personal feelings and practical needs so that they could moderate the role anti-abortion ideology played in his life. He explained,

> What I've learned after all this experience is that we do not live in an ideal world. We do need to have ideals as such, but they need to be in their proper place . . . I was able to sustain myself in that ideal world for quite a while. I was terrified.

The strong emphasis on social responsibility and the neglect of close personal ties in his family of origin inclined Dylan toward an idealistic, almost obligatory pursuit of social justice. With few mediating constraints his activism intensified until he had created a heroic persona through which he related to others. While seeking to care for unknown, unseen others, Dylan appears to have denied his own need for nurturance, and the emotional protection and personal acceptance he could not gain while enacting an assumed persona. In attempting to do what was "right" according to the external standards he had adopted, Dylan neglected to meet internal demands. According to Dylan's narrative, when the conflict between his internal and external needs overwhelmed him, he withdrew from all social contacts, relinquished all responsibility toward others, and addressed his own needs.

Dylan made this transition by means of a core religious experience that replaced his earlier juridical notion of divinity with a concept of God as a companion who would walk "every step along the way and . . . was a buddy" (Kaiser [1991] presents a typology of God-concepts that includes both types: juridical and companion). Dylan described this as a "personal relationship" he could "tap into." Working outward from this new perspective based on connectedness, Dylan redefined his relationships and responsibilities to others. His new understanding recognized equal moral value in diverse demands, rather than the single unmitigated demand of "the unborn children."

Dylan's activism was deeply rooted in a morality that merged "justice" and "care" styles of moral reasoning (cf. Rogers 1987). His intense sense of responsibility to care and respond to "the preborn" as individuals was tied to rulelike moral imperatives that superceded the rest of his personal feelings and guided his decisions. Dylan emerged from his social withdrawal with his attitudes toward abortion and direct action intact. However, his moral imperative to care and respond was moderated by an ethic of balance that precluded destructive self-sacrifice and isolating hierarchical relationships, such as his former leadership role. His new conception of God-as-collaborator (cf. Kaiser 1991) supported this morality of self-inclusion. Like Rick and Jan, he experienced a substantive change in the way he viewed himself. No longer the lonely, heroic leader living mainly through public projections of one aspect of his identity, he became a more private, whole, and integrated person.

CONCLUSION

The activists interviewed for this study described their progressive disapproval of abortion and their increasingly radicalized response to it. Their accounts provided chronological descriptions that suggested linear causality. However, like the people discussed in this chapter, most activists also indicated the importance of shifting spheres of influence in their lives. The factors that appeared crucial to participation in direct action were ideological conviction, personal need, and practical opportunity. Convergence between these factors leant meaning to events and to the options available to the individual. Such meanings determined what established ethics implied about behavior, and so were crucial to interviewees' involvement in direct action. Private symbolism wove together their intellectual perceptions, emotions, social backgrounds, personal experiences, and moral understandings to produce their activism.

Because interviewees understood direct action in different ways, they responded differently to the adverse consequences activism often entailed. Through the lens of these private meanings, activists interpreted, and so subjectively defined, the costs of sitting-in. These dynamics were evident in the stories Rick, Jan, and Dylan told about the thoughts and circumstances that surrounded their adoption and abandonment of direct activism.

When these crucial factors converged, they could counteract the potential inertia posed, in part, by the costs of direct action and, in part, by the general human tendency toward habitual behavior (that resists change). Most interviewees would not have joined direct action without the combined impetus of: 1) emotional or psychological needs thought to be resolvable through activism; 2) an ideology that pointed them toward pro-life direct action for resolution; and 3) material circumstances that afforded at least some minimal opportunity to participate in sit-ins.

CHAPTER FOUR

COPING WITH BEREAVEMENT

THROUGH ACTIVISM:

REAL GRIEF AND

IMAGINED DEATH[1]

It is important to realize that in the sociological field as elsewhere, aver-ages, and hence average types, can be formulated with a relative degree of precision only where they are concerned with differences of degree in respect to action which remains qualitatively the same. Such cases do occur, but in the majority of cases of action important to history or sociology the motives which determine it are qualitatively heterogeneous. Then it is quite impossible to speak of an "average" in the true sense.
— Weber 1978:20–1

We must . . . respect equally rationality, emotionality, and the conative or wishing and driving side of our nature. — Maslow 1970:271

The motives underlying pro-life direct action were, indeed, heteroge-neous, and drew variously upon the disparate aspects of human nature Maslow indicated – the intellect, the emotions, and the "wishing and driving side of our nature." In the previous chapter, Rick's, Jan's, and Dylan's stories illustrated the varying influence of these three dimen-sions of humanity on activists' behavior. I will explore them more fully in this chapter, but in relation to grief. Not only is grief an experience well suited to stirring thought, feeling, and desire, it was an experience that surfaced in many of the activists' narratives in connection to their decisions to sit-in. I was prompted to investigate the connection be-tween grief and direct action after observing a young woman respond in an emotionally violent manner to what seemed, to me, a minor event. I had seen the same response, years before, in my childhood home. I will

---

[1] This chapter was developed from an article published in *Ethos* 23:4:437–52.

begin by relating what I saw at that time, in order to illustrate the depth of emotion activists sometimes connect to what observers might construe to be political experience.

I remember waking up one morning when I was nine years old and walking as far as the entrance to my kitchen. From there I saw my parents' friends, Big Bill and Phyll, come up to the sliding glass door which my mother opened. After they spoke to her I remember seeing my mother's face twist in emotional agony; her mouth stretched into a silent scream as she folded over at the hips and wrapped her arms around her stomach. They had told her of my father's sudden death during an emergency at work. Years later, when just beginning to observe pro-life direct activists, I was surprised to see a young activist make the same dramatic, silent gesture, then begin crying, when she saw a woman she had been speaking with enter an abortion clinic rather reluctantly. I wondered why she responded so acutely, when to my sense, little had happened to warrant it. Upon learning of the recent deaths of that young woman's husband, mother, aunt, and other relatives, I wondered what role grief might play in this activism.

I found that personal loss and vulnerability were prominent themes in the quiet conversations conducted along picket lines during my two years of fieldwork. Several activists said they suspected that familiarity with grief underlay many individuals' direct activism. A long-time activist remarked,

> One thing I've noticed from talking to hundreds of pro-life people, there seem to be a lot of them who have had significant losses, or in one way or another had more difficult lives than your average. And I think that, for some reason, has made people more empathetic . . . Just the value of the individual and that we're not replaceable.

Many activists spoke of addressing lingering or intense mental anguish through their participation in direct action. Activism helped these people cope with their anguish by providing them an opportunity to engage in acts of compassion, anger, or assertiveness.

ANGUISH AND ACTIVISM

Most people joined direct action in response to their perception of God's wishes and in response to their own personal needs. For about one fourth of the sample, those needs included coping with death and the grief it generated.[2] In addition, many more activists associated grief with abortion. All the pro-lifers I contacted considered abortions to entail deaths. Many activists thought abortion epitomized unjust, and therefore, tragic death. Pro-life rhetoric reinforced this association by depicting abortion as damaging women, children, families, and society in general.

American society provides rather inadequate mechanisms for coping with grief. Rosenblatt and his colleagues, analyzing cross-cultural data, found evidence that "...people everywhere build long-term, interdependent relations" and "the termination of these relations produces considerable distress and personal disorganization" – that is, grief (Rosenblatt, Walsh, and Jackson 1976:14). They concluded that, "Americans typically experience grief intensely and have considerable difficulty adjusting to the changed situation" because "Americans often suppress emotional reaction in a way that disrupts their lives and that prevents or delays their return to a normal life without the person who has died" (1976:105). In other societies, higher levels of "ritualization of death activities" and high death rates "provide strong education for grief and mourning" that, in turn, help people experience grief and move beyond it. Americans, however, have "deritualized" funeral activities and attained longevity that leaves American adults "less likely to know what to do when bereaved" (Rosenblatt et al. 1976:114). Uncertainty regarding proper bereavement behavior and the consequent tendency to grieve in private can create a vicious circle increasingly diminishing social support for the bereaved. Social pressure toward stoicism may also mask the potentially persistent nature of grief.

Activists drew associations between anguish in their own lives and the presumed experiences of aborting women and their fetuses. These perceptions of others' pain, echoing activists' own experiences of grief, helped stimulate a sense of sympathy and anxiety that moved recruits to action. Personally identifying with women about to abort, or with their fetuses, helped activists develop the perception that death and sorrow were imminent and intervention was not only justified but a moral requisite. For some activists, the death of a friend or relative triggered an attempt to try to "save someone from death" by sitting-in.

A long-remembered loss was integral to other individuals' desire to act against death – or the anguish they associated with abortion. For

---

[2] Personal experiences of grief were prominent themes in the narratives of at least 23% of the sample.

example, Bailey's prolonged experience of grief, common in our society (Rosenblatt et al. 1976:96), figured prominently in her activism. She explained that, "I was really mad at God for most of my childhood because of my mother dying. I mean He was in charge of that . . . There are just losses that you feel for your whole life." She related her own enduring grief to the prolonged traumatic reactions several of her closest friends had to their abortions, and wove the losses she experienced as a child and young adult into her impulse to undertake direct action.

The activists' narratives not only showed that grief can be an enduring experience, they also illustrated the diverse ways that grief can be integrated into life events. Direct action appears to have provided people what was, for them, an acceptable way to "act out" while coming to terms with the changes death (and other traumatic experiences) made in their circumstances, attitudes, and feelings.

LOSS OF PERSON, PAST, AND FUTURE

In their crosscultural analysis, Rosenblatt et al. (1976) found mourning to be a lengthy and complex process. Pearlin (1992) argues that mourning includes a sense of loss of the past (that is, the loss of part of one's biography that can never be regained), loss of future possibilities (for a jointly experienced future), and loss of the person (because a particular personal relationship and opportunities for intimate exchange are lost along with the individual who dies). Grief is not just for the deceased loved one, it is for all these losses. Pearlin notes that the more such losses are recognized prior to a death, the less the bereavement.

Some activists were caught unprepared by a death, or were overwhelmed by grief. Direct action appears to have helped them cope with grief by allowing them to reconstruct the emotions evoked by a death within a more impersonal and elective arena, through the concern they generated for aborted fetuses. Activists developed vivid images of death, dwelt upon them, and grieved. They experienced a reaction to the deaths of imagined individuals. These emotions could be felt quite deeply, then relinquished along with participation in direct action.

Loss of past, future, and person were prominent themes in pro-life direct activists' informal discourse. In private conversations, most prolifers expressed a concern about future losses due to abortion. For many activists, these were not mere intellectual exercises, they were expressions of fear, anger, or dismay. Some activists argued that abortion would stress the FICA tax base by downsizing upcoming generations. They worried that a disproportionately small younger generation would be unable and unwilling to care for them in their old age. Anxiety over loss of the future also surfaced in arguments about the potential loss of individuals who would have made significant personal contributions to society. Activists commonly buttressed this fear with the image of Moses's and Jesus's narrow escapes from death in infancy, and reflected upon the magnitude of their social contributions. Activists feared the social and economic effects of a massive loss of future workers, consumers, inventors, and leaders. Anxiety over "loss of the person" was reflected in quiet conversations that depicted abortion as permanently rupturing personal relationships and destroying opportunities for generativity and unconditional affection through parenting and grandparenting. Abortion symbolized a threatening breach of norms and values that, in the past, had held individuals in relationship. Pro-life picket lines provided regular social interactions where activists shared such concerns.

Formal pro-life rhetoric inscribed loss of the past, the future, and the person onto abortion. Anxiety over such losses was evident in poetry and newsletter articles that warned of and mourned the loss of siblings, offspring, or friends, never to be known, to love or be loved, and the loss of upcoming cohorts, never to materialize and function in society. The soundtracks of some videos presented at rallies were performed by weeping narrators who mourned the loss of an individual "child" killed by abortion. Activists held up the abandoned past as a cherished lifeway, mocked by the frightening prospects they believed abortion posed. This imagery (like that prominent in private discourse) illustrated the concrete and personalized conceptions direct activists developed of women and "children" involved in abortion. This powerful imagining allowed direct activists to construe abortions as real deaths, real losses, and helped them respond emotionally to those mental constructs.

The imagined death of thousands of "babies" was instrumental in moving individuals to undertake direct action. This imagery helped produce a perception of death and a grief response. Imagined deaths could generate grief despite their inherently detached nature. Not only have Rosenblatt et al. (1976:116) pointed out that "it is by no means clear that love is a necessary prerequisite to the experience of very intense bereavement," but pro-life rhetoric encouraged recruits to personalize the "children killed by abortion," and to perceive their deaths as tragic losses. For example, rally speakers urged listeners to name each fetus, imagine their hair and eye colors, hopes and preferences, the joy they would experience discovering life as they grew up, and their contributions to the lives of others. (Perhaps in response to feminist support of abortion rights, such guided imagery often featured female fetuses.) Pro-life speeches, literature, and audiovisual materials drama- tized "babies' " deaths and overtly promoted mourning as an appropriate response. By transforming the unknown fetus into a named and minutely described individual child, pro-life media reinforced death imagery and intentionally stimulated a sense of grief, while suggesting the appropriate response to such feelings – the appropriate form of mourning – was direct action.

In St. Louis, as elsewhere, special pro-life events included conven- tional signs of mourning such as funerals (conducted by clergy) held for fetuses or fetal body parts, or videos showing such funerals. Some PLAN activists wore mourning bands, walking slowly to a funeral march, as they approached an abortion facility to sit-in. Many Operation Rescue rallies featured late-term fetuses displayed in coffins. Coffins were sometimes borne in a pro-life march, or a "cemetery of the innocents" constructed, in which crosses were erected on a lawn to represent the number of abortions performed in one day, one year, or since the Supreme Court's *Roe v. Wade* decision. These images of death and mourning helped po- tential recruits develop clear mental images of fetuses as people, and such powerful concepts, in turn, made funerary imagery in direct action events seem natural and evocative.

One of the most pervasive concerns expressed by direct activists both privately and publicly centered on the loss of purposes that had been widely accepted previously in our society. Despite their socioeconomic diversity, many activists were distressed by our society's diminished fo- cus on forming and nurturing a family as an essential personal goal for both men and women. The loss of former purposes causes the loss of old, established understandings of morality and roles. Altered pur- poses and understandings change responses to familiar occurrences, such as adolescence, romance, and pregnancy. People witnessing such changes may experience grief (Rosenblatt et al. observed these dynamics in their crosscultural research on grief [1976:119]). Some individuals appear to have joined direct action in response to the anguish such changes caused them. In the minds of some activists, such concerns, along with grief over actual deaths, linked abortion to loss of the past.

Linking Affective and Cognitive Responses to Abortion

The conviction experience most direct activists described was both affective and cognitive. Through this transition activists developed an ideological opposition to abortion and a moral, emotional commitment to stop abortions from taking place. The circumstances that induced such conviction varied from one individual to another. For some activists, conviction derived mainly from personal experience, for others, it was stimulated largely by imagined experience. The narrative of the woman I call Loren illustrates the way some people used activism to cope with grief over "actual" deaths. Kelly's narrative illustrates the powerful role anti-abortion death imagery played in linking individuals' personal concerns to activism, even in the absence of preexisting grief.

IMMINENT AND REMEMBERED TRAGEDIES (LOREN)

Loren's activism stemmed from distress over changing social roles and morality, coupled with a distinct mental image of fetuses and their deaths. Her emotional distress and intellectual opposition to abortion increased as she came to think of abortion as death and killing. But Loren also linked her activism to the pervasive sense of grief she felt following a series of emotionally taumatic events that preceded her activism.

Despite an upbringing that taught her abortion was wrong, Loren remained uninvolved with the issue until she came to perceive abortions as individual deaths. She began describing the roots of her activism by explaining,

> I always was just brought up to know abortion was against the law and that abortion was wrong. Before . . . I didn't really think of abortion as killing a human being. That was something that I guess really didn't come to me until after I had a baby of my own.

Simply having a baby was not sufficient to associate abortion with actual deaths; her interest in abortion arose after the birth of her fifth child. Loren recalled,

> I never really thought about it with my other pregnancies . . . I really never had to think about it before because abortion wasn't

legal. I knew people were getting abortions, but, it was kind of the same way somebody murders somebody is illegal. You'd like to stop it, but, it's not legal . . . Because abortion was made legal, that's why I thought about it. That such a horrible thing could be made legal.

Neither did the legal status of abortion alone atune Loren to the issue. But it did give rise to a suasive social context. Loren's husband, a lawyer, urged her to join the activists he was defending in court, and brought them home to meet her. She remembered that,

> We were becoming more aware of it in church through religion and through friends. I guess it was just the time, too, the timing of when she was being born just happened to be a time when abortion was being brought up in the public eye.

Her last child's birth set the stage. This daughter, Nina, was born prematurely with cerebral palsy. In the days following the birth, doctors told Loren her daughter would not live (at that time, they also told Loren's husband that his wife probably would not survive, either).

The circumstances of Nina's birth resonated with Loren's contemplation of abortion. She explained that,

> Having her born the way she was born and to just to watch her fight for her life, I mean it just turned my stomach to think that there were people out there who actually took the lives of their children. And the fact that she was so tiny, it just completely related to what was going on. She was so cute, like a little Kewpie doll . . . I never thought about the human they were taking being this tiny little baby. [Nina's birth] just brought it all out into the open for me.

Even so, Loren did not become an activist at that point. Nina's fragility added weight to the grief that had inundated Loren's life over a two-year period, as one dear relative after another died. She enumerated her losses, and recalled how she reached out to God for security, recounting that,

> During that same period I had a mother die, a brother die, a brother-in-law die, a father-in-law die and Nina was born with cerebral

palsy... and we loved her so much, and she almost died. They told me she wasn't going to live... And this was like a two-year period... Just everything bad was happening in my life... I'm not saying I had a big religious experience, but it's kind of like you do turn to God for support and help because I mean everything just keeps happening to you, and so I guess that's when I got involved in the pro-life [movement] too, after all this happened... I was keying in on more important things in life.

Nina's birth precipitated five years of intensive care taking and forced Loren to maintain an outward normalcy that suppressed her grief. Loren subjugated her grief to her role as caretaker, but the anguish of her losses did not go away. When Nina was old enough to attend school, Loren was freed from the consuming caretaker role she had played. (Pearlin [1992] discusses the role captivity was often experienced by people who care for seriously ill or dying family members.)

Loren waffled between pragmatic and emotional, symbol-rich explanations for her entry into direct action. On the one hand, she explained that the natural progression of events in her life freed her to become involved outside her home just when her husband and friends urged her to join direct action. She explained,

It was just the right time for me to do something... There was a big gap from the time she was born until the time I got active... I think it was probably just because she was a lot of work... Nina was probably about five when I got started... The kids were all in school, I had the time to do it... [My husband] had been trying to talk me into it for about a month before that... That was just the right time of life for me then to do it.

On the other hand, Loren described her increasing sense of chaos and ambiguity. She saw some parents struggling in anguish to avert their children's deaths and others actively causing their "children's deaths." She saw doctors as both healers and killers, the parents' hope for their children's lives and for their deaths.

Loren explained that through the struggle to save Nina she had discerned the fragility of life, especially prenatal life. By contrast, abortion seemed to disregard the very life Loren sought to preserve. The contrast between the vulnerability of new life, and the threat to that life posed by abortion, made Loren aware of the dissonance in the multiple missions of doctors. She found this dissonance deeply disturbing. Loren recalled that,

> To see the doctors trying to save the lives of these little babies, then somewhere else, snuffing their life out. It just really blew my mind . . . I spent a lot of time in the 'preemie' nursery, and it really made me think, 'I don't believe, I mean here we are trying to save this little baby's life in here, and in other hospitals and in abortion clinics, they're killin' them.' I found absolutely no rationality in it at all. I mean I just couldn't comprehend what was going on. I don't know how anybody could comprehend saving one child's life and then killing another's life.

Loren's distress over what she saw as doctors' irrational agenda both to save and to end lives was agitated by pro-life literature that depicted abortion as brutal death. She found her mind consumed by images of death. Rosenblatt et al. (1976:89,105) point out that "the mere passage of time does not guarantee [the] change and commitment to change" that eliminate grief, and suggest that, as noted above, bereaved Americans "often suppress emotional reactions in a way that . . . prevents or delays their return to a normal life"; they add that "some people do get into serious difficulty as a result of unvented emotion."

As Loren became increasingly absorbed in the abortion issue, her response to it became angry and aggressive. This emotional response to abortion entailed sentiments characteristic of bereavement (as summarized in Rosenblatt et al. 1976:4,6). Early on, a friend gave Loren some pro-life books, and she recalled,

> I read every book on abortion I could . . . and the different types of abortion and I mean, that just turned my stomach . . . and then you see the horrible pictures. Those were being passed around freely, and they're true . . . this child has feelings . . . being burnt with salt and being chopped to pieces is a pretty gruesome way to die . . . I just got madder, and madder, and madder . . . at the people doing it.

These graphic images conjoined with the personalized concept of "little babies being killed" that Loren had developed while spending time with "little preemie babies." Together, these images intensified her opposition to abortion. While constrained by the need to care for her severely ill daughter, Loren's distress over abortion mounted. She remembered,

I had a real deep call for it . . . It's what's going through your mind, too, it's not just timing as far as convenience . . . that was just something that my whole mind was consumed with at the time . . . That was when I started getting active in pro-life. I mean it just ate at me. I was obsessed with it. The fact that one doctor would be trying to save them and the same doctor would be aborting them.

Initially, Nina's premature birth and near death exposed Loren to the complexity of social experience. In particular, Loren saw the ambiguous construal of fetuses implied by the intense efforts to save her child, contrasted with the routinized termination of other pregnancies. This exposure raised essential moral questions that remained unresolved while Loren immersed herself in a care-taking role. Later, Loren's exposure to anti-abortion imagery revived this consternation and the lingering anguish of her unresolved grief. The pressure of Loren's care-taking role, her unresolved grief, and her personal ethics (of nonviolence and sanctity of life) gradually coalesced to make abortion an urgent moral concern, for her, rather than an abstract issue. As Loren developed a consistent pro-life ideology, it joined with her emotional distress over death to form a coherent ethical and emotional opposition to abortion. Once Loren's view of abortion became coherent and the opportunity to act on her beliefs arose, Loren said she "realized" she had to do something – abortion seemed too horrible to ignore.

This sense of coherence created a basis from which she could direct her impulse to actively fight against the agony of her lingering bereavement. Through her husband, Loren made social contacts that exposed her to direct activism. Direct action happened to fulfill both her need to act and her desire to stop death. However, despite her consistent ethical basis supporting activism, her strong desire to undertake activism, and the opportunity to act on her desire, Loren still had not begun.

The precipitating event that catapulted Loren into direct action entailed a return of the terror, confusion, grief, and anger she felt at the near-death of her fifth child. This was brought back by the impending death of her godchild, the daughter of her best friend, a woman who, like Loren, also was raising a large family that included a severely handicapped child. Loren wept as she recounted,

The first day I went out and got arrested, my best friend, the one who has a handicapped child, she had a little girl six years old and she was my godchild, Anna. She left her in the car at school while she was delivering cookies for the girl scouts and the car popped out of gear and the child was killed. She jumped out of the car and got killed. She got run over by the car. She was in a coma for three days and I knew these people were just going to pieces. I've never seen anything like it. I was torn to pieces. It was horrible. I get all emotional when I talk about it. Emotionally I felt so sorry for them and it just tore me apart that these people were fighting for the life of their little girl and people were out there killing their babies. It had a tremendous effect on me. The day that Anna died, I went out [to sit-in]. She hadn't died yet, but they didn't expect her to live through the day. And I went and I said, 'This one is for Anna.' That had a tremendous effect on me. You see these people and they love this baby so much, and she's going to die and the doctors in there are just torn to pieces. And you just think of these little girls [clinic clients] on Saturday afternoon going out there with the giggles and getting an abortion when they [my friends] were in the hospital waiting to hear when their child was going to die. It was just awful. So that probably had a big effect of getting off my duff and doing something. I think we did save one baby that day, and I felt, 'This is for you, Anna.'

Loren had already spent long weeks in a hospital waiting for her own daughter to die, but when that child lived, she was immediately absorbed in care taking. Later, when her friend's daughter lay dying, not only was Loren free to act on her feelings, but direct action provided a format for fighting against death. Loren's activism was a direct attempt to defeat death and to compensate for loss. By saving one child she compensated for the anticipated loss of another and thwarted that which had terrified her when her own child's death seemed imminent. Through direct action Loren felt she not only *could* but *did* actually stop the deaths of children.

The intensity of Loren's activism hinged on her highly developed conception of fetuses as distinct, whole individuals killed during abortions. She argued that,

They're individual little human beings and they're no different than a baby that needs to nurse or take a bottle. They're just living in a different environment for a while . . . Just a normal little baby that somebody would have loved, even if the mother didn't . . . It's just so unfair . . . This baby, another human being, will never have another chance to live, ever . . . that's this little child's one chance

to life and . . . it's over with and they never got a chance to be
born . . . I just really hated that . . . The defenselessness, I mean this
poor little baby can't defend itself. Then you start thinking of them
as being a little toddler.

Once she understood fetuses to be individual people, Loren took the
next step and granted them individual autonomy (in accord with the
high value placed on the individual in American society [cf. Bellah
et al. 1985]). As "defenseless babies," they deserved care and protection
at a minimum. When threatened by death, like any other individuals,
they deserved societal protection. Loren explained,

I don't believe that that child is hers. I don't believe that my
children are mine . . . They belong to themselves, and . . . a mother
doesn't have a right to harm her child . . . We're here to take care of
them until they become responsible enough to take care of themselves, but we don't own them . . . If that mother isn't responsible
for that child, then somebody else has to do it.

Loren found political change too slow. Conceiving of fetuses as babies threatened by imminent death, direct action seemed not only warranted but required. She remembered that, "We knew it wouldn't happen
overnight. We felt like, well, what's going to happen to the babies in
between? Something had to be done."

In addition, Loren's religiosity reinforced the intimate, overt link she
made between her bereavement and her activism. Throughout her narrative, Loren juxtaposed the remarkable series of deaths among her close
kin to Nina's premature birth and near death, and her own subsequent
urge toward activism. Loren explained that her religious orientation im-
bued activism with selfless meaning. Because she grieved, she turned to
God through prayer and by increasing her general religiosity. (In this way,
Loren exemplified a correlation many statistical studies illustrate, that is,
that abortion attitudes correspond more to degree of religiosity than to
denominational affiliation, per se [cf. Cook, Jelen, and Wilcox 1992].)
Believing that God helped her cope with her grief, she sat-in to thank
God. In this sense also, her activism was part of her mourning process –
reciprocity for help received. Loren summed up her experience by saying,

My mom died, this all happened. This all happened like in a two-
year period. It was just like, 'I don't believe this is happening,' . . .

And because all these things were happening, it made me put my religion in perspective and God in perspective . . . You're not so self-centered, you want to do things for people. You want to do something. This was my way of doing something for somebody . . . I guess probably I felt like [God] got me through a very hard period and if I had not turned to Him and prayed, I would not have gotten through that. It was terrible. It was like six months didn't go by when somebody in my immediate family or very close died. I was having health problems at the time that I didn't know about, and they decided I had MS a couple of years later, but that started to creep into my life. I didn't go wacko or nuts because I was praying. I just felt like, this one's for you today. I'm going to do this for you. You got me through a hard period. I don't think it was Catholic influenced, but I guess the fact that my religion was very strong influenced it.[3]

IMAGINED DEATHS: LOREN'S REVIVED AND REJECTED ANGUISH

Unfortunately Loren's activism aggravated the anguish she wanted to overcome. She conceptualized clinic clients as taking frivolous and cavalier attitudes toward their abortions. She was haunted by an image of beautiful, young, laughing women jeering at her as they entered clinics to abort. The deaths she imagined horrified her, making her perception of patients' and pro-choicers' responses to her anguish seem inappropriate and grotesque. Abortion patients and their pro-choice escorts seemed to her to be collaborators in death, so that Loren's image of their laughter struck her as incomprehensibly callous and vindictive. Absorbed in the agony of death and bereavement, Loren interpreted this laughter as trivializing the deaths of the women's own children.

Loren's angry response to her perception of aborting women indicated the proprietary attitude she held toward "little babies about to be killed." Pearlin found that caretakers of terminally ill relatives interpreted changes in family members' attitudes toward invalids as loss of respect for the ill; caretakers resented such changes. Caregivers became angry, not depressed, that norms were being breached (Pearlin 1992). Similarly, Loren was incensed by what she perceived to be mothers'

---

[3] Several individuals argued that their activism derived from the strength of their religious commitment rather than from their particular theology, or that their activism was moral rather than religious. Their conclusions accord with several scholars' quantitative analyses of abortion attitudes (Cook et al. 1992).

attitudes toward their children's deaths. Where Loren felt anguish, she saw them as expressing gaiety and nonchalance. Loren repeatedly described these women in derogatory terms. She recounted that,

> You would get your silly little giddy 18-year olds. These girls would come in with their girlfriends and they were laughing about it. What I'm trying to say is these people were not poor . . . They were just people that just . . . they do something, they'd just get rid of it, 'It's not my responsibility' and this is the easy way out . . . laughing about the whole thing . . . I don't even think they thought about what they were doing . . . I guess the fact that Nina had cerebral palsy, and we loved her so much, and she almost died, they told me she wasn't going to live. And I'd see the pro-choicers and these girls that were going to have beautiful babies, going out and killing them. It just absolutely turned my stomach, and I've got so many friends that can't have babies of their own. I'd tell these girls at the abortion clinic, 'Hey, come with me and I'll take care of you. I'll take your baby. I've got friends that want a baby.' I just thought it was a very selfish thing . . . The ultimate in selfishness.

The behavior Loren attributed to these women aggravated the anger she felt in response to the deaths she imagined and those she witnessed. Despite any inaccuracy in her perceptions, Loren's anger was real. Her anger impelled an aggressive response that fed upon itself (Rosenblatt et al. observed similar dynamics in their crosscultural research on grief and mourning [1976:31,47]). The more she "sacrificed" for the "babies" by sitting-in, the more she resented others not making similar commitments. In response she spent more time at abortion clinics and, so, increased her exposure to the very interactions that upset her. Loren recalled that,

> It would make you so mad when you went out there . . . I would come home, and you just couldn't get it off your mind because you knew that you were out there and the day you were out there five or six babies had been destroyed, and destroyed by people who came in laughing. They just didn't even care what they were doing. Just like it was a routine dentist appointment or something. And you would go back and I would think, 'Why am I getting so mad? I don't know these people.' But you just realized what was going on behind those doors. And it made you just sick and you couldn't

think about anything else. You would be upset and then you'd try to talk to the girls and they would laugh in your face. That's just a way I spent my Saturdays for three years. Every Saturday, and then the kids would come to jail and bail Mom out with Dad . . . It was horribly depressing. It was just terrible. You would go home and you would think about what was going on and all the things that were said to you and how mad you'd get when the girls would come in laughing and joking and jeering at you and calling you names. It would eat at you because you were so serious. You'd get into it so heavily and you'd think about what was going on in there, and to see how lightly they took it . . . I mean, it was like it was just nothing to them, and it was so much to us, what they were doing to their babies. But it didn't phase them at all.

The incongruity between what Loren understood herself to be doing and the way she understood others' responses to her actions exacerbated her anguish. She, in turn, immersed herself in a coherent view of abortion and her responsibilities, one in which she was right and others were wrong. Over time, she became more deeply entrenched in an anxiety-producing relation to her own social world (one that literally nauseated her). She came to resent not only the "uncaring mothers," but anyone who was not helping her protect the "babies." She explained that,

You start thinking on it and dwelling on it so that it just consumes your mind 24 hours a day, and makes you sick to your stomach and mad that you're living in a world of intelligent people that are letting this go on. And you don't like the world that you're living in. You don't like your friends because they're not out there doing it. You get mad at them. You hate the world you're living in. Your whole life becomes very negative, I think. And you see, what you're doing isn't doing any good . . . You get so personally involved with it. You see that girl at night. You see her face in your sleep. You think about what she's just done. I mean you're that close to the person and you're actually touching the person that's going in to have it done . . . It puts a face onto a body. Makes a person out of a shadow . . . It becomes a personal thing. It's no longer something that is a political thing . . . Even knowing how long it's been, ten years, I still see some of those faces of the girls. They were so mad and just screaming and yelling and so abusive . . . They're abusing you verbally and pushing you and everything, and you're spending your time out there trying to save their baby! They'll just have their abortion and go to the mall . . . It's pathetic.

Loren's perception of the behavior of these women played against her "selfless activism" to echo a dichotomy Loren grew up with. As a child, she saw the deep feeling people in her family suffered from the behavior of the emotionally shallow and abusive person – her father. She described him as verbally and physically abusive, and her mother, whose death precipitated Loren's grief, as the emotionally deep, calm, reasonable parent.[4]

Loren's feelings of rage were directed toward women pursuing abortion, abortion clinics, and abortionists. Her fellow activists also expressed varying degress of anger and distress. The early activists spoke of becoming consumed by their concern over abortion. The mental im- ages activists formed of endangered "babies" and "defrauded women" deeply distressed them and encouraged impassioned commitment to ag- gressively stop abortions. Their first organization, PAZ, devoted much time to controlling that anger.

Loren described the consuming nature of direct activism, explaining that,

> You just become consumed in it. Well, this is so much more im- portant than going to work today. This is so much more important than cleaning my house today. This is so much more important than picking my kids up from school. Nothing is important to you anymore but this. [My husband] got that way, too. You can't do everyday things on Friday afternoon and then Saturday morning go out and maybe save a life, and not have that control your life. You think to yourself, I should have been out here Friday, too. Maybe I could have saved somebody's life then, too. You want to be Joan of Arc or something . . .
>
> I mean you do go out there and you really don't want to be peaceful, because you know what's going on in there . . . To be quite honest, I would have done worse if I could have, but they didn't want us to be violent. When you think about the violent acts that are going on, I wanted so bad sometimes just to drive by that place at night and throw bricks through the window or just destroy the

---

[4] Both her mother and brother died from drug addictions, suggesting the unhappi- ness they experienced.

place or hit the man that's doing the abortion. I don't think we did enough . . . You don't want to kill anybody, but you would just get so mad. And you can see where the build-up . . . That's why we had the meetings was to calm people down and tell them they couldn't do this, it would be nonproductive.

She emphasized the intentional efforts early activists made to counteract the distress activism engendered, recalling that,

We went to meetings just to make sure that everybody conducted themselves in an orderly way. Now there were some people that came out and got out of hand . . . which we totally opposed . . . If anybody did not behave properly, they were really reprimanded and asked not to be associated with that group. I mean they were really strict about our order . . . We wanted to be peaceful . . . We would sing religious songs and we would just very peacefully stand by the door and then there would be picketers outside. I mean you could hear a pin drop, it was just very organized and very peaceful . . . We were not out there for violent reasons. We felt the violence was going on inside of the clinic.

Despite these measures, the anger and obsession eventually became destructive to Loren's physical and mental health. She continued, saying,

It would make you so mad when you went out there. And that's why [my husband] said, 'You have to stop' . . . I was getting to the point when you do this day in and day out, and, I mean, you're associated with something you appall so much, you become obsessive about your behavior. I was beginning to worry about myself . . . We wanted to go out and save every baby that was being aborted. We couldn't do it. We were just becoming irrational about everything . . . It became a more personal thing. I felt like these babies were my responsibility.

Loren's anguish over abortion increasingly dominated her life until it reached the point that she had to turn away from it or be destroyed by it. She and her husband both felt her mental and physical health and her social relationships were severely threatened by her intense absorption in activism. In 1984 Loren was diagnosed with multiple sclerosis; because of that and the mental stress she was under she stopped sitting-in. She left voluntarily, but retained an ideological commitment to direct action. The remnant thoughts and feelings that had underlain her activism continued to distress her somewhat. She explained,

> I feel guilty because I'm not doing it, and I feel like I should be doing it . . . I wish I could do more . . . but if I ever got like I was before, I would just go crazy . . . I hate [confrontation]. It upsets me so much, I would go home with my stomach in knots after that.

LOREN'S ESCAPE

Loren's overtly anguished, but elective absorption in activism appears to have provided her a cathartic experience. The consuming agitation she felt during her activism may have made the first historically based grief tolerable by comparison. Although Loren's activism did nothing to replace the family members she lost through death, when she stopped sitting-in the life she returned to was more serene than her life had been as a direct activist. Loren elevated her real grief and consternation to an exaggerated level by imagining the deaths of dozens – even thousands – of babies. She turned from being a conscientious homemaker and care-taker to being a radical activist and social maverick. Loren acted out against death in a public manner, then relinquished activism and the agony it entailed, and returned to her former social roles to find in them a more desirable life than the one she had left behind.

Loren's activism appears to have provided a public way for her to express her outrage at death, and then to renounce her commitment to, and identification with, that anger. After examining mourning practices around the world, Rosenblatt et al. (1976) concluded that making a public commitment to relinquish grief is effective in helping individuals dispense with anguish following a death. They summarize theory on commitment by stating that "commitments are greater when they are public rather than private, voluntary rather than involuntary, and effortful rather than easy"; they point out that such conduct is reinforced by cognitive dissonance that pressures people to "drop old dispositions and take on new ones" (1976:88). Loren left direct action after a prolonged struggle to persist, and only when she realized that her own well-being was seriously threatened by her involvement. Her exit was difficult, although she recognized that it was voluntary. Her high level of involvement in activism up to that point made her exit public.

Loren's conscious, effortful, voluntary, public cessation of direct action may have helped her form a lasting commitment to move beyond mourning and reorient her life away from issues linked to death and grief. Leaving direct action may have provided Loren with a tangible action designating an end to her absorption in death that American mourning practices lack (cf. Rosenblatt 1976:49,50).

In sum, Loren entered direct action to address pressing personal needs – the consuming pain of unresolved grief from earlier losses, the anguish of an imminent loss, and consternation over society's attitudes toward individual life and social roles. She expressed her anguish repeatedly in a public manner. The intensity of Loren's involvement in activism created a crisis in which she perceived her mental and physical well-being to be pitted against her rejection of death and her commitment to those threatened by death. When this involvement threatened to overwhelm her self-identity and her social relationships, she chose to relinquish the fight against death and restore balance in her life.

IMAGINED GRIEF (KELLY)

Direct activists' literature, rhetoric, and events depicted living, individualized children threatened with, or undergoing gruesome deaths. These imagined deaths transformed abortion from an issue and a generalized "shame"; they gave it a sense of eminent reality and urgency. A corollary to "children's" imagined deaths was the presumed torment of their "mothers." Recruits responded to such conceptions by taking personal responsibility to stop abortions.

These decisions entailed both thinking and feeling that abortion was murder. Many people who adopted direct action had long opposed abortion intellectually. Conviction altered the cognitive perception of abortion to either *enhance* or *produce* an affective response to it. Imagined deaths encouraged some recruits to *integrate* pre-existing affective responses and intellectual conceptions of abortion. Imagined deaths helped other recruits reconceptualize abortion in ways that *generated* affective responses to it. As Loren's story illustrates, people augmented these processes by extrapolating from their own experiences to the presumed terror and pain of "children" being aborted. Kelly's story shows how the anguish evoked by the specter of death and grief linked a recruit's personal experiences to the presumed suffering of aborting women, creating a commitment to actively oppose abortion.

The woman I call Kelly "never had an opinion on abortion" until she went to a Debbie Boone concert while a freshman in college. Kelly recalled that the Direct Action League (DAL, discussed in Chapter 2) was there with Americans Against Abortion (representatives of a conservative Christian group called Melody Greene's Last Days Ministries). Kelly remembered that they had brought four preserved human fetuses, which they called "the Baby Chances" in tiny open caskets. She explained that Americans Against Abortion displayed these fetuses at public events around the country. Kelly described the visual impact of the fetuses and the more impressive memory of meeting women who grieved over the loss of the "children" they had aborted. She remembered,

> They were out where you could see them, and you just [sighs and stutters] . . . I saw a lot of people who had abortions, and they said, this is what happened, this is what I killed. It was a very emotional experience for a lot of them.

The jolting experience of viewing corpses and listening to women mourning their losses created an emotive and thought-provoking crucible that altered and intensified Kelly's attitudes, that is, her thoughts and her feelings. Kelly adopted an anti-abortion ideology for the first time by linking her own yearning to be valued with the neglect and agony she presumed had led the grieving women she met to abort. She generalized those feelings to imagine what other women felt when they aborted. Kelly remembered,

> What I really saw was a lot of hurting people . . . I mean, the mothers is what really got me. When I saw all these women who were going through post-abortion syndrome, and then most people don't even recognize it as a real disease. I saw people that were really hurting and millions and millions upon millions more are doing this over and over . . . Seeing the babies – that made an impression on me that will probably stay with me forever – but I don't think that that was it. I guess a lot of it was hearing people's stories . . . I was opened up to just really what abortion was doing to people. Especially to the mothers. So I decided that something needed to be done.

Direct activists manning the display booth at this concert channeled her into sit-ins. Kelly concluded that,

> This is something that's hurting people, and it's something that's abominable, and something has to be done. So I just got involved . . . I picketed one week and rescued the next week.

Kelly participated in direct action for most of her college freshman and sophomore years. When DAL began to disintegrate, she was repelled by the antagonism activists expressed toward one another, stopped sitting-in, and found other means for pursuing her goals – but those goals persisted. At first she concentrated on talking to women entering clinics. Later she organized a home for pregnant teenagers and operated a day care center. Through all three endeavors she pursued a single goal, to get people "to know that they're still people that we value, that we deem worthy of helping."

Through her activism Kelly specifically addressed a problem she experienced growing up. Kelly's childhood familiarized her with the pain people felt when they were not valued. She attributed abortion to a lack of self-worth and valuing of others, arguing,

> I think that we do not value people and we do not value ourselves. We are not taught to value ourselves, we are not taught to value others . . . That's part of why we have all these women killing their kids. They don't think they're important, and they don't think their babies are important.

Through her activism Kelly addressed issues of self-worth and nurturance that were integral to her own experience and personal needs. She explained,

> My mother is a very dominative person . . . I think she's schizophrenic, maybe paranoid schizophrenic, and she tends to be abusive . . . I do not feel valued and I think that all people should feel valued. And I guess that that has made me want to help more with women . . . I felt an emotional conflict. I just don't want people feeling that way, I don't want people treated that way. And I want people to feel valued.

Kelly's theology increased the empathy she felt and reinforced the way she directed her feelings. Kelly believed that women endangered themselves by aborting, which she considered to be "commiting a sin." She was less concerned with aborted "babies," since she believed they were ultimately safe in heaven (after being aborted). With this in mind, she emphasized the need to tell women they would be accountable for aborting. Kelly concluded,

> I guess that's the most important thing that we have to get through to them because some day they're going to end up in Heaven or Hell. Those are the choices. I'd much rather see them in Heaven. Eternity is forever, pregnancy is for 9 months. You only spend 78, 80 years on earth, tops, but eternity is for ever and ever . . . Maybe that's why I have more of a burden for women than for babies. Because I feel more for the people I know are feeling the emotional conflict than I do for the babies, because I know they're going to go to Heaven when they die.

The strong connections Kelly drew between her own life and abortion were evident in the solutions she sought. When Kelly described the mind-set of women about to abort and outlined her strategy and goals for aiding those women, she might have been recounting her own personal experiences, feelings, and needs. Her concept of the circumstances leading to abortion echoed the unhappy relationship she had with her mother, just as her concept of aborting women's distress echoed the anguish emotional abondonment had caused her. Kelly recognized her own grief in the mourning women she met at the concert and in those she imagined helping. Her activism grew out of this empathy. She reasoned that "children" would be helped best by healing damaged and destructive mothers, and explained that,

> When I go to rescue, I'm trying to save people from hurt, trying to keep people from ruining their lives . . . I don't think people know what the abortion is going to do to their child's life and to their life. And to show them they are valuable. Because people just do not feel valuable . . . When I see the women coming in. They're thinking, 'What about me? The most important thing is what situation I'm in, people aren't going to help me, people aren't going to love me, I'm going to be abandoned.' That's really the first place to start. From there you can help the baby . . . It is a family problem, a social problem that can only be solved by dealing with the whole family . . . Not just to help the mother, but

to help the whole family. Because if she's going to keep that child, and if I don't have a healthy mother, the child's not going to feel good about themselves either. So by helping her, then I can help everybody.

Conclusion

Conviction appeared to wed direct activists' ideological and affective opposition to abortion; anguish evoked by both lived and imagined exposure to death or loss helped stimulate this convergence. Although concern over social control was evident throughout the pro-life movement, an emotional response to "individual deaths" brought about by abortion was one of the most powerful motives to direct action. Pro-life rhetoric and events depicted abortion as tragic, horrific death. Such imagery fostered cognitive and emotional experiences that encouraged participation in direct action.

I do not mean to make too great a distinction between memory, imagination, and observation or experience. Among pro-life direct activists, all three generated more or less distinct mental images to which adhered emotional experiences. Together, they guided behavior. Nor do I wish to suggest that death and grief alone motivated pro-life direct action. People sat-in when a convergence of ideology, opportunity, and personal understandings impelled them. However, for many people an awareness of death was integral to their activism and activism was a component in their individual strategies for coping with grief – grief literally felt, although generated by variously proportioned amalgams of lived, remembered, and imagined experience.

CHAPTER FIVE

ABORTION EXPERIENCES[1]

Pro-life picket lines and direct action groups often included women who had had abortions themselves. All of the direct activists I interviewed who reported having had abortions emphasized the dramatic role their own abortions played in their decisions to sit-in. Their narratives repudiate facile explanations for their involvement (which generally attribute it to hypocrisy) and suggest a link between individuals' understanding of salvation and their participation in direct action.

When these women sat-in, they not only addressed problems they associated with their own abortions; their often brief participation provided their companions with truncated exposure to aborted women's experiences. These partial views helped perpetuate direct activists' beliefs about abortion. Pro-life rhetoric foregrounded these inherently dramatic stories – expressions of anguish and remorse.

The narratives of women who had had abortions illustrate the dual role life histories played in motivating political activism. As fluid stories about oneself, life histories or, more precisely, transitory interpretations of the past, impelled individual activism. As fixed stories about other people, life histories served as evidence to confirm storytellers' and listeners' beliefs and shape their values.

RESEARCH ON THE PSYCHOLOGICAL SEQUELAE OF ABORTION

In order to put activists' experiences into perspective, I will review current research regarding the psychological effects of abortion on women.

---

[1] This chapter was developed from an article published in *Social Justice Research* 7:4:401–13.

Prior to the mid-1960s, research on abortion's psychological sequelae focused on women suffering psychopathological responses to abortion, and relied on clinical research and theory. More recent research centers on "stress and coping" studies that plot the range and frequency of responses to abortion (Alder, David, Major, Roth, Russo, and Wyatt 1992; Stark, Blum, Resnick, and Bearinger 1986). "Stress and coping" research documents the types and incidence of reactions rather than exploring their nature or treatment.[2] More recently, studies also have sought to identify factors that place women at risk for negative outcomes (Arthur 2001; Lee and Gilchrist 1997).

Studies focusing on abortion as a potentially stressful life event concluded that legal abortion is unlikely to cause "severe negative reactions . . . in the immediate and short-term aftermath" but that,

> women who are terminating pregnancies that are wanted and personally meaningful, who lack support from their partner or parents for the abortion, or who have more conflicting feelings or are less sure of their decision before hand may be at relatively higher risk for negative consequences

and that "some women experience severe distress or psychopathology after abortion" (Alder et al. 1990:248,249). Subsequent studies suggest that emotionally immature teenagers, women with previous psychiatric problems, women with strong philosophical objections to abortion, women undergoing late abortions, and women coerced into aborting are at risk for negative sequelae (Arthur 2001). Former Surgeon General C. Everett Koop indicated the importance of the caveat, testifying before Congress that, despite the "minuscule" threat abortion poses to the public, "such responses can be overwhelming to a given individual" (Alder et al. 1992:1202).

Researchers have disagreed on the psychiatric and psychological sequelae of terminating pregnancies because findings have been inconsistent, studies have tended to be methodologically flawed, a broad base of data has been unavailable in most countries (including the United States), and because researchers' biases concerning the moral status of abortion influenced the assumptions guiding their choice of theoretical

---

[2] The American Psychological Association appointed an expert panel to review the literature on "theoretical, methodological, and substantive findings on psychological responses following abortion" (Alder et al. 1992:1195). This panel reported its conclusions in the Alder et al. articles.

approaches and in some cases biased conclusions (Alder et al. 1990, 1992; Arthur 2001; David, Rasmussen, and Holst 1981; NAS 1975; Simon and Senturia 1966; Stark et al. 1986).[3] Nonetheless, diverse studies concluded that most women undergoing legal abortions were not harmed by their experiences – but rather may have benefitted from them – and that a very small percentage of women experienced severe psychological responses. These findings are a strong accolade for legal abortion.

Unfortunately, few studies followed women for more than two years after their abortions, and most studies examined only brief periods of time immediately following abortion procedures.[4] The small window of observation most researchers employed could not determine the existence, extent, or nature of any long-term psychological effects associated with abortion. Also, studies based on questionnaires may underreport grief, distress, and depression related to abortion experiences; such effects are more likely to become evident through in-depth interviewing

[3] Methodological concerns weakened findings regarding abortion sequelae. For example: 1) studies were based on volunteer samples that may have underrepresented women prone to finding the abortion experience stressful; 2) many studies focused on women during and after their abortions but did not gather baseline data on women's mental health prior to the abortion experiences; 3) due to the lack of long-term follow-up studies, very little data exists to suggest the validity of short-term responses in indicating long-term responses to abortion; 4) little attention was paid to interviewer bias; 5) many studies lacked control groups, others did not fully consider what constituted an appropriate control population; 6) terms for mental health outcomes were vague or inconsistently applied; 7) ill-defined or ambiguous measures (such as "seeing a psychiatrist") were used to assess mental health; and 8) researchers used questionnaires to gather information on "well-suppressed feelings and conflicts" (Alder et al. 1990:43; NAS 1975:90–1; Ney and Wickett 1989; Simon and Senturia 1966; Stark et al. 1986). In addition, 9) many early studies paid insufficient attention to the linkage between the legal and social contexts in which abortions occurred and their psychological effects, and 10) researchers' personal convictions often colored their conclusions (NAS 1975: 91;94; Simon and Senturia 1966). In 1966 Simon and Senturia observed that, "Deeply held personal convictions frequently seem to outweigh the importance of data, especially when conclusions are drawn" (387) and this problem persists.

[4] The majority focused on periods that varied from one hour to three weeks following the abortion experience; several studies conducted one- to two-year follow-ups and one study completed an eight-year follow-up. As recently as 1990 the longest follow-up was two years (Alder et al. 1990). Most scientifically valid studies measured effects women experienced for hours, weeks, or up to one year after their abortions, but little research was done on effects occurring beyond that point (Alder et al. 1992; Cohen and Roth 1984; David et al. 1981).

(cf. Ney and Wickett 1989).[5] Consequently, Alder et al. conclude that "no definitive conclusions can be drawn about longer term effects," although research on other life stresses indicates that "women who do not experience severe negative responses within a few months of the event are unlikely to develop future significant psychological problems related to the event" (1990:43).

This comparative note is encouraging, and supports the conclusion that few women will suffer negative abortion sequelae. However, the severity of reactions experienced by that very small minority of women who do report negative outcomes calls for more conclusive research on abortion's potential long-term effects. Adequate endeavor needs to be directed toward assisting women who do experience psychological distress after aborting, whether such outcomes result from their abortions, the circumstances surrounding their abortions, or pre-existing psychological problems.

While the percentage of women adversely affected by abortion is very small, the sheer number of abortions performed annually can be associated with a large number of women experiencing undesirable sequelae. The annual number of abortions in the United States peaked around 1980 and gradually declined to 1.61 million in 1990 (according to the Alan Guttmacher Institute [1998] which provides a less frequently tabulated, but more thorough assessment of abortion rates than that of the Centers for Disease Control). Abortions may have fallen to 1.37 million at the turn of the century, but this decline may be a function of underreporting due to the 1996 Personal Responsibility and Work Opportunity Act, a federal program that offered a $20 million bonus to states that, among other things, could show a reduction in their abortion rates (AGI 1997). Armsworth's (1991) review of the literature on abortion sequelae suggests that 2–5% of abortion patients experience severe psychological reactions. This would mean, minimally, that between 27,000 and 69,000 women a year are confronted with significant psychological problems following their abortions.

In their widely cited study, Cohen and Roth (1984:144) concluded that "abortion patients are similar in their stress-response patterns to other stressed populations." Women's responses tended to vary according to the social support they received during their abortion experiences,

[5] In addition, some research suggests postabortive women (and especially teenagers) experience a lack of affect that is, in itself, an adverse psychological response (Kent et al. 1978). Sometimes such symptoms are quite severe.

how they understood themselves to have come to the point of aborting, what meanings they attached to their abortions, and the strategies they employed to cope with their abortion experiences (Alder et al. 1992; Bracken, Hachamovitch, and Grossman 1974; David et al. 1981). Pro-life direct activists' narratives explained how they coped with the grief, guilt, anxiety, and depression they associated with their abortions.

Perhaps the firsthand accounts of long-term psychological distress considered here can further inform the medical, political, and social work communities of the complex ramifications of untreated negative abortion sequelae. Activists spoke of the effects their abortions had on their lives many years after the actual procedures. In the format of a qualitative interview, they were able to articulate the connections they drew between their abortions and both prior and subsequent experiences and feelings.

Abortion Experiences, Private Paradigms, and Public Discourse

In the sample of 80 activists, 6 women reported having had at least one abortion, and 1 man spoke of paying to abort "children" he considered his own. All seven individuals described in forceful detail the abiding deleterious effects these experiences had on them. The six women considered their abortions important factors in their activism (although the man did not consider his abortion experience to have had a bearing on his activism).[6] Most direct activists knew women who experienced emotional or physical difficulties immediately after aborting. However, in some cases the negative consequences they observed did not appear until years (and even decades) after the abortions took place. Women reporting delayed distress consciously and causally linked their anguish to their abortions, and this linkage was reinforced figuratively by the nature of the problems they described. Observing such experiences, direct activists concluded that abortion had long-term negative effects on women.

[6] Although the percentage of activists who had aborted was modest, the relative proportion of men to women was suggestive. Rosenblatt and Burns (1986) found that mothers were significantly more troubled by perinatal and abortive losses than were fathers, and direct activists' narratives reflect this dynamic. Past abortions were crucial factors in women's activism, but not so in men's activism. Rates of abortion in the St. Louis and Wichita samples were nearly identical. (See Appendix I for details.)

The consequences of both firsthand and observed experiences multiplied when they became the topic of direct activists' public testimonies and private conversations. Personal experiences were generalized into the abstract realms of debate and myth when they entered activists' public discourse as stories. As such, they formed arguments about the nature of abortion and moral rectitude.

STORIES

Along with tales of miracles and abuse by police or pro-choice demonstrators, stories of harm done by abortion permeated both rhetoric and informal discourse during activists' events. Such stories punctuated picketers' conversations and traveled widely from state to state along the direct action grapevine.[7] They were not offered casually; speakers used them as proofs or highlights. People usually told such stories when a rapport had been established, often toward the end of a picket, among a group that stayed on to talk after others had left.

Although stories were purported to have a basis in fact, they often differed substantially from the incidents that inspired them. For example, on several occasions activists told me that Joan Andrews "hears the babies laughing" when she goes into court and that she saw the "babies all around her, laughing" from time to time. Such "experiences" have been reported in print. But her actual experience and the broadly disseminated rhetorical material differed dramatically. The "baby vision" myth began in a Florida courtroom. Joan Andrews had just received a five-year prison sentence for entering an abortion clinic and occupying a procedure room where she tampered with a vacuum aspirator. Andrews (Andrews and Cavanaugh-O'Keefe 1989:189) explained that,

What really happened was that I said to [my sister], 'Can you imagine all those little babies who have been killed? They die, and no one's at their death camps. Can you imagine how they must feel if someone does try to stand up for them? We can't betray them. We can't say that we won't rescue them, because that would offend

---

[7] By contrast, print media such as direct action newsletter articles, more commonly carried stories of personal heroism either literally or metaphorically linked to anti-abortion activism. Such stories often focused on people confronting abortion despite physical abuse or social rejection, or depicted heroic acts nominally unrelated to abortion (such as resisting Nazi control) that authors likened to opposition to abortion.

their dignity. I love these babies.' I said that when I thought about the babies, it made me feel good about what was happening, even when the judge found me guilty and sentenced me to five years in jail. I painted an imaginary picture to explain how I felt, but [my sister] thought I was describing what I saw.

The story circulated that Andrews had "seen the babies," although she affirmed "in fact, I did not see babies all over the courtroom or feel them" (Andrews and Cavanaugh-O'Keefe 1989:188). Andrews' denial of any such visionary experience was printed and widely read before my fieldwork began. Even so, several people I interviewed recommended I read a book of hers that was supposed to contain the story. (I did, but could not find that story in the book itself.) Nonetheless, a perfectly rational, empirically mundane experience had already been transformed into a fictional metaphysical experience and generated an ongoing myth, a myth that effectively verified the existence of life after death, illustrated the concreteness of the "unborn children," justified direct action, and created a prominent mystical figure for the pro-life movement (and especially for direct activists).

While individual experiences of abortion may not have generated such romantic myths, in the aggregate they formed a powerful argument that helped radicalize direct activists. Women working through the aftermath of stressful abortion experiences sometimes joined direct action, then left it as they began to resolve their distress. Direct activists observed such women before they began to mend, and concluded that tragic consequences inevitably followed abortion. For many, this conclusion helped justify radical means for interrupting abortion practice.

Women's experiences of abortion dominated narratives of their activism. In their narratives, these women placed their abortions at the core of their motivation to sit-in. Fellow direct activists attributed such women's activism solely to their abortion experiences.

I will examine the link "Carrie" made between her abortion and her activism, and expand this account through the narratives of the five other women in the sample who had abortions.[8] Carrie had been married once and bore one child when she found herself pregnant by the man who eventually became her second husband. She aborted that

---

[8] Demographically, the people who had aborted a "child" mirrored the sample as a whole, with the main exceptions being that all seven of them had had religious conversions and a larger percentage of them had sat-in more than three times.

pregnancy. Carrie's narrative incorporated the abortion experiences of her sister and a friend in church, to support the conclusion she drew about her own abortion, just as Carrie's story reinforced other direct activists' beliefs.

RESOLVING AMBIGUITY

Women linked diverse problems in their lives to a vilified concept of their abortion experiences, and this linkage appears to have helped women resolve complex and long-standing difficulties. Through regretting and compensating (or "atoning") for their own abortions, women resolved ambiguous feelings and were able to alter behaviors they found undesirable or self-destructive. This connection became an ongoing schema that helped such women cope with subsequent problematic feelings. For example, years after designating her abortion the source of diverse problems in her past, one woman remarked, "Even now I'll realize something I do that is a defense connected to abortion."

Many of the women in this sample intended to compensate for their abortions (in part) by sitting-in. Carrie explained, "I had to do something for that baby that I had killed . . . I knew it wouldn't bring that baby back, but I felt like it would help me, too, to do something." But a long process led Carrie to this approach. Carrie said she first addressed the grief her abortion caused her, years later, by speaking to other women. They directed her to Women Exploited by Abortion (WEBA), an organization that pointed her toward a religious solution to her distress.

Consequently, Carrie began to cope with the irreversible nature of her past by addressing her spiritual state. Although she "was not a Christian at the time," Carrie began to consider how she might safeguard her spiritual salvation, "just in case" God existed. She tried conventional activism but it did not satisfy her need to compensate for her abortion. Just as she was putting her abortion into a cosmic frame of reference, a WEBA contact introduced Carrie to a poem that further solidified her concept of the specific fetus she had aborted, heightened her grief, and intensified her need to make amends. At that point Carrie found WEBA's approach inadequate to cope with the emotions it stimulated. Carrie wept heavier and heavier as she recalled,

And finally when I talked to someone . . . I read that poem and I wasn't a Christian or anything, but I read that poem and I freaked out. I cried for hours and hours . . . The first line says that if I knew then what I know now, you never would have died. It talks about how the mother would have nurtured this daughter and kept her right by her side instead of doing what she had done. And then the very last line, it says, in Jesus' name I ask you, hear my plea, take my baby, hold my baby. Oh, man! . . . I never really put an afterlife onto that child until that day. And I thought gosh, what if? If this baby is real, I want you to pick her up and hold her . . . I guess you can see the emotion, it's been years.

Carrie channeled the religious quest WEBA initiated into direct activism. She remembered,

I was just hurting, I knew I had to do something to make up for what I'd done. I didn't feel like doing this newsletter was enough, and I didn't feel like picketing was enough, so I called Dylan. And he was direct action, big time.

In the grip of her grief, Carrie needed to act. She explained that, "WEBA brings out the feelings, but doesn't take you beyond them a lot . . . Rescue helped me. Rescuing was totally different than WEBA, it helped me."

Through direct activism Carrie performed actions that she considered to be on a par with her abortion. She recalled thinking that she actually could prevent the act that she had "committed." Carrie said she,

felt like if I helped somebody else not make that mistake too, that I would have done something else that would have been so important, it would have been so important to me. And I did. I did stop people.

Direct action apparently helped other women by giving them a way to act against abortion. For example, Lila had been pro-choice but ambivalent about abortion when her partner convinced her to terminate a pregnancy. She resolved her conflicting feelings about abortion when she was "saved" and became pro-life, but she continued to grieve for her lost "child." Twenty years after her abortion she solaced that grief by sitting-in. Lila remarked, "Just to feel I could actively go down and do something . . . Just that feeling that you can actively keep somebody from going in there and making the same mistake I made." She laughed and added, "It changed me forever!"

Carrie made her rescue activities personally relevant by doing most of her sit-ins at the clinic that had performed her abortion. She also wrote to her abortionist, then later picketed his home. This approach exacerbated the alienation she remembered feeling during her abortion. Carrie tearfully explained that,

> I would think they would understand more because they were the ones that did my abortion. I went back and talked to them, and they basically told me, it was Terry [the director of the clinic] basically told me I was crazy. I said, 'Do you talk to all your customers like this?' I told her, 'I had problems! Don't you care?' She said, 'Frankly, no!' They didn't care about me, it was money, that's all it was ... When they took my money, I asked what was this fetus, and she said, 'Oh, you don't have to worry about that; it's just a little blob of tissue. Did you bring the $250?'

Carrie pointed to proof that, through direct action, she was indeed compensating for one "child" by saving another. She explained,

> I knew I couldn't stop everybody. If it was some. If it was some ... And people have come back to me and said, so and so had her baby. Man that's neat! I got to see a baby once that wasn't aborted. That was so neat! The mother was crying, she couldn't believe she almost aborted that baby. It made it worth getting slapped around [by police].

Carrie's experience reinforced several mainstays of pro-lifers' conception of abortion. First, she decided to abort quickly, while under duress, and against the wishes of a partner who later became her husband. In other words, pro-lifers could readily imagine an alternative scenario in which carrying the pregnancy to term would have been feasible. Second, although clinic personnel described Carrie's fetus as a blob of tissue, she later saw physical evidence that it was a "baby," when she passed a limb into her toilet the morning following the abortion. Third, the clinic staff showed disdain and antagonism for Carrie when she returned to them in her search for resolution, thus reinforcing direct activists' impression that abortion was heartless and profit-driven, an "exploitative industry." Picketers told me about Carrie's experiences long before I met her.

The women considered here (as well as those in a controversial study by Reardon, described below) thought of their abortions as final and irreversible acts.[9] This concept hinged on their belief that they killed

---

[9] Reardon's (1987) strongly anti-abortion biased study of abortion sequelae drew upon 252 responses to a survey he conducted among members of WEBA in 42 states. He chose 20 accounts to represent the types of circumstances he found

children by aborting (regardless of fetal age) and that those "children" were irreplaceable. Although, in crosscultural perspective, these concepts are not universal perceptions of pregnancy and abortion (Devereux 1979; Rylko-Bauer 1991), all of these women expressed them. One woman explained,

> I might not have been as radical as I am . . . if I hadn't had an abortion . . . The pain is knowing you've destroyed a life, and that was something that was given to you by God. That's the pain of knowing you can never undo it. That's what I try to tell these [women considering abortion].

Pro-lifers concluded that women who aborted must suffer because pro-lifers believed that abortion was wrong and that wrongs bring about hurt or punishment (Peterman 1991). A corollary to this paradigm was that wrongs can also be forgiven, and so absolved. This philosophical connection appears to have helped women cope with the grief and guilt they felt for having aborted.

Severely censuring abortion appeared to help these women resolve the ambiguity surrounding their own experiences. They remembered the contradictory thoughts, emotions, and pressures they had felt when deciding to abort. They described concurrent, yet conflicting desires to keep and to end their pregnancies, to feel and to stop feeling, and to do both as they wanted and as they thought they should. These feelings surrounded their abortion decisions both immediately preceding their abortions and for years following. In retrospect, women remembered why, at the time, they had thought they could not (or should not) continue a pregnancy, then reflected on their actual ability to have done so, and agonized over their decisions.

Censure drew clear lines between "right" and "wrong," and so may have helped these women experience remorse and anguish in a cathartic fashion and then move away from agonizing ambiguity and toward a stable resolution. By repudiating their abortions, a lifetime of accumulated regret and despair was gathered into one event, explained, repented, and then either transformed or expunged.

---

surrounding abortion decisions in his survey results. These 20 women described how they came to abort, the effects their abortions had on them, and how they coped with those outcomes. Given his sample, I have used Reardon's study as a description of *damaging* abortion sequelae, although he presents it as a generalizable description of the impact of abortion on women's lives.

Most of these women explained that they came to see their abortions as central causes of diverse, severe problems in their lives, including a marked loss of self-esteem. One woman in Reardon's study (1987:87) recalled,

> I started to think about my life then – something clicked in me. I began to realize that everything I had done – the abortions, drugs, affairs, depressions – had all been a result of the circumstances of my first abortion . . . My decision to abort distorted my ability to make other decisions.

The activist I call Karen told me, "I got real messed up because I had an abortion at 17 . . . It totally contaminates every part of your life . . . My whole life was haywire after the abortion." Eventually, she "got into alcohol and drugs" and "stopped feeling." Karen associated a series of tragic events with her abortion. Within a year of her abortion, she had what she described as a "replacement baby," Mark, who died of Sudden Infant Death Syndrome at 38 days of age. Six months later she was gang raped by three men, two of whom were her coworkers; she blamed herself and "felt filthy." Shortly afterwards, she married "the first man who came along" because she "just wanted to have babies." When that man became physically abusive, she divorced him and married a man who emotionally abused her. Karen said she had been a "very sensitive warm person but I went to being a very hard, insensitive person." She recalled, "I didn't feel. I didn't have any self-esteem." She became depressed and did not "bond" or "relate well" with her children. These subsequent traumas contributed to the anguish Karen later resolved by adopting Christianity, repenting her abortion, and feeling absolved.

Carrie equated her abortion to murder and, through this extreme construal, explained to herself why she felt devastated by her abortion. Like other pro-lifers, Carrie emphasized the need to suffer for aborting. She wept many times as she explained that aborting agonized people because it was the same as murder, declaring,

> I know that those people who eventually come to their senses and realize that they killed somebody that they could see, being drunk when they did it or whatever, when they come around and they realize what they did, they never really forget it. Well, it's the same thing with the abortion . . . On the TV they showed this guy who threw his baby down a trash chute into a compacter, to crush his

baby. He knew what he was doing. Only difference is, he seen his victim before he did it. I didn't. You can't separate it. The feelings are there, no matter what. That I did that . . . It's just that I didn't see mine before I did it. I hired someone to do it . . . It would be no different than if I took $250 and told someone to kill my son. There really would be no difference. It's just that one is more helpless.

The nature of her own abortion experience not only reinforced Carrie's concept that she had killed a person, it also reinforced other direct activists' belief in the humanity of fetuses, and the consequent anguish they believed abortion must cause women. Carrie wept again while she explained that,

It was an incomplete abortion. The next day I passed pieces in the toilet. It was real strange because you know it's human. What was I going to do? Give it a burial? And I remember a million thoughts flashed through my mind . . . I just wanted it out of my life . . . I didn't want to talk to anyone . . . I didn't want to talk to my husband about it when we finally got together.

Carrie's abortion preceded a prolonged depression during which she attempted suicide several times. She also became depressed during pregnancies she carried to term both before and after the abortion. Carrie's physician suspected a chemical imbalance and treated her with "almost every drug" available. As Carrie put it, they had only one or two drug therapies left to try before they ran out, and none had alleviated her depression. Despite this medical diagnosis and her prior and subsequent depressions, Carrie attributed the distress that precipitated her suicide attempts to her abortion, saying, "I could pinpoint the depression to the abortion."

Carrie's depression affirmed the model posed in pro-life rhetoric and repeated in direct activists' informal discourse. Pro-lifers argued that, sooner or later, most women would suffer after aborting, but that some women (particularly those who had already carried a pregnancy to term) were predisposed to suffer more or sooner than others. Carrie recalled,

I had the abortion and went crazy immediately. Within minutes I was . . . like a roller coaster emotionally . . . I knew what I did. It was obvious what I did. Any time you know about development . . . it's awful.

Sitting-in landed activists in jail, where they met women who reinforced their conception that abortion nearly inevitably harmed women.
The activist I call Cynthia had a legal abortion at age 18 and suffered
medical complications that eventually left her sterile. She grieved for
the child she lost by aborting and for her inability to conceive subsequent children. Time and again, while in police custody for sitting-in,
Cynthia found herself engaged in intimate, emotional conversations
with inmates – conversations stimulated by her presence as an activist.
Cynthia found her own grief mirrored in these women. She drew out
their sorrow through her expectations, yet many direct activists who
had never aborted reported similar encounters. The grief expressed by
inmates who had aborted reinforced direct activists' beliefs about abortion. Cynthia's arguments typified those of other activists. She insisted
that,

> Post abortion syndrome is so real, I just can't emphasize how real
> it is to you. I could get you a lot of girls to talk to, that have gone
> through what I've gone through that had abortions . . . The emo-
> tional trauma that comes along with abortion can be so buried
> in your conscience to where you have all these problems but
> you're in such denial in your mind that you'll never relate it to
> abortion . . . Some of the things that [they do], the drinking, the
> drugs . . . you're trying to bury that pain. I've sat with girls and
> they've said, 'My abortion doesn't bother me, my abortion doesn't
> bother me,' so many times that they start crying . . . I was locked
> up in the fishbowl in the county once and this girl started cussin'
> me out saying, 'I've had five abortions and none of them bothered
> me.' Real tough, you know. And I said, 'Yes they do, I know they
> do.' And she broke. She started crying. Because I didn't yell back
> at her and I just said, 'I've had an abortion. I know it bothers you.
> I know at night when you're by yourself and you think about that
> baby and then when you're around other children, I know how it
> bothers ya.' And then they'll break! . . . Abortion is not a friend
> to women, it's not a friend to children, it's not a friend to female
> fetuses – it's not a friend!

Over a third of Reardon's sample (1987) iterated Carrie's contention
that the "wounds of abortion" healed when women talked about them,
that is, when they ceased keeping their experiences to themselves. However, even those women who did not talk to people about their abortions

said they found solace when they talked to God.[10] In a sense these women let God into their abortion experiences instead of bearing the experiences, and the consequences they associated with them, alone.

Religion played a salient role in many women's recoveries.[11] Through a religious reinterpretation of their worldviews, women reconstructed their life histories, reconstrued their current states, and so, alleviated their distress. Like other direct activists who had aborted, Karen argued that repentance removed a barrier to happiness. After repenting her abortion, she redefined her self-identity and her relationships. Karen recounted that one morning, shortly after she "became a Christian," she was getting into her car when,

> A voice spoke to my heart and said, 'Remember that abortion you had?' I had denied it for years. I was pro-abortion, I was a member of the ACLU . . . I said, 'Lord, I never confessed to you that I had an abortion, and I had an abortion and I ask you to forgive me. I'm really sorry I did it. It was wrong and I'm sorry I did it.' And every muscle in my body relaxed! It was like for years I was holding those muscles tense. It was such a relief to confess this to the Lord.

This confession removed a depression of many years standing. Karen remembered that, "It was like a cloud that was over my mind; when I was delivered from that depression it was like a cloudy thing was removed." She said that this transition allowed her to resolve the grief she felt over the deaths of her infant son and a miscarried child. She recalled,

> When I had Mark and he died . . . I didn't allow myself to grieve so I was carrying around a lot of despair. When I said goodbye to

[10] Similarly, Reardon noted that, "in the years that followed [their abortions], most felt increasingly isolated from others by the pain and doubts associated with their abortion experiences" (1987:30).

[11] Seventeen of the 20 women in Reardon's sample reported resolving the distress they felt after aborting, although resolution required many years. Fifteen of those 17 women said that they recovered because of God's acceptance of them. God either forgave them, loved and accepted them unconditionally, or simply "was there" for them. WEBA's program probably helped shape the resolution these women found. Like Alcoholics Anonymous, WEBA "encourages aborted women to draw on that same Higher Power, rebuilding their lives around the spiritual message of forgiveness, hope, and eternal life" (Reardon 1987:30). However, many of the 20 women were "born again" *before* joining WEBA. Although WEBA encouraged women to resolve their abortion experiences through religion, other women unaffiliated with WEBA did so on their own.

this [aborted] child, and said I'm going to see this child in heaven some day, I was able to forgive myself...I said I'm really sorry I took your life...I was able to grieve for Mark, and I realized I was never able to grieve for the child I miscarried.

Afterwards, she was able to tell her seven children for the first time that she loved them, and she and her husband (who also "was saved" around that time) became "two different people" and rebuilt their marriage.[12]

Women clarified the ambiguity of diverse acts, decisions, and patterns of behavior by attributing them to one central cause – an abortion – then resolving the abortion experience. Vilifying abortion reclassified it, removing the ambiguity surrounding the abortion decision so that it "had" to be rejected. Moreover, that rejection could only be done by something outside the woman herself (removing the onus from her). Unlike "lesser deeds," amenable to various correctives, the extremity of the irreparable act found a "natural resolution" in God's forgiveness.

These women redefined their personal experiences of grief by placing them in the larger framework of salvation. In that context, they solved the seemingly intractable problem posed by an irreversible past.

SALVATION

The women considered here explained that their concepts of salvation initially pointed them toward direct action to resolve the torment they associated with their abortions. Some women spoke of sitting-in to compensate or atone for the "child" they killed, others said they sat-in to be saved through "good works." Still others said they sat-in because they knew abortion was "wrong" and harmful, and they felt they had a responsibility to stop other women from "making the same mistake" they had made.

Women's commitment to activism rose and fell with changes in their concepts of salvation. For example, Carrie began to address her abortion experience before she was "born again." At that time she questioned the

---

[12] The connection Karen made between abortion and the difficulties she had in her life, and especially those related to her children, might have stemmed, in part, from a negative association she made between abortion and mothering long before her own abortion experience. Throughout her childhood, Karen's own mother threatened her, beat her, and reminded her that she had been an unwanted child. Karen recalled, "I got a lot of abuse from my mother. She told me herself that she tried to abort me herself and wasn't successful. I didn't have to do anything bad to be beaten."

existence of God, but decided to safeguard her future by atoning for her abortion through "good works," that is, through rescuing. She explained that she sat-in because,

> I thought I had to work my way to salvation, if there was a God, I had to work my way through good works. I wanted to know God. Since I did this horrible thing. If He's the creator, He created us, and I did this horrible thing and killed His creation, I had to make it up . . . It was something I felt like I had to do. I felt like I had to work my way into heaven. I felt like it was on merit.

After hearing about direct action, Carrie recalled, "I thought, why didn't they do that when I went for my abortion?" Direct action allowed Carrie to express her regret, make amends, and promote her potential salvation.

But direct action did not resolve the anguish in Carrie's life. Although rescue addressed Carrie's distress, it also caused her to relive the pain she associated with her abortion. She explained that,

> When I was rescuing, you see the women. I remember walking back in to one of the procedure rooms and getting kind of sick . . . It's a sick room. The first time I walked in it was like panic; I wanted to run out . . . Psychologically, it was too much. You go through it, and then you have to keep living it over and over and over. Every time you go to one of those clinics to sit-in, you know those women go in there to have abortions and you go through it . . . I used to cry constantly. And I would re-live it and I would re-live it over, and over.

Sometime after she began sitting-in, Carrie experienced another depression. Upon narrowly surviving one suicide attempt, she became wildly despondent and contemplated yet another. Her depression vanished instantaneously when she was "saved." She wept as she recalled,

> I tried to kill myself, actually I did die, and they revived me a couple of times, and they said it was a miracle I was alive . . . They released me and I went home and was into it with my husband . . . That was the last straw. I just broke down and I was gone. And I said, I just can't do this any more, if you don't take care of these problems for me I would just as soon die . . . I just thank God for it. It was then that he poured out his spirit and I felt it. It was like warm

electricity all around me. And I knew that God was real, and I always thought before that the Bible was just a book. And I knew that God was alive. And so I remember it was like joy! A joy, almost like schizophrenic, it was limitless. I was so happy, I just couldn't believe. God was real and I knew it right then.

Soon afterwards, her husband was also "saved," stopped drinking and verbally abusing her, and their marriage was restored. (Like Karen, Carrie's first marriage had ended because her husband was physically abusive.) Carrie's understanding of salvation and the course of her involvement in direct action were altered by that religious experience.

Once she no longer felt her salvation depended on earning "merit" Carrie turned away from the pain direct action caused. She concluded that her recovery required moving beyond sit-ins and explained,

I don't get involved [in rescue] the same way that I used to. It brought back so much . . . Somewheres along in the line of life you got to put it on the shelf. You got to start being able to be more objective, and I couldn't because I was so involved and so emotional . . . Almost what I'm doing now, just talking to people, is enough . . . But it's enough. I can't do so much that I get wrapped up in it emotionally.

Carrie first conceived of direct action as a means to obtain salvation, and salvation, indeed, relieved her of her anguish – and her motivation to sit-in. Carrie had become a direct activist to safeguard her future by atoning for her abortion through "good works." Once her doubts about God's existence were resolved, she came to feel her salvation was secured through divine grace. At that point, which came after several years of involvement, Carrie withdrew from direct action to relieve the continual distress it caused her. She returned to conventional anti-abortion activities that centered on talking. Carrie explained that she continued "talking to women" to help them avoid pain such as she had suffered following her abortion.

TALKING

Carrie said she measured a woman's pain (and to some extent, her mental health) by her ability to talk about her abortion. She concluded that such discourse was an essential part of coping with abortion-related stress. Throughout Carrie's narrative, talking about one's abortion experience symbolized well-being, or at least progress toward recovery. Carrie's narrative was frequently punctuated with the comment that women were hurting and she recognized their pain in their inability to talk about their abortions. She repeated this theme, saying,

> I don't think it's just me because I know too many people that, they don't want to talk about it . . . The women out there who have had the abortions, you can't get 'em to talk. When you think about that, you can draw the conclusion that it bugs them.

Carry related the harm abortion did her, her sister, and a friend in church through this trope. At the beginning of the depression that followed her abortion, Carrie could not talk about her own abortion. Her continued inability to do so when the depression diminished proved to her the need of further healing. Then, Carrie indicated the extent of her sister June's distress by recounting June's unwillingness to talk after ending a pregnancy. Unbeknownst to Carrie, June had become pregnant in her early teens by a married neighbor her father's age; she aborted that pregnancy. When, some time later, Carrie disparaged abortion, June refused to speak to her in any way for a three-year period, while they were living together in their parents' home.

Carrie also told me the dramatic story of a friend and member of her church, who became a fellow direct activist. Carrie said this woman, Rosanne, was in the military when she became pregnant by a high-ranking, married officer. Rosanne told Carrie that she had been six-and-a-half months pregnant and planning to carry to term when military physicians convinced her she was carrying a "retarded, deformed baby." Rosanne felt coerced and deceived when she delivered a live, well-formed female child during her saline abortion. Rosanne apparently repressed the memory of her abortion experience for 13 years. In the interim she gave birth to two daughters. Carrie told how, when Rosanne recalled the experience, she grieved deeply, participated in direct action for some time, then withdrew from activism altogether. Carrie was present the day Rosanne remembered her abortion; she recounted Rosanne's experiences, recalling that,

> She gave a live birth to a saline abortion. The nurse went out of the room and she delivered real quick. And she sat there and rocked the baby. Six-and-a-half-months pregnant. She said she was perfect and the doctors said she was deformed and convinced her to have the abortion. You know, 'You're going to have a retarded,

deformed baby.' And they kept telling her that. And she gave birth to a beautifully shaped, perfectly healthy little baby girl, except for the salt poisoning . . . She was six-and-a-half-months pregnant and she went crazy. Literally crazy. For 13 years she forgot about it. She forgot she had one. She rocked her baby until she died. She was really hurt. She remembered it while she was in church. And she freaked out. She screamed right in the middle of the church service and ran out of the church building. She ran home, locked herself in her room. She was in there for two days and they finally broke the door down and got her out. She won't talk to anybody about it now. She went into it for a while. She was to the point though, that she would hit someone that would say abortion is OK . . . She got hostile. Oh man. I felt sorry for her . . . You could tell that her every waking moment she had a picture embedded of that baby and what that baby looked like. It was like her every waking moment. She had nightmares. She just ate, slept, woke to this baby, this other daughter of hers. But she didn't remember that abortion for years. It was so weird. It was like her mind just couldn't take it, couldn't handle what she had done. It's murder, what she did was. She just couldn't handle it. And when she talks over this, the whole time, every time, [she] is shaking. Because, she just can't get rid of it.

When direct activists recounted Rosanne's story, she was caught perpetually in the agony of her grief and guilt. This frozen glimpse into Rosanne's life convinced activists that she remained so, remembering her dying daughter to the exclusion of all else, her mental health ruined by that single past experience. Rosanne's story illustrated the inevitability of suffering as a consequence of abortion. Rosanne, a would-be mother rocking her dying daughter, escaped that experience through 13 years of "denial," only to be revisited by the knowledge that she had "murdered" her own "perfect child," and then live on, unable to escape that consuming "fact." Furthermore, Rosanne's story thoroughly vilified her partner and the physicians who aborted her fetus. She had reluctantly aborted at the urging of corrupt physicians and a self-serving, adulterous partner, who duped Rosanne and sacrificed her child to hide his own guilt and shirk his responsibility. In Rosanne's story, abortion was an irreversible, grotesque, and damning act.

When Rosanne picketed during sit-ins, her presence gave direct activists firsthand exposure to the trauma she associated with her abortion. Her sudden and complete withdrawal from activism, and from talking about her abortion experience, left direct activists with an ominous story of tragic exploitation and perpetual suffering in the aftermath of abortion. The circumstances of Rosanne's abortion amplified direct activists' images of abortionists as heartless, immoral, and corrupt, and of women as vulnerable and damaged. Rosanne's experience supported direct activists' contentions that legal abortion allowed men to exploit women they would otherwise be forced to support, and that abortion killed healthy children and devastated women in the process.

The way rescue was conducted enhanced the impact of such stories. Rescue drew women working through past abortion experiences; consequently, direct activists tended to meet such women when they were in the process of confronting negative aspects of their abortion experiences. However, as Carrie demonstrated, women tended to leave direct action as they resolved their grief. The ephemeral nature of most participation in direct action gave activists only partial views of such processes, suspended the women's experiences in time and, so, provided activists ample anecdotal evidence of harm done by abortion.[13]

The narratives of direct activists who had aborted suggested that, over time, many lessened or resolved their distress, whether through activism or salvation. Like Carrie, most saw themselves undergoing a healing process that would eventually take them beyond the anguish they felt at any given point – including the point at which other direct activists knew them. Lila said that before she joined direct action she would cry "when it just welled up within me that this was my child. I would never see him." She cried again as she explained,

There's been a real healing process. The rescue where I counseled, I spent the day crying. I just feel like God was really healing, really bringing out all that pain and hidden hurt. It's a gradual thing.

CONCLUSION

Cohen and Roth (1984:142–3) found that women who thought and talked about their abortion experiences (despite the upset such contemplation caused) were less depressed and anxious than women who avoided such processing. Depression and anxiety tended to persist among women who avoided talking and thinking about their abortions, and

---

[13] The discussion of "Bailey" in a previous chapter showed how people who never aborted were powerfully influenced to become pro-life by watching friends and relatives suffer after aborting.

such women generally continued this approach over time. These findings lend credence to Carrie's observation, that women who refused to
talk about their abortions tended to be hurting.

The symptoms described by postabortal women in the St. Louis sample were within the range of symptoms reported in Callahan's (1988)
summary of literature on the controversial topic of Post-Abortion
Syndrome (PAS) and Speckhard's (1985) doctoral research findings on
PAS.[14] These authors suggest PAS is indicated most clearly by feelings
of loss, sadness, regret, guilt, and the need to grieve, often accompanied
by "anxiety, depression, and hostility."

The narratives of activists who had aborted suggested that these feelings resonated with the emotional consequences of other stressful events
in their lives – events that occurred both before and after their abortions.
These women addressed the distress they associated with their abortions
through their activism. They designated that single event as the cause of
their anguish, and then resolved that experience, in part through direct
action, and more permanently, through redemption and salvation.

The meanings these women gave to their abortion experiences were
linked to the coping strategies they employed. As a consequence of
developing clear concepts of their aborted "children," these activists
thought of themselves as having cooperated in their own "children's
murders." Consequently, they felt intense grief, remorse, or guilt that,
in turn, impelled their activism. They sat-in either to atone for having
aborted or to fulfill their "responsibility" to other women, to "children
threatened" by abortion, or to God.

While still an active "rescuer," Hillary illustrated the synergy created
when women's desires to save "babies," atone, protect other women from
aborting, and serve God, converged. Such convergence created a consistent ideology that resolved ambiguous feelings and impelled direct
activism. In her late teens and twenties Hillary had been an ardently
liberal activist. She had joined Students for a Democratic Society, rejected conservative sexual mores, helped organize a commune, protested
nuclear power plants, the destruction of the environment, the Vietnam
War, and the Kent State massacre. However, when pressured to abort by
her partner, her liberal intellect had warred with her emotional opposition to abortion. Her decision to abort left her with unresolved conflicts.

---

[14] Speckhard's dissertation research focused exclusively on women who experienced
traumatic reactions to abortion. Callahan's paper was directed toward public
healthcare providers and policymakers.

Years later, this ambivalence was eradicated when she became an evangelical, and established an unambiguous position opposing abortion. In conformity with her new concept of salvation and in response to her abortion experience, she joined prolife direct action and argued that,

> Guilt is a very healthy thing. It is the vehicle that brings a person to repentance . . . The only thing that causes healing is repentance. There has to be an acknowledging of the sin, and a turning away from the sin. Rescue is basically doing what Christ did for us . . . We remove a woman who is in imminent danger of spiritual death and a child who is in danger of imminent physical death, and put them nearer Christ . . . It's the real stuff of the Bible come to life. It was the most powerful experience. To suffer for the cause of Christ is an amazing experience . . . What your captors mean for evil is experienced for good.

While also still an active "rescuer," Cynthia expressed the consuming nature of this powerful nexus of thinking, feeling, and acting. She declared, "I would be violating my entire being if I didn't speak out. I would be violating my entire existence if I didn't speak out right now." Cynthia, too, indicated the linkages between her emotional turmoil, her concept of salvation, and her activism, saying,

> I probably would have made a great proabort if I hadn't found the Lord. You can't live with that pain without making some sense of it all . . . I was convinced God would never forgive me for the abortion [until] I heard about this merciful, loving God . . . That God's there to forgive us. I just said, 'I want to know God and I want him to forgive me' . . . I really believe I was born for this . . . I believe I am called according to his planned purposes. And I really believe all this garbage that happened to me, He's turned around and He's restored, and now I can make a difference.

As one woman after another addressed her abortion-related distress through activism, other direct activists saw slices of these personal experiences of abortion. In the aggregate, these encounters formed a powerful argument, encouraging activists to contend that tragic consequences inevitably followed abortion. For some activists, this perspective justified radical means for interrupting abortion practice. The powerful role women's concepts of salvation played in their decisions to engage in direct action shows how integral private symbolism was to commitment.

CHAPTER SIX

PRO-LIFE CONVICTION

Listening to activists tell me how they came to sit-in, as they strolled along picketlines, I was struck by how often they would conclude their stories by saying, "And that's how I became convicted to pro-life," or by asking me, "And how did you become convicted to pro-life?" (giving me the opportunity to explain my role as researcher). Most activists told of personal experiences or social roles that exposed them to the abortion issue. They placed those experiences within an intellectual and emotional progression that many labeled "conviction." Over 80% of the activists interviewed described such a process.[1]

Activists described conviction as an obligation placed on them from an external source. Among all three cohorts, conviction provided a divine unction that helped overcome recruits' reluctance to incur the costs of direct activism. Such experiences strongly related to high levels of participation in direct action.

---

[1] Twenty interviewees (25%) actually used the term while describing the process, 45 interviewees (56.25%) described the process but did not use the term, and 13 interviewees (16.25%) neither used the term this way nor described the process. Two interviewees (2.5%) appeared to describe the process, but did not do so clearly or completely; I classified them as uncodable. I did not classify interviewees as having described a conviction experience if they said they acted on their convictions (moral acts they chose to do), or if they felt compelled to become activists but did not mention an external source, such as God, as the motivating force.

While "conviction" was important to activists in all three cohorts, it was far more pervasive in the second and third cohorts than in the first. Sixty-seven percent of activists in the first cohort were "convicted" as opposed to 78% and 88% of activists of the second and third cohorts, respectively.

Some activists recounted instantaneous, and often emotionally over-whelming, conviction experiences. Several individuals said they cried uncontrollably upon becoming convicted and concluded that, "Nothing else mattered." Such convictions usually entailed a precipitating event. For example, pro-life videos radically altered the perspectives of many recruits. One activist recalled, "I saw that movie and came out of there a changed person."

Other activists described a slower, stepwise progression toward con-viction that, ultimately, established an equally emotionally intense commitment. Such slower progressions usually began when individuals conceived of fetuses as concrete individuals, then strengthened when they conceptualized abortion as agonizing to both fetus and mother, culminating in an intense commitment to stop abortions.

Whether their convictions had been slow or immediate, interview-ees made equivalent or even identical statements when describing their conviction experiences. In either case, individuals might describe a "stir in the heart," or remember that "the Lord pierced our hearts with the conviction" or that they received "a leading from the Lord." Some remarked, "It tendered out my heart," or "God prepared my heart."

Conviction was essentially a divine unction that created a moral commitment. Many activists agreed, "We have the moral imperative from God." A few interviewees spoke of "God's angels going to and fro throughout the nation marking people" who were to become active. Most interviewees said they became active because "God convicted" them or because "the Lord calls me to do it," not because of intellectual efforts, through study, or by their own doing. One person explained, "I realized, *that* is what God wanted me to do." Others remarked that, "God tells His children what to do," and, "This would be a step of obedience," or that, "God revealed to me that I needed to do more on this issue." Several interviewees remembered that God gave them a sign that directed them to become active. One woman, who had resisted activism until she experienced an instantaneous conviction, explained that "God just zapped me! You don't argue with the Lord; that's stupid!"

The divine guidance they attributed to conviction reassured inter-viewees. One activist remembered thinking, "I should do this, it's OK, I'm under God's protection." Others spoke of receiving "a holy boldness." The divine mandate strengthened activists' commitment; several agreed that, "By conviction, you'll face death." Another remembered that, "It broke my heart when we started actively doing more than picketing;

it was fearful, yet I felt the pleasure of God."[2] Several recalled "the feeling that this was pleasing to God."

Many interviewees explained that God intervened to teach them about abortion, thereby obligating them to become active against it. Some said, "the Lord shows you," or "the Lord spoke about the abortion issue." One activist concluded, "I had a personal responsibility to act on behalf of these helpless people." In essence, they were made aware, and so responsible. Some individuals related this responsibility to their personal salvation. One woman explained that, "The spirit said this is what you should do to make retribution," another activist sat-in "knowing I have to face God one day."

Yet attitudes do not necessarily dictate practice. Some interviewees described a conviction experience (and even used the term) but did not sit-in. Although they felt impelled by God to assail legalized abortion, they did not necessarily understand that injunction as a mandate to sit-in. They either felt "called" to some other aspect of activism or another factor in their lives outweighed the obligation they felt to sit-in. For example, one woman was repelled by the conflict, danger, and undignified treatment direct action could entail. She said she did not sit-in because the "police abused" direct activists too much; she preferred "carrying signs about lifting up Jesus" which she thought was "a nicer way to let people know this is wrong." A small group of interviewees who maintained a regular presence at particular abortion clinics over a period of years, said they were "convicted to pro-life," but they were not "called" to sit-in.

Conviction was a transformation of attitude and daily life orientation that usually preceded participation in direct action. Conviction appeared to be a form of conversion, often founded on religious beliefs or described as an intensification of religiosity or commitment to acting upon religious beliefs. However, conviction was not necessarily linked to a change in religious affiliation or the advent of a religious life. Although voiced in a religious idiom and prompted at least in part by religious beliefs, conviction appeared to be a form of secular conversion. It entailed both cognitive and affective changes that resonated to alter the individual's self-concept, worldview, and behavior.

Eric, one of the most active figures in St. Louis's early pro-life direct action, described his own conviction, saying,

---

[2] Direct activists spoke of their hearts being broken when their resistance or apathy toward something was replaced by willingness or empathy, not when they became sad or dejected.

I think I was very similar with a lot of pro-life people in that there was an event or a series of events that occurred that brought them to not only be against abortion but to be involved in the pro-life movement, and particularly to be involved in rescues or to be very involved in lobbying and like that.

For most people active in pro-life there is an event, I call it a conversion experience, not in the sense of a religious conversion, although sometimes it's tied in with that. But there's a definite before and after. The before may have been, yes, they're opposed to abortion. It may have been that they were in favor of abortion. But the after is, they are personally committed to do something to stop it. It may be rescues, it may not be. But there's a personal commitment there, and there is a conversion experience there.

And it comes different ways. For many people it's being at the abortion clinic and visually seeing women going in, contemplating what's going to be happening to that woman and her unborn child. If you were to picket... there on the second floor you can hear the vacuum aspirator... Seeing someone getting arrested at an abortion clinic or going to jail... Or because they read about me and some of the people who were going to jail... For other people, they'll see the dead baby pictures and they'll just be horrified. They'll say, 'I didn't know this was what was going on. I didn't know. I didn't realize. What can I do to stop it?' Sometimes it will just be a friend or they'll know somebody who had an abortion. And more and more nowadays, someone who had an abortion themselves, and realized how terrible it is and how awful it's been to themselves, will do that. It's those types of visual things.

I find it is something that will trigger that. It's very similar to people who have been brought up in a mainstream Catholic or Protestant church but eventually will come to some sort of a spiritual awakening. It's very similar to that.

What Is Conversion?

The push-pull (or deprivation-ideology) theory of religious conversion describes conversion as a diachronic process and explores the causal relationships between social and psychological preadaptation of individuals and their consequent involvement in religious movements (Cohn 1961; Galanter 1982; Kidahl 1965; Simmonds 1977; Taylor 1976; Ullman 1982). Although preoccupation with preadaptive processes dominated the literature on conversion (Snow and Machalek 1984) for much of the past century, the adequacy and relevance of this model have been challenged more recently (Cucchiari 1988; Heirich 1977; Stark and Bainbridge 1980). Research increasingly focuses on the social means that bring about conversion and the psychological processes involved, toward the process itself – the nature of conversion and how it occurs.

Researchers have increasingly shifted away from a view of conversion as pathology, social deviance, or coping mechanism to see conversion as a creative process (Cucchiari 1988). It is conceptualized as a "religious quest" or biography reconstruction, a "paradigm shift" or a changed "universe of discourse" or "root reality." This approach frames conversion as a universal human potential, not a process limited to the socially or psychologically pathological.

Conversion may be conceptualized as a singularly powerful and significant instance of the continually emergent process whereby all individuals impose order on the flux of experience (cf. Berger and Luckmann 1966; cf. Whorf 1956). People continually interpret experience according to their own individual histories, knowledge, values, and cognitive processes (McCombs 1985). In conversion, the newly established order constitutes a perceptible shift from former interpretations of reality and may noticeably alter the individual's attitudes and behavior.

Conversion may be seen as a process of maturation and enlightenment based on a changed understanding and appropriation of social and material conditions. The individual reinterprets past experiences to fit into a newly learned worldview, redefines the self, and accepts the moral responsibility inherent in this new moral order (Cucchiari 1988). The individual's self-identity emerges as a new, restructured whole, encompassing past understandings, interpreted, however, from a new perspective (cf. Kegan 1985:189).

THE PERSPECTIVE CLARIFIED

Above all, conviction clarified one's perspective and foregrounded the moral demands that new understanding placed on the individual. But what was being clarified? During this period in American society, emerging gender contructs challenged the naturalness of traditional male, female, and familial roles and labeled them cultural constructions (Ginsburg 1989; Luker 1984). Harding (1981) describes two competing family ideologies that related to these changes and informed opposing approaches women took toward issues such as abortion. One ideology stresses "equality, individualism, and reason"; the other stresses "hierarchy, wholism [sic], and morality" (1981:58). Harding labels these two ideologies (and the strategies they generate) "egalitarian" and "hierarchical," respectively.[3]

The egalitarian strategy (Harding 1981:59) emphasizes the individual and,

> The personal well-being, fulfillment, and prosperity of family members. An equitable division of rights and responsibilities is idealized as the best means of expressing individual ability and inclination. Secular authorities, such as psychologists and doctors, are relied upon to justify arrangements and deal with crises in an individualized manner.

The hierarchical strategy (Harding 1981:58–9) defines one's place within the family,

> In relation to the whole, in terms of a family role, the emphasis is on conformity to standards of right and wrong. Wives and husbands, mothers and fathers, children and parents naturally have unequal rights and responsibilities in the family, and the symbolic authority and prestige of the father are stressed. Kin and religious authorities are relied upon to justify arrangements and to handle crisis situations by appealing to a shared sense of moral behavior.

Harding's (1981) typology encompasses the dichotomies that Luker (1984) and Ginsburg (1989) used to describe pro-choice and pro-life activists' conceptualizations of women's social roles and the strategies activists employed to improve women's material and cultural options. According to Luker and Ginsburg, pro-life women tend to value the ethics underlying a hierarchical strategy more than those entailed in an egalitarian strategy. Such preferences form the basis from which individuals draw their self-identities and their material security (Harding 1981).[4]

---

[3] Harding (1981) refutes the idea that Americans share a common ideology regarding the family, and argues that conflicts between feminists and conservatives cannot be understood without acknowledging these differences. Similarly, analysts misinterpret the basis of violent activism when they assume that radical activists and mainstream society share common conceptualizations and ethics regarding law, order, and violence (Rose 1969).

[4] Harding, however, questions the determinative link between socioeconomic position and family strategies that Luker emphasized.

These models are ideal types; most individuals employ both strategies in varying proportions. But these models help explain activists' conceptualizations of abortion, their opposition to it, and their willingness to escalate the assertiveness of their opposition. Conviction appears to have clarified the ambiguity inherent in a blending of these two ideologies, privileging one ideology over the other. I was struck over and over by the calm certitude active rescuers evinced. They seemed reasurred by the consistent ideology they had adopted.

I would like to extend Harding's model beyond family strategies to consider a broader range of personal conduct and social relations. In doing this, I will refer to relational strategies rather than familial strategies. Harding's model corresponds to the thoughts and responses direct activists described, just as it helps explain the beliefs and actions of pro-lifers more generally. Like pro-lifers in Luker's (1984) and Ginsburg's (1989) samples, direct activists favored hierarchical rather than egalitarian relational strategies.

Legal, political, and lifestyle changes begun in the 1960s placed the egalitarian strategy in ascendence. Throughout the 1970s a backlash formed against this incipient ethical hegemony (Faludi 1991; Ginsburg 1993; Ginsburg and Tsing 1990), and pro-life direct action was part of that backlash.

Collective action in opposition to a dominant regime reaffirms the actuality of an alternative group's identity. Rebellion reaffirms existence; as Albert Camus argued, "'I rebel, therefore we exist'" (quoted in Rose 1969:39). Radical activism arises out of a conflict between divergent ethical perspectives. Activism that brings about "crisis and drama" aims not only to control others, but to illuminate a conflict of ethical values. Violent activism attempts to change the very norms that existing forms of social control are designed to defend (Rose 1969).

Direct activists expressed a sense of exclusion from mainstream society, and this perceived marginalization helped push them away from conventional political activism. Conventional means for attaining political change hold appeal only "when a commonly shared view exists concerning the ultimate possibility of change *within* a system" (Rose 1969:xiii). As confidence in their ability to participate effectively in conventional political processes fades, groups tend to adopt more radical forms of activism (Rose 1969), and this dynamic characterized pro-life direct action, especially in the 1980s.

Theories of political violence focus on the attempts of disenfranchised groups – especially the poor – to gain access to resources through violent means (and reciprocally, on regimes' violent attempts to maintain a status quo). Demographically, direct activists did not fit this profile; they were not excluded literally from political or economic power. However, the ideology supporting abortion excluded their preferred relational strategy. Legal abortion threatened the hierarchical way of life, affirmed an ideology that undermined traditional gender roles and not only defined identity independent of parenthood, but as a matter of individual choice. These complaints were not novel to direct activists, conventional pro-life activists voiced them, as well.

Direct activists' private discourse expressed a more alarming concern, and suggested that their subjective understanding was equivalent to the attitude theorists recognize as conducive to violent activism. Direct activists clearly indicated that they feared exclusion from scarce resources, and that they felt the ideology supporting legal abortion threatened them, personally. This perception encouraged a radical defense of their beliefs and lifeways. This is not to say that pro-life direct action was undertaken solely as self-defense, but rather that such perceptions linked the individual and the contention over abortion, pointing the individual toward direct activism.

The Process of Conviction

Conviction either drew upon or reformulated activists' existing ethics to validate a novel perspective. A few individuals gained new perspectives on themselves, their fellows, God, or society through contemplation. However, conviction more often followed personal life crises, sometimes only tangentially related to abortion. (Rick's and Loren's stories illustrated such experiences.) Pro-life organizations provided a social context and a forum for rhetoric that encouraged and reinforced individuals' conviction experiences.

CHANGED PERSPECTIVES

Most activists explained that traumatic experiences such as divorce, bereavement, or dramatic changes in the way they viewed the world or their relationships to other people, played important roles in their decisions to join direct activism. Many activists' narratives centered on such experiences. The variety of these instigating experiences was reflected in activists' anti-abortion discourse, as well, in that the imagery and issues such experiences entailed permeated their arguments against abortion.

Two themes dominated these stories of changed perspectives: first, and most pervasive, the compelling demand of others' needs; second, the threat of impending chaos. For example, activists sometimes argued that abortion interrupted the "natural" order of society, and would lead to cut-throat competition over scarce resources, exclusion of disenfranchised groups, and even involuntary euthanasia. Other times, activists pointed to personal experiences such as seeing their own newborn children, watching a child die, or realizing that they could have been aborted themselves. They explained that these experiences helped them con-ceptualize "children threatened by abortion" as individual people in danger of an agonizing death – people in need of help they could not refuse to give.

FEAR OF EXCLUSION

Direct activists expressed intense concern over changing attitudes, social practices, and material circumstances. As noted above, the pre-eminence given egalitarian notions of identity, relationships, and com-munity impelled some individuals to join direct action. Like conven-tional pro-lifers concerned over changes in gender roles (Ginsburg 1989; Himmelstein 1986; Lo 1982; Luker 1984), some rescuers argued that abortion broke down the differences between male and female sexuality by allowing women to adopt structurally male approaches to sexual-ity based on pleasure, individualism, and ambition. These activists ex-pressed concern that such rationalization, epitomized by abortion, would dismantle the sanctity of motherhood, place it under human control, reduce male responsibility for reproduction, and threaten the viability of women's nurturant roles. Ginsburg (1989), Lake (1984), and Luker (1984) describe identical concerns among conventional pro-lifers. Many (but not all) direct activists advocated differentiated gender roles that subordinated women to men. This inequality made men (who accepted responsibility) a resource for women, who relinquished equality for se-curity (Harding 1981; Klatch 1987; Luker 1984).

Several studies follow Luker's (1984) logic, arguing that pro-life ac-tivists fear changes abortion would bring because such changes threaten their socioeconomic niche (Ehrenreich 1983; Harding 1981; Luker 1984). As you will recall from Chapter 1, Luker (1984) found that many of the pro-lifers she interviewed were marginal to the wage labor market, because they lacked either work experience or extensive education. She suggests their concerns derived from their dependent social sta-tuses. Klatch (1987) echos Luker's conclusion. However, Himmelstein

(1986:12) contests this interpretation and argues that activists' "beliefs about abortion . . . depend less on self-interest and personal circumstances and more on long-standing values and collective judgments." The broad socioeconomic spectrum presented by the St. Louis sample strongly suggests that their relational strategies, their acceptance of differentiated gender roles, and their sense of vulnerability did not derive from their socioeconomic positions.

Direct activists often expressed fear of an elemental conflict over the basis of social organization, but they focused more on the potential for exclusion than on gender roles per se. As one activist put it,

> There's a desensitizing of the general populace about human life, period. Abortion, euthanasia, and the right to die. All of those cases are the same issue – how valuable is human life, versus society.

Direct activists almost universally contended that communal compassion and respect for individual life had been replaced by utilitarian ethics that devalued the individual and threatened the individual's access to scarce rescources.

Most of the activists I interviewed argued not only that abortion threatened the "imperfect," "unwanted," and "unborn," but that abortion set a precedent that would allow other categories of people to be classed as expendable. Like many others, one activist insisted, "Hitler had that down pat, the propaganda war . . . He desensitized them to certain classes of people and that's what's happening with abortion." Referring to the Supreme Court, another man argued that,

> In truth, the judge was promoting anarchy by disenfranchising a whole class of our citizens from their rights of constitutional protection, that's the unborn child.

Direct activists anticipated that more and more categories of people would be endangered with time. They speculated that invalids, ethnic minorities, the elderly, poor, or handicapped, might be classed as "undesirable" and so become vulnerable to enforced euthanasia. Several people suggested Catholics might be targeted, and quite a few people echoed the fears of one activist who said, "Persecution of Christians could be an end result." One activist articulated the reasoning behind this fear when he said,

I think, this is my own view, I think if we don't ban abortion in this country, I think if there are still Christians left that you'll see more and more people involved in direct action. Where you see a hundred now, there'll be thousands. It will become as big as the Civil Rights crusade of the 1960s. I think that, because in our society they don't want to have anarchy, because the end result is that when you have thousands of people breaking the law, even when it's an unjust law, you have anarchy. The only way to fight that anarchy is to use police-state type weapons. I think that if Christians are unwavering in their opposition to abortion and they refuse to heed the penalties for breaking those unjust laws, I think that someday it will just mean persecution of Christians in general.

Over and over, activists reiterated the fear that abortion was a "slippery slope." As one man warned,

A society that has such a low value on life, it goes into other areas ... When life itself is not valued, but the quality of life is measured, you slide down hill on a slippery slope.

Activists almost unanimously argued that this slippery slope led to forced euthanasia. One activist explained that,

They say it's a human being but it's not wanted; simply kill on the basis of wantedness. Once this is accepted to a complete point, then the idea of killing unwanted elderly is accepted very easily. So, that's the point we're getting to.

Since pro-lifers almost unanimously argued that such treatment would be extended to the elderly, they saw themselves as virtually inevitable victims. One man commented that,

The kids are going to be taking care of us one day. I'd rather have them look at us kindly than to look at us as useless pieces of meat. I do believe you reap what you sow.

Through these fears, direct activists included themselves in potential target populations and conjured images of personal exclusion resulting from the breakdown of community values.

Any sense of security afforded by their social statuses (that is, their education, access to the wage-labor market, or household income)

dissipated in the face of forced euthanasia. Although most people in my sample lived in households with incomes above the national median, many had advanced education, and most had work experience, fear of impending exclusion (via euthanasia) was rampant among them. In fact, one activist with a personal annual income of over $200,000 concluded that:

> This will lead to my death. I'm a goner; I'm as good as dead. They're going to kill me just as sure as I'm sitting here. The numbers are all there, they have to. They can't support me at age 75 because of the demographics. The children that are being born and raised today being exposed to the morality they are, are they going to have better morality than the generation before them? . . . You're going to have very tough demographics that will force the issue. Do you want 10 or 15 percent of the quality of life that people have had for the last 50 years, or do you want to start knocking off these old jerks? It's not going to be hard to decide. That was the [story with] Nancy Cruzan, let's face it. [A court decision allowed caretakers to cease giving food and water to Nancy Cruzan, a young woman in the St. Louis area who was in a coma.]

Activists' own words suggest that social position was not the basis of their anti-abortion attitudes. As Himmelstein (1986) argues, individuals' perceptions of vulnerability affect their attitudes toward abortion more than their actual social positions. He contends that such fears need not relate to the individual activist on a personal basis, but rather to perceptions of societywide vulnerability or threats to certain groups within society.

Many researchers have interpreted a disparity between activists' "actual" vulnerability to a given threat and their opposition to it as indicating a lack of self-interested motivation (summarized in Himmelstein 1986). However, this interpretation assesses individuals' perceptions on strictly empirical grounds – from the analysts' perspective. Direct activists' intellectual and affective responses to abortion were informed by their subjective perceptions of vulnerability and self-interest. Sears and his colleagues (Sears, Lau, Tyler, and Allen 1980) illustrate the general depth and honesty of political attitudes; they found that,

> Political attitudes . . . are formed mainly in congruence with long-standing values about society and the polity, rather than short-term instrumentalities for satisfaction of one's current needs.

However, such values are set within a worldview that may create a subjective sense of shared vulnerability, despite material circumstances.

Direct activists argued that a pro-life ethic combated exclusion from scarce resources by repudiating differentiation between categories of people: the born and the unborn, the healthy and the deformed or diseased, male and female, young and old, wanted and unwanted. They spoke of the pro-life ethic as a matter of self-defense, a way to maintain a humane order and avert moral chaos. They argued for the inclusive aspects of hierarchical relations and against an individualism that they saw as threatening to the individual.

OTHERS' NEEDS

Ginsburg (1989) linked abortion activism to women's personal struggles to reconcile stressful life-cycle transitions with available gender models. The conflicts Ginsburg analyzed most often related to women's reproductive experiences. While direct activists noted that the births of their children contributed to their activism, they did not focus on the incongruity of our society's simultaneously ascribing nurturant roles to women and devaluing those roles. Both male and female direct activists focused on their children's births as the mechanism through which they came to recognize the worth of others. One man, moved to tears at the birth of his daughter, recalled being overwhelmed by the preciousness of another's life in God's eyes. A woman remembered that gazing at her own firstborn had played a crucial role in her activism. The compelling effect she (and other direct activists) described was not ambivalence over social roles but strong, concurrent, and complementary feelings of attraction and revulsion. She remembered that the "warm, fuzzy" feelings her own newborn evoked caused her to be revolted by the idea of abortion. She made such a strong link between those feelings and her own experience of pregnancy and childbirth that she wondered how men and nonparous women could be brought to the point of sitting-in, since (she assumed) they would not have experienced what were for her, crucial, motivating emotions.

But this was not the case. Activists' conviction stories encompassed a wide range of experiences; some stories related to birth, others did not. But references they made to births mainly voiced their identification with threatened others and indicated fear of exclusion from society.

For example, some individuals identified with "the unborn" because they themselves had been adopted as infants and they suspected that their birth mothers had contemplated aborting them. Several adoptees echoed the sentiments of one woman who declared, "I was lucky to be born at all." Other activists said they opposed abortion in solidarity with "children" who, like themselves or their ancestresses, were conceived in rape. Like adopted activists, one child of a rape victim concluded that she had been spared from death-by-abortion. She explained that,

> Everyone has something in their family line. I don't know what it is. In my family line there's rape . . . [weeping] And the Lord let that person have her baby, and so I'm here and I'm grateful. So I'm standing up for the unborn.

Several activists identified with the "unborn" because they themselves were born prematurely. Similarly, other activists reflected on the changes legal abortion had brought, and noted that nowadays children possessing disabilities such as their own were liable to be aborted. Such activists often concluded that they would have been likely candidates for abortion had amniocentesis informed their parents of their disabilities. Like the adopted activists and the raped women's descendents, they felt akin to "children threatened by abortion." One such activist explained that,

> Now everybody's going to fertilize all their eggs in a test tube and test them to see if they're defective and destroy them if they are. I'd be destroyed that way, because, you see, I'm manic depressive. They can detect that in the embryo now, and I would have been destroyed.

Apparently, one common avenue to pro-life conviction opened when people perceived themselves to have narrowly escaped into life through channels routinely closed by abortion. Like the people mentioned above, another woman reasoned that,

> My mother's had two abortions, which killed three children. She had twins . . . One day I realized I was convenient. I happened at the right time, I had a brother that happened at the right time, and the other three didn't. Their timing was poor, so they're dead. And it really gives you a sense of, if I would have been conceived two years later, I wouldn't be here. She got those abortions before they were legal. That tells me I would not have had a shot! [laughs]

Another common theme in activists' discourse was concern over the fate of their grandchildren. They said they wanted to outlaw abortion so that their own grandchildren would not be aborted. Like many others, one woman remarked, "I don't want my grandchildren to be up for grabs. I want to do everything I can do to protect them, and that's why I'm involved."

In one way or another, many activists thought of abortion as a personal threat and they routinely passed that conceptualization on to their children. Activists proudly exclaimed that their children understood themselves to be survivors. Several activists noted that their adopted children understood themselves to have "escaped abortion." One man recounted his daughters' response to the story of an aborted "baby," saying he had,

Heard of a baby born at [a local clinic] – full term – they slaughtered him. My adopted daughter was born there, too. She said, 'Daddy, that could have been me!' If that don't break your heart strings, you don't have no heart strings left.

People pointed to diverse aspects of their personal life histories when explaining why they adopted direct activism. Such links portrayed abortion as a threat, whether to the narrator or a helpless Other. For example, several nurses said they became aware of the "deaths" involved in abortion after they worked with premature infants, assisted during hysterectomies performed on pregnant women, or worked on actual abortions. All of the women who reported having had abortions emphasized the role their abortions played in their decisions to sit-in. One man asked energetically,

What if you had a woman that was only 20 years old, had a child eight years old, one six, one five, and one in the womb. You have no job, husband's gone, single parent, no visible means of support. Would you abort it? If you'd abort it, you would have aborted my brother Mike, cause that was my mom! Well, at the time my mom had throat cancer . . . My mom couldn't take care of us so she put us in St. Louis's Orphan Home.

An elderly man explained that his great-grandmother was eight years old when she became sick and was left beside the Trail of Tears to die. As we sat on a low wall, watching federal marshalls pull plastic handcuffs tight around activists' wrists, he described the horror of the Trail of Tears, and concluded that,

> That was the best the federal marshalls could do for that little eight-year old. People cried out then that this was unjust and an outrage, but those things happened because they weren't citizens and there were people greedy for the land.

His grandmother survived because, "A white family found her and you might say they rescued her." This man equated the experiences of his ancestress with those of "abortion-bound babies," and concluded that, "Now rescuers sacrifice. We need to profit from the mistakes of the past. This is the same as when they persecuted the Indians and the Blacks."

In diverse ways activists linked their own lives to abortion. They emphasized the role such connections played in their decisions to engage in direct action. Procreation-related stories referred, not to crucial changes in their awareness of gender constructs, but to new awareness of the value of others and a sense of connectedness with those others. Activists explained that from these new perspectives arose a need to respond to the needs of others.

REFORMULATING THE IMPLICATIONS
OF EXISTING ETHICS

Conviction employed pre-existing ethics within the field of vision offered by activists' new perspectives. Activists reorganized their view of authority, responded to an ethic of extensivity, employed deontological metaethical reasoning, and generally viewed human nature as weak and fallible. Care and justice ethics powerfully converged during conviction, and an apocalyptic worldview reinforced the moral demand and practical need to rescue.

EXTENSIVITY AND THE NEED TO ACT

When new interpretations of their own pasts linked activists to "those threatened by abortion," activists saw "the preborn" as people like themselves. This perception is termed "extensivity." Prior to joining direct action most individuals developed a concrete and often personalized concept of fetuses. Typical of many others, one activist explained that,

> Once I started focusing, this baby is no different than you are right here, sitting here. I started focusing on that idea of this unborn

child being a person, no different than I am. Then you take that focus and focus on the idea that somebody over here is killing that person, and wouldn't I rush out there if that little child were a three-year old and try to tear that three-year old away from this bully? Why wouldn't I go and try to tear this three-month old away from this bully? So, the focus became more intense on what this unborn child really is. It's a person. Once I got that point, then I had to say, well, you can't stay away from rescues . . . In other words, in my mind the unborn child becomes an equal to a six-month old or a three-year old child, and once you see that equality, you cannot stand there and over and over again watch that child, no matter what his age is, being destroyed without doing something physical about it.

This sense of extensivity, coupled with an ethic that demanded one act on one's beliefs, pervaded activists' narratives. Together, they prompted an emotional and intellectual commitment to accept a personal moral responsibility to defend those potential "victims." Many activists explained that such connections between their own lives and the lives they imagined were essential to conviction. (Other activists emphasized their concerns about society.)

MORAL IMPERATIVES REDEFINED

Before they could sit-in, most activists had to overcome a longstanding aversion to thwarting authority, particularly legal authority. To do so they reframed laws as social conventions, that is, as arbitrary and relative rules intended to promote social orderliness (cf. Berk 1989:515). Social conventions could be subordinated to divine law, which activists held supreme. By redefining pre-existing moral imperatives to be social conventions, conviction not only mandated but justified behavior that individuals previously would have considered aberrant.

Participation in direct action reorganized individuals' experience, weakening old habits and the attitudes attached to them (cf. Bentley 1987). This reorganization created new possibilities. Like others, one man articulated these changes, saying,

Also, see, I grew up in a family and in a church that stresses authority . . . To counter [a policeofficer's] authority was almost like being against my total nature . . . Even though I know abortion is wrong and that this is an evil here, it's still legal and I'm doing something against my total nature . . . I have to go against authority, which I've always assumed to be totally right . . . But now I see . . . those policeofficers there, of course, should always be right, but now I'm seeing that he's not always right . . . This temporal authority here is right on to the extent that it obeys a higher authority that I recognized, which is God, of course.

While some activists came to question, distrust, or even despise legal authority, other activists amplified their respect for law officers and their self-identity as law-abiding citizens, even while privileging obedience to God's law and accepting abrogation of "man's law." Another activist explained,

I have been in jail and have broken the law, even though I would say I haven't broken the law, I would say I have kept the law of God. I have a higher respect for the existing law in our land because of that. I really do. I speed less . . . If I see a policeman, I have great respect for him to support him and pray for him, since I have, in a sense, kept a higher law. I didn't break the law, I kept God's law.

Activists' religious beliefs supported this transformation. Many interviewees described a theory of government in which each individual's primary responsibility was to govern themselves according to the Scriptures. Beyond that, they argued that God authorized three institutions: family, church, and government. Individuals were personally responsible to submit to each institution insofar as it followed God's law and to correct any institution that varied from divine law. As one activist argued,

Government is a very weak sister when it comes to moral leadership . . . Government is something God has appointed . . . but I think it has a very limited function, a very limited role in our lives. It's basically to keep the peace, and to promote justice. But that justice is never going to be something which springs from government as an institution. It's going to be something that springs from individuals and citizens, and it's only to the extent that citizens are active and let their voice be heard that government can even come close to resembling a true promoter of justice.

Another interviewee illustrated the inherent political aspects of personal morality and social norms. Like many direct activists, he framed these in Biblical terms, explaining that,

What the Bible says to you is, and this is the ultimate question that every person and every nation faces. It's the question of power. That is: Who is the boss? You have two choices: Either you, as the human being, are the boss of your own life; or God, the Creator, is the boss. The bottom line comes down to, who's going to be boss of your life, and as a country, who's going to be boss of our country? Is it going to be man or is it going to be God? And that's where the struggle is and that's where the war that's going on inside America. It's the war of sovereignty, it's the war of power, and it's a war that goes on in every individual's life.

Conflict between divine and secular authority formed a salient theme in activists' narratives and echoed the conflict of progressive egalitarian versus conservative hierarchical ideologies that Harding (1981) proposed. Activists resolved this conflict by honoring God as the highest authority and subordinating civil law to divinely sanctioned conduct. Family, then church, superseded government in this model of authority.

APOCALYPSE

An apocalyptic worldview linked many activists' personal fate to that of the nation, enhanced the impact of activists' personal stories, and reinforced the superiority of God's law over "man's law." Many direct activists feared that society's acceptance of legalized abortion would bring about a national disaster. As one activist concluded,

America won't continue with the abortion situation for too long. Ultimately it's going to stop. The only question is how is it going to stop? It will either be stopped by God's judgement, which will be quite violent and very painful, and ruin your whole day. Or it will stop because people like the rescue people finally manage to wake up the conscience of the nation. It's one of those two alternatives . . . We're at a crossroads.

According to these activists, abortion was a threat to all, not just a personal matter for those engaging in it. On the one hand, direct activists expressed much horror at the "cruelty" of abortion. They talked about the fate of "defenseless, little quiet, innocent babies" and "the exploitation of women" – the cruelty of the process, the injustice of the practice – and the inevitable consequence – forced euthanasia. On the other hand, many direct activists spoke of concern about their personal salvation and a judgement on the United States that would cause its demise or, at least, its political or economic failure. As one activist argued,

> Abortion is the focal point. It is so much to the crux of it all . . . That one person there is a faithful presence, as long as you're there for the proper reasons. You're not there for glory; you're there because of the killing and because of the witness for Christ. By their presence they're standing in the gap. The Lord will honor that. The spiritual battle will still be conducted. That one person will stem the tide for the day and lay the foundation for something to come . . . If we don't do something about this and the moment that the few remnant stop standing in the gap, I think there'll be a judgement comes upon this country, and mankind in general, that will be awesome. And we'll all get burned by it, the good, the bad, and the like. If you're talking about physical judgement, there's not going to be anybody that's spared the travail here. But when that's over, the real judgement is going to be before the throne of God. And there again we get back to the fact that if I know, then I have to be faithful to God. If I'm faithful to that, then I will probably hear, 'Well done, good and faithful servant.' At least that's what I'm striving for.

Somewhat less dramatically, another activist feared that if abortion were not stopped, "the United States will crumble. It will not be a world power, and a world leader. Because of that more people will suffer. We'll economically crash."

The logic behind these fears was founded on activists' religious beliefs, but cut across denominational lines. In response to these fears some direct activists took radical stands against abortion and performed acts counter to their otherwise mainstream lifestyles. For example, they routinely risked lengthy jail sentences instead of paying fines, admitting guilt, or promising to abstain from activism. Many activists incurred repeated arrests while continuing to speak of themselves as inherently law-abiding citizens. One activist explained,

> I just felt the privilege of being arrested for obeying the Lord, and it's just like the Bible says, 'Rejoice when you suffer persecution for

righteousness' sake' . . . We felt we were obeying the Lord, so there was great joy in our hearts. There was no guilt. There was great clarity of conscience. People who do this are the most law-abiding people. In fact, they'll even go beyond the law; they'll see what God's law is.

CARE, JUSTICE, DEONTOLOGY, AND HUMAN WEAKNESS

The connections that comprised the conviction experience formed within a framework of deontological metaethical reasoning. This means that, like conventional pro-lifers (Harding 1981; Lake 1986:480), direct activists tended to subscribe to a "theory of duty and moral obligation" that emphasized discrete right and wrong absolutes (as opposed to gradations of good and bad).[5] For example, one activist remarked, "There should be a right or a wrong about abortion. I don't buy the argument that it's good for somebody . . . I believe there is a true wrong." More explicitly, another activist argued that, "Abortion's wrong and it's wrong because God says it's wrong. It's a law of God; it's not that we decided it was wrong." Similarly, another activist argued,

I shouldn't say, 'You shouldn't engage in premarital sex because you might get pregnant.' You shouldn't engage in premarital sex because it's wrong. Say, 'I'm going to do it because it's right,' or 'I'm not going to do it because it's wrong.'

Yet another activist explained that, "It's not like, 'I have my opinion and you have your opinion.' It's 'This is what God has said.'" Deontological reasoning pervaded activists' narratives, conversations, and rhetoric.

From this basis some direct activists harshly denigrated compromise. One man argued that,

You don't compromise one inch with these people . . . They're evil . . . You take a glass of water and put just a little bit of dirt and what happens? You can pour gallon after gallon of clean water in it but it still has dirt in it. It's the same with this place. [Referring to the abortion clinic we stood by.]

[5] A deontological perspective may be contrasted to teleological metaethical reasoning that entails an adjustable scale of good and bad, open to personal evaluation.

Such codes foregrounded prescriptive and proscriptive moral rules, often corresponding to Biblical themes and emphasizing legalistic reasoning (Lake 1986).

Activists' notions of community incorporated these moral rules. In essence, they construed interpersonal relationships (especially those linked to family and gender) according to absolutes rather than personal interpretations, and discredited the notion that relationships and behavior are subject to personal or situational interpretations or evaluation. These aspects of their moral reasoning made community the unquestioned basis of social order, and individualism a hazard. In this way, activists' statements regarding personal relationships, social roles, and community accorded with Harding's (1981) description of a hierarchical family strategy.

Activists repeatedly argued that abortion undermined a collective responsibility to care for women who were in need. They insisted that abortion resolved a woman's crisis only by "damaging" her and killing her "child." They explained that a woman's crisis resulted from diverse pressures on her, not from her pregnancy. Consequently, they reasoned that if, by acting together, they could resolve those pressures, most women would "recognize" that their pregnancies were not their problems. Given a new perspective, they expected women to respond with a "natural desire" to carry their pregnancies to term. From this perspective, availability of abortion set aside collective responsibility to care for women and "abandoned" them to "heartless individualism" (Garton 1979:74).

Most direct activists argued that abortion denied crucial interpersonal relationships. Through abortion, the trust necessary for an individual to be born and grow up was broken. The fetus was betrayed by its genetrix, its genetor, and society. Pro-lifers worried that children who learned their mothers had had abortions would feel insecure and fear that their parents would emotionally reject or physically harm them. Activists also feared such children would hate or reject their parents. To direct activists, abortion meant love and solidarity became contingent and death prevailed over birth. The continuity between generations and across time symbolized by sexual intercourse and reproduction (Schneider 1980:116) was broken if its products were discarded. Because abortion denied the symbolic meaning of conception and its products, it threatened human relations and society. Abortion privileged the biological and mechanistic, and denied the social and relational.

Both men and women in the sample voiced a need for nurturant support systems and nurturant social roles. (Luker 1984 and Ginsburg 1991 noted this desire, as well.) Activists tended to essentialize community, and idealize and cherish the individual as an indispensable component of the relationships that composed community. Because they also employed legalistic reasoning (Himmelstein 1986; Lake 1986), they tended to employ ethics of both care and justice. Such convergence of moral reasoning styles may indicate the intensity of the conviction experience and its pivotal nature. Gilligan suggests that such convergence "marks times of crisis and change" (Gilligan 1993:209).

Both male and female direct activists' rhetoric and narratives illustrated this convergence.[6] Activists' desire to respond to the needs of specific individuals and their emphasis on being connected to others (including God) rather than addressing the larger, more abstract issue of abortion, evidenced a key characteristic of "care" reasoning. Direct action also provided the opportunity to make a concrete difference – to exercise real power. Most individuals spoke of direct action as enabling. Activists reasoned along the lines of one individual who declared, "I may not be able to end legalized abortion, but I can stop *this* abortion." In this sense, sit-ins were a response to the outrage pro-lifers felt at having their standards of fairness, equality, and right abrogated. Their outrage stemmed from moral considerations associated with "justice" reasoning.

One activist demonstrated the blending of thought and feeling that accompanied these two ethical perspectives, saying,

> I guess your love for God has to be pretty great . . . when you love a person like God, you have to appreciate your own very existence, your own self. Then this is, I guess, what's transferred to this less fortunate individual. This individual is being denied what was given him. He was given life. He was given the same opportunities, but then these opportunities are being unjustly denied, and this life that he has a right to live out, in a manner that I've been able to live out, this was all being denied. So this was a matter then, of justice, that I have to be there to help this person.

Pro-life conviction resolved a state of disequilibrium, a crisis, of sorts, during which former ethics, and behavior based on them, were called

---

[6] I relied on Rogers's (1987) coding method for identifying justice and care reasoning; it was developed in conjunction with Kay Johnston and Nona Lyons, students of Gilligan. A growing body of literature suggests care and justice moral orientations are less gender-linked than originally suggested (Larrabee 1993). Several moral philosophers argue that care and justice are only two among many moral orientations (Flanagan and Jackson 1993). They also suggest this division between moral orientations may be artificial.

into question. Upon conviction, lawfulness was recast as a social convention and abortion was designated a moral violation. An ethic of response and care converged powerfully with an ethic of rights and justice to impel action. In other words, pro-lifers felt responsible to care for "their preborn brothers and sisters," and outraged that abortion "unjustly" abrogated an individual's "right to life."

Activists' concepts of human nature reinforced the need to care and to help. Many direct activists spoke of human beings as naturally self-centered and prone to wrong-doing (cf. Himmelstein 1986; cf. Lake 1986). Consequently, they concluded that without moral absolutes, society degenerates. As one activist argued,

> We read about all these civilizations that used to do child sacrifice publicly and cannibalism. I used to read that stuff and say, 'Oh, God, that was horrible. That was way in the past and I'm glad man has gotten better.' Man hasn't. And if we don't stop abortion now, we're going to end up in that place.

Many activists insisted that current socialization aggravates this tendency. As one man argued,

> The whole next generation is being taught that how you feel is the deciding factor in situations and that life doesn't mean anything. You can shoot if you want; you can kill if you want.

Inclined toward selfishness, people would tend to abuse the option of judging the rightness or wrongness of an act according to the relative good or bad effects that act might have on others (Lake 1986). Along this line, Himmelstein (1986:9) argues that, "Underlying anti-abortion opinion, in short, is a concern for protecting the coherence of the private sphere against the corrosive effects of individuation."

From this perspective, people benefit from unquestionable rules. Many activists argued that without such rules, society becomes chaotic as people inevitably devolve toward various forms of socially sanctioned killing. One activist repeated the arguments of many others when he told me,

> You see there is a death agenda. You talk about abortion, that's one end of the spectrum; euthanasia, that's the other. The elderly, they've got no quality of life – get rid of 'em. The comatose, they've got no quality of life. Get rid of them. We've got a new death ethic and that's what happens. You get away from the Bible, you get away

from the word of God which says that we're to love one another, we're to take care of one another, we're to respect our parents, we're to treat the elderly with respect. Thou shalt not kill. We get away from that, what do you have left? A new death ethic in America. People finding ways to kill one another for convenience.

Most direct activists argued that "secular humanism" has eroded the former ethical basis of the United States and replaced it with a moral relativism that gives free rein to selfish tendencies inherent in human nature. Direct activists described the United States as a world trend-setter and, so, highly culpable for "failing" to maintain the "right" moral standard on abortion. Consequently, many saw the United States as existing on "borrowed time." They wanted to see the nation restored to its "original state" – a "tolerant Christian community."

Because they perceived their own Christian ethics to be "natural" and "God-given," not chosen for human political purposes, they saw their absolutes and their symbols as simply "right" and therefore innocent rather than manipulative or controlling. Thus, they understood their persuasion to be enlightenment, intended to preserve community, and so cast as a caring rather than a dominating activity.[7]

In sum direct activists spoke of moral issues surrounding abortion in distinct, unequivocal terms, and their conviction experiences appear to have been crucial in eradicating ambiguity and producing a uniform perspective on abortion. Conviction left recruits with consistent log-ical, moral, and social strategies.[8] Pro-lifers marshalled deontological metaethics to support a hierarchical relational strategy (thus opposing an egalitarian relational strategy and teleological reasoning). (Teleolog-ical metaethical reasoning entails an adjustable scale of good and bad, open to personal evaluation.) Generally, individuals described convic-tion as having awakened them to their roles in relation to others, either by stimulating "awareness" of others' needs, or by depicting the individ-ual as vulnerable to a morally chaotic society. This heightened sense of community, coupled with activists' action ethic, helped promote partic-ipation in sit-ins.

---

[7] Such assumptions are not unique to social conservatives, nor do they make their tactics more palatable to their opponents.

[8] Philosophical consistency is arguably dangerous. If life is more complex than any one philosophy, consistent approaches may lead to moral travesty, great or small (Pedro Cavalcanti, personal communication 1991; Flanagan and Jackson 1993).

RHETORIC AND ORGANIZATIONAL CONTEXTS

Direct action organizations provided social contexts that nurtured conviction. Like conviction, fellowship among activists prepared individuals to experience sit-ins, trials, and jail time as inspiring or meaningful opportunities. Organizations promoted special language use, countered legal discourse relating to abortion, disparaged highly visible advocates of "choice", and encouraged individual efforts to challenge pro-choice ideologies.

ORGANIZATIONS

Conversion cannot succeed in isolation; it requires a like-minded community in which the convert can live out the newly reorganized self (Cucchiari 1988). Like religious conversion, conviction to pro-life was facilitated and sustained by social interactions. Pro-life groups provided social contexts that helped move a convert from conviction to participation and then helped sustain involvement in direct action. Identification with a social collectivity (such as a direct action group, church congregation, or pro-life committee) helped many individuals reformulate their self-identities.

The prospect of joining a group of like-minded companions promised inspiration and fulfillment during sit-ins and jail time. This dynamic helped overcome individuals' aversion to the personal confrontation sit-ins entailed and time-consuming aspects of trial and jail experiences. The prospect of belonging to a group and being at the center of the action helped lure people away from the security of a "normal" life. Conversely, group dissension or lack of group support strongly suppressed participation in sit-ins.

Kelly (1955) describes individuals as "construing" reality by developing "theories" and testing "hypotheses" and evidence in order to discern the meaning of personal experience and formulate a personal notion of reality.[9] Such notions vary from person to person, in their myriad details.

---

[9] McCombs (1985) suggests that social groups operate in the same manner to produce collective notions of reality that result in shared norms and values. Building upon Berger and Luckmann (1966), Kelly (1955), and Sherif (1936), she argues that common frames of reference are formulated through contact and interaction of individuals within a community. These frames of reference are valued and accepted as real when they produce attitudes and behaviors that appear to accurately interpret and express reality and facilitate individuals' adjustments to their environment. McCombs suggests that when such common frames of reference come to guide the behavior of each community member in everyday life they produce

Social norms and values (emergent by nature) may serve as much to bridge the divergences among individuals' concepts of reality as they serve to express actual consensus. Pro-life organizations maintained an appearance of consensus, but, in other contexts, such appearances have been shown to be conscious social constructions. These constructions may mask social actions that both conflict with and manipulate ostensibly accepted norms (espoused by an apparent consensus) (Bailey 1983; Murphy 1990).

From time to time an apparent consensus opposing abortion and supporting direct action emerged among various congregations in St. Louis. However, when activism precipitated unexpected negative consequences, what had appeared to be a consensus on norms and values dissipated, leaving congregations distraught. Under duress, the mosaic of consensus separated, as the various beliefs individuals held polarized and factionalized congregations. When consensus failed, most individuals opted out of direct action. Because group contexts were important in sustaining conviction and participation, this dynamic lent a fragility to rescue groups that undermined the sit-in movement.

Groups such as St. Louis's direct action organizations, were not organized along "rational" bureaucratic principles. They operated through categorical obligations, rather than contracts. Consequently, their hold on members was normative, involving the total selves of members rather than only those aspects of the self associated with specialized roles (cf. Cohen 1974). This relationship between organizational style and the nature of individual involvement may explain why pro-life direct activists often found their group interactions intensely engaging and highly emotional. It may also help explain direct activists' all-or-nothing approach to involvement.

The political manipulability of norms suggests such organizations need to develop stabilizing mechanisms that will combat fragmentation or individual domination. Lacking coercive force, direct action organizations often relied on religious ideology to unite supporters and control leaders. Direct activists frequently stated the "will of God" and then defined the proper human response to that will (often concluding that rescuing fulfilled that obligation). By framing their arguments within religious themes, direct activists shifted the realm of discourse away from

common or collective knowledge and form the psychological basis of social norms and values. In short, she argues that a shared notion of reality produces shared norms and values. Such consensus may not exist among pro-lifers (or any other community).

contested issues and toward broad, overriding points of agreement (such as God's love for children, omnipotent guidance, and righteousness). Such themes resonated with the beliefs and feelings underlying direct activists' conviction experiences.

RHETORIC

Spokespeople generally employed "assertive rhetoric" to persuade pro-lifers to join direct action. Assertive rhetoric is characterized by the invocation of authority or danger, the presentation of a moral self, a focus on personalities, and vivid examples (Bailey 1983). Pro-life rhetoric was more than a medium of communication and persuasion. Like sitting-in, speaking was valued as an act in itself, a witness that helped fulfill one's responsibility to God. By pronouncing inescapable truths, pro-lifers' rhetoric defied argument (Condit 1990). Typical of assertive rhetoric, it relied on emotional force, rather than rational evaluation or cool reason.

Many direct activists explained that, prior to conviction, they were confused about their attitudes toward abortion, activism, or personal issues they contemplated addressing through their activism; rhetoric helped assuage this confusion. Assertive rhetoric can privilege emotion, and so support, alter, or displace existing normative patterns (Bailey 1983). Such argument is well-suited to cope with paradox and confusion. It supplements rational evaluation with emotional "evidence." Direct activists' narratives suggested that such evidence excited conviction by simplifying complexity and overcoming the inertia of indecision. Emotional evidence reassured, and so comforted, attracted, and compelled potential recruits (cf. Bailey 1983).

1. *Emotional force.* Pro-life rhetoric not only relied on emotion, but called for an end to questioning (or reasoning) and a commitment to action. Many direct activists disparaged indecision and rejected qualified condemnations of abortion. Their writings and speeches overtly encouraged audiences to respond emotionally to "the murdered children and exploited women" and to a "grieving God." Direct activists' expressed strong feelings in response to such imagery. Although they explained that their choice of imagery stemmed legitimately from their own understandings and sentiments, they also said they yearned to stimulate an emotional response in their audiences.

2. *Danger.* In discourse directed toward pro-life audiences, speakers and authors frequently implied that people who heard their messages should fear the consequences of not rescuing. Some speakers insisted that people who chose not to rescue were deliberately opting to fail in

their duty to God. One direct activist asked, "Have I committed murder? No. Am I complicit in the murder? Yes, by not speaking against it."

Not surprisingly, people who were intensely involved in direct action made more radical statements than those less involved. Some punctuated their discourse by warning that people who were informed of their duty to "their pre-born brethren" and knowingly refused to rescue were willfully disobedient and so would incur more fearsome penalties than those who "ignorantly" failed to respond. Direct activists acknowledged the legitimacy of pursuing other avenues for "being a light and the influence in society that God wants us to be," but such opinions were voiced more commonly by those who no longer sat-in.

Direct activists often depicted the pro-life movement as a phenomenon poised between attaining imminent success or falling into shameful and disastrous failure. They warned that the outcome would be consequential for all Americans since individuals, as well as the nation, would be "judged" by their stand on abortion. In contrast, they also emphasized that they rescued, not to attain salvation, but to "save that baby."

Overtly, direct activists opposed abortion "for the children's sake," a selfless stance and a self-sacrificing task. By implementing pro-life ideology with an intensity that even some other pro-lifers considered extreme or misguided, direct activists pursued a covert project of personal salvation. They redefined pro-life norms by intensifying them. While in some arenas, people covertly abrogate or manipulate norms behind a facade of normative concensus in order to skirt a human system, fear of divine judgement placed direct activists on a divine field. This may explain their inclination to succeed by intensifying rather than defying existing norms.

3. *Moral self.* Direct activists' rhetoric defined the nature of the relevant universe and its implications for their audience. Activists drew lines that sorted individuals depending on their understanding of and response to abortion. Their schema placed informed, obedient (direct activist) Christians closest to God, and informed abortion proponents furthest. Through their rhetoric, pro-lifers claimed to "clarify" areas others considered gray, resolving them into black-and-white domains. Characteristic of deontological reasoning, this simplification encouraged pro-lifers to become judgemental and confident.

4. *Personalities.* Direct activists validated their tactics by associating rescuers with groups of acknowledged culture heros such as Nazi resistors Corrie Ten Boom, Deitrich Bonhauffer, and Franz Jagerstatter; Martin

Luther King, Jr. and other civil rights activists; and nineteenth century abolitionists. Less ambitiously, authors encouraged recruits to liken themselves to a select group of well-known activists by freely describing how these prominent figures struggled with fear, bigotry, and ambivalence while deciding to sit-in.

Direct activists frequently tried to evoke clear images of fetuses-as-individual-personalities through allusion to both fictive and real kinship. A case was made for personal responsibility toward individual fetuses, "our tiny, preborn brethren." Some speakers urged each member of an audience to name an individual fetus and pray for it, personally. Speakers and authors described fetuses in detail, including their eye and hair color, gender, and personality characteristics. Rhetoric often recounted the agony of grandparents seen crying for their lost progeny at clinics, pleading with their daughters not to abort. This focus on imagined personal identities encouraged listeners (potential recruits) to place their decisions in a social, rather than a private, domain.

5. *Vivid examples.* Although conversion may occur in a context of pre-existing emotional distress (Cucchiari 1988), people can also be brought to a state of conflict (and consequently to conversion) through discourse that causes hearers to feel they are in a desperate and lost condition they were previously "unaware of" (Harding 1987). Direct activists' rhetoric addressed the sense of self their audiences had established and challenged its propriety, attacking their security and motivating them to act. Direct activists recounted tales of successful rescuers and faithful boyfriends who begged women not to abort (posited as ideal gender roles). They also told of overbearing boyfriends and callous mothers who herded pregnant women in to abort (modeling antithetical gender roles). Their ideal models were caring, self-sacrificing, and principled; antithetical models were violent, controlling, self-serving, and shallow. Such contrasts dichotomized behavior, ignoring the existence of ambivalent feelings or implying that they were unacceptable.

The vivid images direct activists used to educate, persuade, and indoctrinate helped stimulate a sense of anxiety or crisis and encouraged conversion. Gruesome pictures of aborted fetuses juxtaposed to aesthetically appealing pictures of living fetuses and idyllic maternal imagery created a jarring effect. Direct activists overtly attempted to shock the public with their imagery, and they expected to turn the hearts of their audiences with it.

6. *Witness.* Rescuers' conviction narratives served as normative statements intended both to persuade and inculpate audiences. Rescuers

explained that direct action was a political tool, a symbolic statement, and a witness. Politically, direct action prevented abortions from taking place, intimidated abortion providers and, more broadly, created political tension that supported legislative attempts to criminalize abortion. Symbolically, sitting-in spoke to direct activists' personhood, their relations to God and to other human beings. But, above all, direct activists said, rescue was a witness, and those exposed to this witness were no longer innocent-through-ignorance. As one activist argued,

> You don't have to be involved in one, but if you see one, your heart will be changed. Whatever your position, whatever your preconceived notion of it is, if you just come, you can stand across the street, you can watch from a helicopter, but if you see it, you'll understand, and you'll be changed. That doesn't necessarily mean you'll become a rescuer, but you'll be changed. It's because you're witnessing spiritual warfare. You can no longer be ambivalent about the issue of murdering innocent defenseless babies.

Harding (1987) linked evangelical conversion to the appropriation of gospel discourse. Such discourse moved the "unregenerate listener" into a state of spiritual conflict that was resolved when the listener became a "regenerate speaker." Speakers appropriated the gospel (or in-group speech) and were prepared to convert others through discourse. This process of exposure, conviction, learning, and speaking appeared to take place among direct activists, as well (regardless of their denominational affiliation). However, among direct activists, persuasive discourse was not limited to personal conversion testimonies or Biblical themes (as was the conversion discourse of Harding's religious converts).

7. *Relexicalization.* Direct activists' rhetoric included a simple substitution of new words for old, and only a portion of the lexicon was reworked. (Halliday [1976] terms this process "relexicalization.") Through the labels they applied to actions and entities, direct activists created an ideologically charged jargon. This jargon iterated a dichotomy between right and wrong, supported traditional gender roles, and opposed moral relativism. In so doing, it resisted currently ascendent norms.

Crucial areas were overlexicalized, creating many terms for key concepts. These terms made strong moralistic comments on whatever they signified. For example: A pro-choice escort was renamed a "deathscort"; an "abortion clinic" was called an "abortuary," "deathmill," "mill," "deathcamp," or "abortion chamber." Doctors performing abortions were termed "butchers" or "killers." Disabling abortion equipment was recast as "disarming weapons," feminists were termed "feminazis," and pro-choice advocates became "pro-aborts," "pro-death," or "anti-women-and-children."

Pro-lifers transformed and responded to pro-choice discourse. Opposition discourses became plastic media. On one hand, direct activists exchanged mainstream or pro-choice terms for metaphoric mutations that conformed to their own perspective. They eclectically appropriated symbols from the past into their rhetoric and graphics (especially abolitionist, holocaust, civil rights, patriotic, and Biblical imagery). These images flowed freely from their convictions. On the other hand, they also adopted imagery and arguments that targeted pro-choicers' arguments.[10] They inverted pro-choice gambits by arguing for the "rights of unborn women," "freedom of choice (for fetuses) to live," and "protection of the health and safety of unborn people." They simultaneously challenged and appropriated pro-choice rhetoric in a rhyme chanted at demonstrations: "Pro-choice is a lie; fetuses don't choose to die."

At rallies, seminars, prayer sessions, and pickets, direct activists presented arguments against their cause, then countered them. While organized events addressed issues deemed important by a hierarchy (of sorts), pickets allowed converts to deal with ambiguities crucial to furthering or maintaining their own personal convictions. They spent hours on picket lines arguing against absent opponents, articulating carefully crafted lines of reasoning to their sympathetic companions.

Direct activists' jargon both embodied and guided their ideology. It was both a model *of* and a model *for* pro-life belief (cf. Geertz 1973). Because of this, their rhetoric itself helped them resolve ambiguities surrounding abortion (Stromberg 1990). For example, the term "abortion clinic" may have aroused dissonance since a clinic was a helping-place and, in the pro-life worldview, abortion did not help the fetus and was thought to harm the mother. Terms such as "abortuary," "deathcamp," and "abortion mill" resolved this ambiguity. "Abortuary" removed the conflictive term "clinic" and replaced it with a negative term that was only a slight modification of "mortuary," making the reference consistently negative. "Abortion mill" substituted an ostensibly neutral term, "mill," for the word "clinic." However, extralinguistic cues suggested

---

[10] Pro-lifers' adoption of portions of their opponents' line of reasoning signaled the strength of the pro-choice movement (cf. Condit 1990; cf. Lo 1982).

"mill" lost its potential neutrality in this usage (as in "a finely-milled soap") and stressed its implication of habituation, routinization, and dehumanization (as in "on the treadmill").

Through relexicalization direct activists underlined the differences between their own and alternative views of reality. Because the perspective they presented *was* oblique to outsiders' reality, their ideology-bearing speech appeared oblique or metaphorical (cf. Halliday 1976).

8. *Core themes.* Direct activists' literature, posters, and audiovisual material blended the secular idioms of biology, history, and statistics with the social idioms of maternity, fraternity, and fidelity. Secular idioms spoke of the "victims of abortion" and the "threat" posed by pro-choice ideology. Social idioms argued for a deontological, hierarchical sense of community.

Both public and private discourse drew concepts from biology, history, and the Bible and supported these arguments with statistical, biomedical, and clinical psychological data. In-group doctrinal materials emphasized the religious and moralistic idioms of self-sacrifice, responsibility, consequences, and obedience to God. Such discourse reinforced direct activists' commitments to their preferred relational strategy and style of moral reasoning. Out-group discourse was persuasive, focusing on victimization, shared notions of moral behavior, and danger.

Direct activists clearly stated that they intended to convict people through their rhetoric and events. Their media seemed designed to promote conviction through a nexus of religious and secular imagery and argument intended to warn, convince, and inspire recruits to act on their beliefs.

Conclusion

Through their conviction experiences, direct activists made a moral commitment to obey God and champion "preborn people" (and sometimes their "mothers"). Concrete concepts of fetuses facilitated the feelings of extensivity and personal attachment underlying conviction. Some direct activists emphasized aspects of their own self-identities that linked them to "victims of abortion." Others focused on the moral basis of social practices they considered unprincipled, harmful, and personally threatening. Whether they depicted their opponents as a usurping minority or described themselves as a remnant group, direct activists argued that they were struggling to avert social chaos and that they were responding to the needs of threatened people.

The dawning crisis evoked by such considerations was resolved, in part, when individuals reorganized their view of authority, privileging divine will over human regulation. They accepted God's laws as moral imperatives and redefined human laws as social conventions. Direct activists villified egalitarian, teleological ethics (based on individual judgement that privileged "quality of life" and "wantedness") and sanctified a deontological perspective that privileged community, based on hierarchical, God-centered ethics. They foregrounded an action ethic (that demanded one act on one's beliefs), and recognized a responsibility to care for others and to contend with injustice.

This convergence of moral considerations may have been less an attained stage of moral maturity (Gilligan 1982) than a temporary response to the pressures involved in conviction. Through conviction, direct activists simplified ambiguity by adopting consistent logical, ethical, and social strategies. The intense convergence of thought and feeling entailed in conviction experiences appears to have evoked relatively altruistic moral reasoning among these activists.

Although they provided reasoned arguments against abortion, direct activists either clearly stated or implied that they contended against more than an unwise policy – they saw themselves to be fighting an evil. Given this perspective, the depth of some individuals' involvement in direct action becomes understandable.

Many interviewees recalled feeling powerless prior to engaging in direct action. By clarifying ambiguity and opting for a side in the "battle," direct activists felt empowered, engaged in an active struggle against something they fervently opposed, and united with a group of peers.

Yet, conviction alone did not necessarily lead one to sit-in. Before they "risked arrest," individuals also had to reorganize their priorities to foreground the responsibility conviction laid upon them. Some people felt "called" to engage in other forms of direct action. In fact, 86% of "independent activists" in the sample (those who did not identify with any pro-life direct action organization) never sat-in, yet reported conviction experiences. Among those people were several of the most persistent activists in St. Louis – people who stood "at the gate to give warning" or "witnessed" one or more days a week for years on end. Unlike such independent interventions, sitting-in almost always occurred as collective action.

Direct action groups not only organized sit-ins, they also reinforced the perspective conviction produced. Rescue groups provided social contexts (such as meetings, rallies, conferences, pickets, and rescues) that allowed converts to employ their loaded vocabulary and make unchallenged arguments in support of their opinions. Participation in activist events encouraged converts to repeatedly reason through distressing aspects of abortion and to arrive at conclusions couched in pro-life ideology.

Direct activists' rhetoric served as a political tool to unite sympathizers and persuade others to join them in a common perspective, reinforce that perspective, and distinguish pro-lifers and their sense of reality and morality from those who opposed them. Through relexicalization and graphics rich in symbolism that both shocked and pleased, pro-life direct activists combined powerful imagery to reconstruct a portion of their audiences' worldviews. Rhetoric amplified recruits' sense of danger, heightened their emotional response to "their preborn brethren," and honored the direct action response. While direct action organizations provided converts immediate social unity, their literature and audiovisual materials dramatized an extended community within the nation "fighting for the children" and against their "enemies."

Human action carries a double burden. It serves to construct or negotiate personal identity or selfhood for its agents and to help them deal with the persistent, universal problems of human existence (such as birth, ill health, death, and good or bad fortune) (Cohen 1974). Answering to these two demands, direct activists' rhetoric and rescue, like other human actions, were at once political and symbolic. Politically, the rhetoric and sit-ins helped negotiate a role for the individual within society (even as they cast others into roles) (cf. Cohen 1974). Symbolically they expressed and refined the self-concept of the individual. Rescuers' narratives clearly articulated these two functions of activism.

Conviction occurred when individuals brought their self-identities, views of social relationships, and approaches to moral reasoning into accord. Their opposition to abortion was a manifestation of the clear, unified perspective conviction provided on the nature of community and their roles in it.

Most direct activists indicated that through rescue they surpassed their normal response to others' needs or to God. Participation in direct action was not a typical instance of their morality at work. It was an extraordinary expression of high ideals that conviction brought to the fore. This very exceptionality helps explain individuals' eventual willingness to stop sitting-in, despite their continuing ideological commitment to direct action.

CHAPTER SEVEN

PERSISTENCE:

A QUANTITATIVE ANALYSIS[1]

While most direct activists described themselves as "convicted to pro-life," levels of participation varied widely. Conviction did not assure persistence in rescue. In order to gain a perspective on the sample as a whole, I looked for correlations between interviewees' attitudes toward direct action and the number of sit-ins they undertook. Their attitudes toward activism had several distinct dimensions: One related to their evaluation of strategies, another related to the objectives they pursued through activism – an aspect of the meanings they attributed to it. Conviction experiences provided a third dimension to interviewees' attitudes toward activism. I coded "meanings," "strategic preferences," and "conviction" in activists' narratives, then correlated these themes with "levels of participation" in sit-ins (my dependent variable). Because of the religious tenor of conviction and the meanings many activists gave to rescue, I also compared the distribution of these themes in the three religious groups represented in the sample. I will describe each of the variables before presenting the correlations.

STRATEGIC PREFERENCE

Direct action made sense to both purists and pragmatists, at least for a time. Purists doubted legal measures would ever bring change and attempted to stop abortions through direct confrontations. They argued that, "Babies are dying today, what good will legislation you obtain three years from now do them?" Pragmatists most often responded, "You may

---

[1] This chapter is based on an article coauthored with Ted G. Jelen and published in the *Journal for the Scientific Study of Religion* 35:1:65–70.

save two babies today, and that is very important, but if you delay legal change, millions will die each year." However, at times pragmatists argued that, by threatening chaos, direct action goaded legislators to adopt pro-life measures; hence, they saw direct action complimenting and promoting the goals of conventional activism. From this perspective direct action was evolutionary in that it incrementally furthered a long-term, multifaceted approach to recriminalizing abortion. From purists' viewpoint, direct action was revolutionary in that it took immediate control of a situation, overturning the status quo.

Most interviewees evidenced both pragmatic and purist leanings when evaluating tactics and describing activism itself. However, they tended to speak either more forcefully or more consistently along the lines of one or the other approach. Although many interviewees made strong statements of both purist and pragmatist convictions, one theme predominated (in all but three cases). Some interviewees unequivocally espoused a single strategic preference. I coded 17 (21.25%) interviewees as pragmatists and 60 (75%) as purists (3, or 3.75% were uncodable).

PRAGMATISTS

A pragmatic pro-life strategy would adopt intermediate demands to gain readily attainable goals, restricting abortion practice with the intent to press incrementally toward an ultimate objective of fully recriminalizing abortion. Pragmatists attached "relatively more value to policies outside the immediate vicinity of [their] ideal point," and so pursued a more compromising, evolutionary approach (following DeNardo's definition of pragmatism, 1985:68,91,92). The quintessential attitude evinced by pragmatists was "I'm not going to go to jail for the sake of going to jail." For them, activism had to be effective (according to their terms) or it was misguided. While they did not discount the value of "a single life saved," they evaluated the effectiveness of time spent saving that one life by comparing it to the number of lives they might have saved through other means over the same period of time.

Pragmatists said their tactics provided "real chances" for "concrete success." They either stated that the tactics they favored were the "best thing to do" or claimed that other tactics were not effective. Some described their own tactics as a way to get their communities involved and persuade authorities; these people often sought publicity, saying that it helped their cause.

Pragmatists placed a high value on maintaining a balance in their lives. They talked about weighing the risks inherent in a given tactic against the hope of success it afforded and their own sense of duty.

A pure, sincere strategy "steadfastly demands the ideal policy of the strategy maker" (DeNardo 1985:42). Pro-life purists would accept nothing less than their ultimate goal, the full recriminalization of all abortions, with exception made only when a woman's life was clearly threatened by her pregnancy. Purists not only focused primarily on "ultimate goals and abstract principles," they had an "intense disliking for policies only slightly removed from [their] ideal point," inclining them toward a revolutionary approach to activism (following DeNardo's definition of purism, 1985:68,91,92). Purists contended that hope and duty outweighed any risks involved in direct action and that risks were not worthy of weighing into a decision. Their activism was a moral imperative; they did not accept a middle ground on abortion or seek publicity. Many explained that their only purpose was to "save babies" and "stand up for children who are being killed"; they said they "put [themselves] between the killer and the victim." One activist, referring to her efforts to "save lives," concluded, "That has to be my first commitment, other things are secondary."

When explaining why they chose to enact their beliefs by sitting-in, some purists stated that they would go to jail or even die for God. As one woman remarked several times during her interview, "That would be the greatest, to die for God!" (Many activists described what they did as risking their own lives both literally and figuratively.) Purists concluded that conventional activism "wasn't enough, it's not really getting into the heart of it."

Purists argued that people needed to "make sacrifices, personally" or at least be "willing to sacrifice." They insisted, "That's that baby's last chance," said they performed their duty at the "doors of hell," and described a need to "change now."

Purists valued symbolic success that lacked concrete evidence. They countered arguments against the effectiveness of their activism by replying that "You never know what good you've done," often concluding that, "If one woman changes her mind, that's enough."

Many purists' activism was a response to an emotional impulse. Some purists cried copiously while discussing their activism or the experiences that led them to become involved. Pragmatists' narratives lacked this expressive dimension. Purists occasionally expressed anger at conventional activists, at public apathy and acquiescence, and at people performing or supporting abortion practice. Some purists (unlike pragmatists) condoned violent means; as one commented, "I have no problems with somebody who wants to bomb a clinic unless someone is in it."

MEANING

A slight majority of interviewees stated that their activism was primarily worship, although they might also hope to "save babies," help women, or arouse the nation through it. The remainder of the sample described their activism as instrumental, tactical, political, moral, or expressive, although many in this group said they were inclined to take such actions because they were committed to religious principles. Activists often mingled these two elements in their narratives, but all stressed one type of rationality over the other. Activism was essentially a religious activity for 42 interviewees (52.5% of the sample) and primarily a nonreligious activity for 38 interviewees (47.5%).

SACRED ACTS

The 42 interviewees who characterized their activism as essentially sacred enactments said they sat-in, picketed, and so forth in order to honor God, thank God, serve God, be obedient to God, let God use them, carry the Lord's message, "proclaim," "lift up Jesus," "share Jesus," or "witness" (either to God's power, truth, or saving grace, or to the hazards and "sin of abortion"). They said these purposes were achieved through the sheer activity of sitting-in, picketing, and so forth, whether or not activists dissuaded women from aborting or aroused their communities. The meaning these interviewees gave to their activism lay in the doing of it – not in ulterior results obtained *through* activism. Rescue was valuable because in and of itself it fulfilled demands placed upon the people who did it. Weber (1978) termed this type of reasoning and motivation "value-rationality."

Many of these interviewees explained that through their activism they were able to live out their religion (that is, they put their religious beliefs into action or lived up to the obligations and standards entailed in their beliefs). One activist remarked that by sitting-in he could "be an upright man of God"; a woman said that by sitting-in she fulfilled her duty in God's eyes. Another activist explained, "I had to act to be a Christian."

Several interviewees said that they sat-in to fulfill their "Godly duty" to follow their religious leaders. A small number of interviewees said they participated because following their religious leaders assuaged the guilt evoked in them by rally speakers. Several activists explained that by sitting-in they could "help the stranger." One woman said she sat-in because she was determined to make her life count. Another woman captured the sentiments expressed by many activists when she explained that, "It's the real stuff of the Bible come to life."

Some interviewees said their activism fulfilled a religious obligation to make personal sacrifices. They described activism as sacrificial giving of the self, a way to sacrifice for another or to suffer for Christ. Other interviewees emphasized the redemptive capacity of their activism. Some said it was a means for obtaining personal salvation or averting damnation; a few said it was indispensable. Several women explained that they first joined direct action in order to "redeem" themselves for having aborted; although their motivations changed with time, they first sat-in because "it was a way to get to heaven." Others (who had not aborted) declared, "I couldn't face God if I didn't do something." Activism was also a way of "setting the captives free" or saving people from going to hell.

Some interviewees described their activism as "spiritual warfare." Rather than focusing on personal salvation, they conceptualized their activism as a means to cope with a threat to "the community," a way to preserve or secure communal good. They said they were engaging in a "spiritual battle against evil," "standing up against evil," "warring against Satan," or "standing in the gap." Through their activism they were "repenting to the Lord and asking Him to forgive our leaders"; they hoped to bring "restoration" to the nation and "prepare for Christ." Along this line, others said they were enforcing God's law, "making a statement that can't be censored," "holding up a standard of God before the public," "taking a stand for God" (for "the Lord," or for "Christian principle"), or attempting to "activate the Christian community."

None within this group said they did not hope to save babies as well, but the sacred purposes they pursued were primary. They avidly affirmed this primacy, and some openly doubted they would deter any abortions or stir a community response.

SECULAR ACTS

The 38 interviewees who characterized their activism as essentially secular in purpose stated that it was expressly intended to "save babies," "stop abortion," or "fulfill their duty to the unborn." Many within this group intended their activism to arouse the pro-life community and pressure politicians into restricting or outlawing abortion as well. They described their activism as a logical and potentially effective "response to injustice." Some said they participated in order to "stop women from hurting themselves" or "to respond to women's needs." One man participated in order to protect his wife (who considered her activism to be a religious expression). These were instumental actions, undertaken to obtain objective results. Weber (1978) termed this type of reasoning and motivation "instrumental rationality." Like those who considered their activism to be worship, many interviewees who emphasized instumental rationality feared that legalized abortion would destroy the United States by distorting its demographics and undermining nurturant values. They explained that their activism was intended to avert the disaster that human folly would surely bring if our society continued to sanction abortion.

FINDINGS

I compared subgroups within the sample of 80 to determine which attitudes corresponded with a high level of participation in sit-ins. I distinguished between activists who did not sit-in ($n = 14$), those who sat-in up to three times ($n = 22$), and those who sat-in four or more times ($n = 44$).[2] (I discuss the rationale for choosing these particular levels in the methods section.) Because of the small number of interviewees in the subgroup that did not sit-in, these findings are suggestive of differences and are not conclusive.

CONVICTION

Conviction appears to have increased the likelihood of extensive involvement in sit-ins. Overall, 81% of the sample reported conviction

---

[2] Four interviewees in the subgroup that did not sit-in were new to direct action and might eventually have chosen to sit-in. All but one of the interviewees who did not sit-in but did recount a conviction experience, attributed a religious meaning to their activism. That one person was intensely involved in promoting the direct action movement over a long period of time, and encouraged his spouse to sit-in. Four of these activists assumed roles in the direct action movement to support their spouses, who did sit-in. Three of those four had not become convicted to pro-life, such as one older man who picketed primarily to protect his wife when she sat-in and, secondarily, to express his opinion on various political and economic points consonant with attitudes that goaded conviction in other interviewees.

experiences (2.5% of the sample were uncodable on this variable). However, the percent reporting conviction in the three subgroups varied. The
rate of conviction increased with the rate of participation. Seventy-one
percent of those who never sat-in described conviction experiences,
77% of those who sat-in a few times had been convicted, and 86% of
those who sat-in the most had been convicted. (One person in each of
the first two subgroups was uncodable.)

As noted in the previous chapter, many activists' narratives indicated that conviction was crucial to their participation in sit-ins. These
qualitative reports were supported by quantitative analysis that found
activists who reported a conviction experience were much more likely
to have participated extensively in sit-ins than those who did not report
conviction experiences (Maxwell and Jelen 1994, 1996).[3] Conviction
was an important part of becoming a direct activist and encouraged
intense participation. However, the high rate of conviction among all
three subgroups suggests that it did not *determine* the manner or extent
of one's participation in direct activism.

STRATEGIC PREFERENCE

All three subgroups included both purists and pragmatists but the proportions of each varied from one subgroup to the next. The group that
sat-in the most had proportionately more purists (86%) than the group
that sat-in a few times (64%), which, in turn, had proportionately more
purists than the group that did not sit-in at all (57%). Pragmatists were
unusually well represented in the group that sat-in a little (36%), and
poorly represented in the group that sat-in the most (14%). However,
this correlation was most often a consequence of the way strategic preference covaried with meaning (Maxwell and Jelen 1994, 1996). That
is, for most activists, a particular strategic preference was coupled with
a particular meaning given to activism, but the meaning of activism,
not the strategic preference, related to activists' persistence – with one
exception.

---

[3] An analysis of variance (ANOVA), well-suited to analyzing a sample such as
this, with small subgroups, showed a very strong correlation between levels of
participation and the conviction experience (significant at .031) (Maxwell and
Jelen 1994).
   My thanks to Dr. Ted Jelen for putting his head together with mine while his
fingers punched in one statistical analysis after another, and to his lovely secretary
who re-entered all of my data so that we could do this!

Among all three religious groups, purism corresponded with persistent participation in sit-ins. However, religion differentiated among pragmatists. While pragmatic Protestants participated at noticeably low levels, pragmatic Catholics were among the most extensively involved activists in the sample. Although pragmatic *non*-Catholics are likely to participate in few sit-ins, pragmatism did not depress participation in sit-ins among Catholics.[4] In fact, 72% of pure Catholics and 75% of pragmatic Catholics sat-in four or more times. In contrast, 57% of pure – but only 23% of pragmatic – *non*-Catholics sat-in four or more times. The notable difference among pragmatists associated with religious affiliation may have masked the influence of strategic preference on levels of participation.

MEANING

The proportions of interviewees who attributed either a religious or a secular meaning to their activism varied sharply from one subgroup to the next. Among those who never sat-in, 71% considered their activism to be worship, as did 73% of those who sat-in less than four times, while only 36% of those who sat-in four times or more described their activism in such terms. (Everyone in the sample was codable on this factor.)

Meaning had an extremely powerful effect on the level of activists' involvement in sit-ins. Quantitative analysis showed a very strong tendency for interviewees who attributed secular meanings to their activism to participate extensively and for interviewees who attributed religious meanings to their activism to participate much less extensively (Maxwell and Jelen 1994, 1996).[5] Although religious and secular meanings neither precluded nor mandated sitting-in, secular meanings predominated among those who sat-in extensively, and religious meanings

---

[4] The correlation (Pearson's r) between number of rescues and pragmatism for *non*-Catholics was $-.25$ ($p = .04$), indicating that pragmatic non-Catholics were likely to participate in few sit-ins; the correlation between number of rescues and pragmatism for Catholics was $.08$ ($p = .36$), indicating that pragmatism *did not* depress Catholic's participation in sit-ins. The intense participation of pragmatic Catholics might have dampened the correlation between strategic preference and levels of participation. Unfortunately, the small number of pragmatists in the sample made a multivariate model inappropriate for further analysis.

[5] An analysis of variance (ANOVA) for this correlation was (significant at .002) (Maxwell and Jelen 1994).

predominated among those who either did not sit-in at all, or did not persist in sitting-in.

STRATEGIC PREFERENCE AND MEANING

In order to better understand the dynamics underlying high levels of participation in sit-ins I looked for links between strategic preference and meaning in the three subgroups. The sample as a whole contained 28 pure secularists (35%) and 32 pure religionists (40%). The pragmatists split as evenly as possible; 9 considered their activism to be a secular activity (11%) and 8 considered it to be worship (10%).

Pure religionists dominated the subgroup that did not sit-in and formed a clear majority in the subgroup that sat-in a few times.[6] Pure secularists formed a clear majority in the subgroup that sat-in the most, while this group's proportion of pragmatic religionists was half that of the sample as a whole.

The directions of change from one subgroup to the next were consistent on all but one comparison.[7] Overall, the proportion of pure secularists increased and the proportion of both pragmatic and pure religionists decreased as the extent of participation in sit-ins increased.

CONVICTION AND MEANING

The combination of meaning and conviction had a very strong effect on levels of participation in sit-ins (Maxwell and Jelen 1994, 1996).[8] However, the predictive value of conviction varied dramatically according to the specific meaning activists assigned to rescue. Quantitative analysis

---

[6] The group that did not sit-in was compromised by its small size and the large proportion of interviewees in it that were not codable. However, adding its three uncodable interviewees to any component of this group would not have created a larger contingent than the 43% who were pure religionists.

[7] The group that sat-in the most had fewer pragmatic secularists than the group that sat-in a little, and slightly more than the group that did not sit-in. Again, comparisons to the group that did not sit-in are suspect, due to its very small size and the large proportion of interviewees in it that were uncodable as to their strategic preference.

[8] The ANOVA for this relationship was significant at .021. The relationship (Pearson's r) between conviction and the number of rescues for secularists was .47 ($p = .0017$) – very strong. The relationship between conviction and number of rescues for religionists was .04 ($p = .4121$) – meaningless (Maxwell and Jelen 1994).

showed a very strong correlation between conviction and number of rescues for secularists, indicating that (instrumentally rational) secularists
who were convicted would sit-in extensively. The same analysis showed
a negligible correlation between conviction and number of rescues for
religionists, indicating that (value-rational) religionists who where convicted were as likely to participate in other forms of opposition as they
were to sit-in.

CONVICTION AND RELIGIOUS AFFILIATION

Activists' religious affiliations did not determine the likelihood of their
experiencing conviction. The proportions of non-denominationals,
Protestants, and Catholics that described conviction experiences were
almost identical to the proportions of those religious groups in the sample as a whole. (For example, denominational Protestants comprised
17% of the interviewees who were convicted and 18% of the sample
as a whole.) Nondenominationals tended to use the term "conviction
to pro-life" much more frequently than Protestants and Catholics, although interviewees with all three affiliations did use the term. While
nondenominationals were slightly more likely to have been convicted,
conviction was not exclusively an evangelical experience.

The high percentage of nondenominationals who indicated they
were "convicted to pro-life" (91% of evangelicals) might suggest that
conviction was a trope drawn from their customary ways of framing
experiences. However, the majority of Catholics (65%) and denominational Protestants (79%) reported conviction experiences as well.
These interviewees might have adopted their nondenominational companions' trope. Alternatively, the high rate of conviction in all three
religious groups suggests that conviction was not merely an extension of
an evangelical worldview or nondenominationals' jargon, but rather a
type of experience that was an important aspect of forming commitment
to a risky, challenging task.

CONCLUSION

Neither the experience of conviction, nor a particular construal of activism was requisite to impel direct action, but conviction increased the
likelihood of persistent participation in sit-ins, as did a secular (instrumentally rational) construal of activism. People who conceived of direct
action as a (value-rational) religious activity tended toward short-term

involvement in sit-ins. I suspect that because religion addresses diverse phenomena – including opposition to abortion – religious obligations or yearnings could be satisfied through means other than anti-abortion activism. In contrast, my observations suggested that both pragmatists and purists who focused on a "baby being torn limb from limb" repeatedly concluded that sitting-in was either justified or necessary – at times inescapable.

The large majority of purists in the sample is not surprising, owing to the nature of the activism under consideration. Direct action, with its immediacy and high personal involvement lends itself to purist pursuits, while conventional activism with its step-by-step processes and incremental successes lends itself to pragmatic temperaments. Purists tended to persist in sit-ins while most pragmatists joined a few sit-ins and then either gravitated toward other facets of the direct action movement or left abortion activism altogether – at least, that was the path taken by most non-Catholic pragmatists.

Pragmatists of different faiths confronted disparate social contexts. The persistence of Catholic pragmatists may result from their church's long-standing, adamant opposition to abortion. Perhaps this overt, unyielding doctrine, in conjunction with the church's complex history of social activism, turned Catholics back to rescue when they contemplated quitting, prolonged their willingness to persist, or normalized unconventional anti-abortion activism – making it more palatable to people with a pragmatic bent, while non-Catholic churches readily offered a safehaven for pragmatic "drop-outs." In addition to promoting an intellectual and emotional atmosphere conducive to anti-abortion attitudes, the layers of authority within the Catholic church created options for grassroots activists that were unavailable to non-Catholics (as discussed in the final chapter). Although the local archbishop discouraged direct action, bishops elsewhere sat-in, and the Pope condemned abortion. This ambiguity in the extensive Catholic hierarchy dampened the impact of the local archbishop's disapproval and allowed Catholics to argue that persistence was compatible with obedience, justifying continued direct action. Evangelical churches lacked higher authorities to mitigate local leaders' positions. Denominational Protestant churches never became officially involved in direct action, and so served as uncondemning, undemanding safe havens for former direct activists.

In the sample as a whole, the conviction experience was more strongly associated with purism and sacred meanings. (Ninety percent of purists reported conviction experiences, as compared to 59% of pragmatists, and 88% of those pursuing religious objectives reported conviction experiences as compared to 71% of those pursuing secular goals.) However, the conviction experience did not necessarily endow activism with a (value-rational) religious meaning or instill purist aspirations. The high proportion of pure-secularists who experienced conviction (82%) suggests that conviction was not simply an extension of religious experience or a function of value-rationality.

The meaning activists attributed to rescue powerfully influenced their persistence in it; the conviction experience also strongly related to persistence.[9] Quantitative analysis indicated that of the variables considered above, only meaning and conviction explained levels of participation. Strategic preference appeared to be related to participation, but this was a function of the way it covaried with meaning (Maxwell and Jelen 1994, 1996).[10]

Such analyses provide no simple explanation of participation in sit-ins. Activists' attitudes were not static. Interviewees indicated that the contexts within which they made their decisions to participate in sit-ins modified the meaning of rescue, the influence of strategic preferences, and the impetus provided by "conviction to pro-life." Such contexts influenced the type of rationality individuals employed in deciding whether to sit-in or not. The narratives in preceding chapters explored the interaction of individual circumstances, conviction experiences, personal understandings, and involvement in direct action. For example, Rick's narrative illustrated the initial impetus of conviction and the subsequent dissipation of value-rational motivation, so readily diverted into alternative sacred channels. Jan's narrative showed how shifts in personal circumstances could allow pragmatic considerations to overshadow purist pursuits, despite her secular objectives. And Bailey's persistent activism demonstrated the stable influence of pragmatic, secular motivations.

---

[9] An ANOVA showed a powerful relationship between the variables for meaning and persistence (significant at .002); conviction and persistence were also strongly related (significant at .031) (Maxwell and Jelen 1994).

[10] The ANOVA also showed that, of all the demographic factors noted in the sample description – including religious affiliation – levels of participation were related significantly only to the number of children activists had.

CHAPTER EIGHT

GENDER DIFFERENCES IN

MOTIVATION[1]

For the past two decades, the issue of abortion has occasioned a great deal of political activity (both conventional and unconventional) by people whose political involvement was previously casual, intermittent, or even nonexistent (Andrews and Cavanaugh-O'Keefe 1989; Cook et al. 1992; deParrie 1989; Ginsburg 1989, 1993; Granberg 1981; Harding 1990; Luker 1984). In the pro-life direct action movement, many such first-time activists were women.

THE INVISIBILITY OF WOMEN'S ACTIVISM

Historically, women's formal activism has largely disappeared. Women's small-scale activism is often crushed before it matures into mass movement. Their more evident activism has been dismissed as nonpolitical behavior or simply not recorded. In either case women's activism tends to disappear from public and historical view (West and Blumberg 1990). Women's informal activism is difficult to quantify because, by simply shaping her life into something other than a socially prescribed role, a woman's very selfhood smacks of political action. Conversely, women can adopt a traditional role to either reinforce or challenge a power structure, and so, become part of a society's politics. Women's activism has been simultaneously long-standing, hampered, vast, and largely invisible or discounted. West and Blumberg note that "academic work on

---

[1] This chapter was developed from two papers coauthored with Ted G. Jelen, one presented at the Annual Meeting of the Society for the Scientific Study of Religion in 1995, and the other published in the *Review of Religious Research* 37:2:117–31 (see Maxwell and Jelen 1995a, 1995b).

social protest" rarely mentions women and even less frequently provides "comparative analysis of men's and women's roles, attitudes, and feelings as social protestors" (1990:7). This has not been the case with women's abortion-related activism, which has been analyzed repeatedly since the late 1960s.

Since political activism in general (like moral reasoning, religious ceremony, and other aspects of human behavior) has largely been defined by men's participation, conceptions of its nature have begun to change as it has been reformulated to include women's participation, or as West and Blumberg put it, "women's lives, experiences, feelings, and visions" (1990:4). Adding this dimension is not merely politically correct, but essential for accurate analysis. Not only is women's participation part of the reality of political behavior, recent studies have shown that "'gender is one of the most, sometimes *the* most, differentiating factor in studies of political behavior'" (West and Blumberg 1990:7). Because of the potential for gendered differences, I will analyze the relationship between men's and women's narrative themes and levels of participation separately, and compare the findings.[2]

Political behavior in general is shaped by the resources and opportunities available to potential actors. Women's activism has been particularly constrained by legal codes, religious doctrines, and cultural ideologies and practices that define politics, who may participate in them, and at what cost (Luker 1984; Nelson and Chowdhury 1994; West and Blumberg 1990). Historically, power structures have afforded women (like poor or marginalized groups of people) few opportunities to assert their claims. They have often incurred high costs for participation and had few resources available to them. Consequently, much of women's activism has involved activities that have been dismissed as "crowdlike, emotional, or deviant." From the 1960s onward, scholars began to argue that opportunity structures and the availability of resources explained such strategic choices as political, rather than psychological (West and Blumberg 1990:5).

Studies of women's activism worldwide show that it tends to focus on either practical or strategic gender interests. Practical interests arise from concrete conditions and address immediate, perceived needs; strategic

---

[2] Both analyses were conservative. For example, all men referred to fetuses as "babies" or "children" and expressed empathy toward them as people. Yet I only coded men on this theme when they specifically noted this perception as a factor in their initial decision to sit-in.

interests stem from an analysis of women's conditions and a formulation of more satisfying arrangements (Nelson and Chowdhury 1994). Women addressing practical interests often adopt an ameliorative approach that may rely on traditional gender roles or norms rather than challenging them. However, such concerns often precede – and stimulate – recognition of strategic interests (Chafetz, Dworkin, and Swanson 1990; Nelson and Chowdhury 1994). Consequently, while these types of interests may be associated initially with different classes, a class-based construction is not universally supported. And, indeed, women in the St. Louis sample ranged from lower to upper middle class, and common indicators of class did not explain their levels of activism (Maxwell and Jelen 1995b).

Direct activists' narratives suggest they addressed both practical and strategic goals through their sit-ins. That is, women sat in both to stop abortions from happening, and to resist aspects of their society that they deemed damaging to both society as a whole, and to individuals. Some analysts suggest that the people who support pro-life organizations, or who engage in pro-life direct action, may exhibit primarily religious motivations (Blanchard 1994; Blanchard and Prewitt 1993; Ginsburg 1989, 1993; Guth, Smidt, Kellstedt, and Green 1993;). This research has produced an emergent, conventional wisdom, in which religous orthodoxy, activity, and zeal is thought to provide the primary impetus for unconventional anti-abortion protest activity. The previous chapter shows the fragility of religious motivation. While many pro-life leaders make explicit use of religious imagery in justifying their activities, this tendency is not sufficient to explain women's activism (Maxwell and Jelen 1995a, 1995b; Wills 1990:318–28). Women's narratives paint a more complex picture of their motivations.

WOMEN'S NARRATIVE THEMES

Like men in the sample, women most often related their activism to their Christianity (73% of women and 72% of men).[3] However, women's

---

[3] Taken together, a number of covariates (parental status, participation in the paid labor force, religious affiliation, and having had a born-again experience) did exhibit significant effects on sit-in participation. But the only single variable with statistically significant effects was the born-again experience. Women who had been born again were much more likely to engage in frequent sit-ins than those who had not. Given the importance of conviction in most activists' narratives, such a result is not surprising, although it is of interest to note that the specific

narratives explicated the rather omnibus explanation that their activism was a consequence of their religiosity. They described their decisions to engage in direct action as expressions of gratitude to God, reflections of their love for God, a way to make a commitment or sacrifice to God, act as a Christian, serve God, please God, or uphold God's righteousness. One woman explained, "I do it because I have been saved, because I love Jesus . . . I sensed God's broken heart over what's happening and it breaks my heart, too." Another emphasized the need for action, saying, "I repented for my sin of just letting it go, but to correct it in my life, I had to do something." She elaborated, asking, "What if I died tonight and I stood before God and He said, 'What did you do about this horrible thing?'" A third woman explained that,

> Probably the most important thing to me is to uphold the righteousness of God. It's like saying God does not like this, this is against God's law, the Commandments. Taking a stand for God. That would please God.

Along these lines, women also described their activism as a way to evangelize, establish themselves as Christians, revive the church, or respond to God's call. One woman concluded, "I guess the abortion issue is just another way to talk to some different people and share with them that God cares about what's going on down here." Another woman said, "The good works that we do are basically to show people our faith. If we sit at home, how is anybody to know? Why would anybody want to become a Chrisitan if they didn't see?"

Women often referred to God leading or commanding them to sit-in. One recalled that, "The Lord really pierced our hearts with the conviction: What are you doing? Why are you sitting back?" Activism allowed her to fulfill a sense of duty and reciprocity important to her self-identity. She explained that,

> Christ laid his life down for us. I feel like I should be able to give my life back to Him. If by giving my life back to him I'm laying it before Him to block the entrance to these killing places. What purpose do I have in life if I don't help save a life? We need to be Christians and stand up . . . not be imitation Christians.

experience of being convicted to pro-life is empirically independent of a more general experience of being born-again. (For more detail see Maxwell and Jelen 1995b.)

Another woman described a "crisis of about 20 minutes" during which she recalled thinking, "I would die if I didn't obey the Lord. It was incredible. It was shortness of breath, it was utterly clear that I had to do it." She explained that, "Every saved person has a mission, something that God wants them to do. And this was it for me." She described direct action as being "basically what Christ did for us," that is, removing "a woman who is in imminent danger of spiritual death and a child who is in danger of imminent physical death, and putting them nearer Christ."

While men distinctly described their activism as sacrifice, women infrequently used this term. When women did make reference to sacrifice, it did not emerge as a separate motivating theme, nor did women speak of sacrifice with the same strident tone men used. They blended it into their descriptions of the religious nature of activism. One woman asked, "Why were these people there? Laying down their lives . . . their safety. It was a real act of love . . . sacrificial love." She went on to recall that, "there was a terrible wrong being committed, and I thought if it would help, I would be there."

Many more women than men were swayed to sit-in by pro-life rhetoric – especially videos, rally speakers, and Christian radio (70% of women, compared to 44% of men). Videos were particularly potent motivators. One woman recalled that after viewing *Assignment Life*, which showed footage of an actual abortion, "I just broke down, uncontrollably broke down, me and this one other girl were holding each others' hands." She felt that, "Nothing else mattered. Nothing else was important. This horrible thing was going on and nobody was doing anything about it." Photos could revive the response initially elicited by a movie. She continued, "I couldn't look at these pictures without breaking down in tears. I felt like somebody ripped my heart out." Another woman concluded that she became involved, "through reading Randall Terry's material and through becoming convinced that he was a godly man. I saw it as a move of God . . . that would honor Him." When women pointed to pro-life videos as the source of their commitment to activism, they usually indicated that the movies shocked, enlightened, and permanently changed them.

Although women did not emphasize their desire to obtain or maintain affiliation with a group, as men did, women often joined direct action with a friend, and sometimes with a group. Women frequently referred to the close, meaningful bonds they felt with other activists. Altogether, 61% of women referred to the value they placed on such social aspects of activism, often without indicating that their participation was dependent on them. Women spoke of these bonds more as an unanticipated benefit or natural, pleasing environment than a causal factor in their activism. This contrasted with men's discourse; 66% of men indicated that they joined direct action to establish or maintain such bonds. Women commented: "I've never had friends like I've had in pro-life"; "I went with a group of people. I never did anything on my own . . . To me, scripturally and every way it made sense, and I knew people who were doing it." Women recalled that at rallies, "You get inspired when you get with other people that are inspired . . . You want to help others that are out there trying to do something about it," and "Some of the closest relationships I've made lately were in jail because I knew these were committed people, they were honest, they loved the important things of life that I loved." More in line with men's narratives, one woman recalled that,

> I became pro-life probably because the people I lean hardest on are really into it and they challenged me with standing up for what I believed. That was the mode they chose at the time. So I thought, it will be showing what I think, and it'll mean something to somebody, I'm willing to do that.

Half of the women said they sat-in to save a life. As one woman put it, "Number two is to plead to God Almighty to change their hearts. Number one should be to save babies." Another woman asserted that, "If it weren't for somebody being killed, I'd be on the other side, clearly . . . I'd be the first person so mad at some guy trying to tell her what to do!" One woman voiced a sentiment many expressed, saying, "I guess I felt for those babies . . . these babies are dying and somebody's got to go in and get them."

While women tended to focus on their desire to save a life, men tended to refer to abortion as a threat to life in the process of explaining why they needed to act, or why activism was Christian. That is, women expressed a desire or need to save a life, while men expressed a need to act, and explained that need by pointing at the threat to life. This is a rather subtle distinction, a difference in emphasis, and certainly some men were intent on "saving a life." Conversely, some women did emphasize the need-to-act, so prominent in men's narratives (41% of women, 66% of men). Such women spoke of the need to bring their actions in line with their beliefs, or of needing to sit-in because direct action entailed all parts of themselves or suited their personalities. A few women emphasized their need to respond to the helplessness or innocence of the "babies" (21%).

Almost half the women (46%) were motivated to sit-in by guilt, although very few used the word. They spoke of sitting-in to avoid hurting themselves, and explained that they sat-in because they would feel bad if they did not sit-in because they "knew" they should "do more," or needed to be involved. The motivating force of guilt was more weakly implied by men's discourse regarding the need to act. A woman, devastated by her own abortion, explained that, "It broke my heart everytime I went to picket." She recalled that, just before sitting-in, "When I saw those three individuals blocking the door with their heads bowed in prayer, I just thought, with what I know, I should be in front of that door."

Several themes were common to both men and women, but showed dramatic differences in their prevalence. In sharp contrast to men, very few women used martial or war imagery (11% of women, 59% of men). (The implications of this difference are discussed in Maxwell and Jelen 1995a.) Martial imagery or a concern with marshalling energy echoed through several minor themes and showed similar gender differences. Men were almost three times as likely as women to describe the contention over abortion as a spiritual battle or problem (14% of women, 38% of men). Again, men were about three times as likely as women to have been inspired by a direct action leader (7% of women, 22% of men), or to have joined direct action to witness, warn people of the evil of abortion, or make the community accountable (9% of women, 31% of men). And men were twice as likely as women to engage in direct action because it was a threat to the nation or to themselves (27% of women, 56% of men). One woman, whose narrative did include this theme, remarked, "I don't know how long God's going to put up with this. I don't think He can stand it." Another woman focused on more empirical concerns:

> We're killing babies and we're killing off our future standing army, future doctors, future inventors, future scientists, future leaders, future educators. We're killing off our future. We're killing off social security, workers. We're destroying the family concept. We're destroying the sanctity of life. We're destroying the idea of children, the preciousness of children.

Women were over three times as likely as men to explain that they engaged in direct action after becoming frustrated with conventional activism (23% of women, 6% of men). Anger, an uncommon factor in men's activism, was so infrequently mentioned by women that it was not scored. Women were twice as likely as men to report joining activism as a response to the horror they felt at seeing aborted fetuses, learning about abortion procedures, or reflecting on the fact that abortion occurred in their society (36% of women, 16% of men).

Men and women showed only slight differences regarding some themes. Men were a little bit more likely than women to explain that they began sitting-in after coming to conceptualize abortion as killing babies (36% of women, 38% of men). Almost equal proportions of men and women sat-in to be in solidarity or communion with the "babies" (14% of women, 16% of men). Grief was a somewhat more common motivator among men than among women (9% of women, 14% of men). Similarly low percentages of men and women joined direct action because they conceptualized it as effective (21% of women, 19% of men).

Several themes appeared in women's narratives, but were nearly absent in men's narratives. Thirty percent of women became active in response to the role abortion had played in their own lives, or those of their family or friends. Fourteen percent of women sat-in to redeem themselves. Nine percent wanted to express love to others as it had been expressed to them in the past. Twenty-three percent joined direct action in order to send a message to the public or lawmakers. They described sitting-in as a strategy that alerted lawmakers to an element in the pro-life movement "that can only be stalled so long."

Forty-three percent of women sat-in because they felt women were being coerced into abortions and they wanted to offer help or information about abortion and its effects on women. Some of these activists had had abortions themselves. Typical of women who had aborted, one referred to, "just that feeling that you can actively keep somebody from going in there and making the same mistake I made." Another described abortion as "the bondage of women to the system that says, you have no alternatives other than to kill your baby." A woman who had not aborted said she sat-in after "I was opened up to just really what abortion was doing to people – especially to mothers. So I decided that something needed to be done." Another woman remembered that, "What I really saw was a lot of hurting people. And the whole message of the gospel is that Jesus came to save hurting people. I mean the mothers is what really got me." An older woman remarked that, "Grandmothers need to take a stand; they need to counsel these women." And another woman explained, "I wanted to be the kind of person that would go the extra mile and help somebody because I grew up with that. I knew what I was going to do without, if somebody didn't do it for me."

About a third of the women considered their direct activism an out-growth of commitment and distress developed through their picketing experiences (34%). One woman captured the essence of this theme, saying,

> But it was very distressful to picket . . . Well, you're there and you're seeing these women go in, and it's not just "Babies are being killed somewhere out there," it's "Babies are being killed several feet away from you." And not just any babies are being killed – that beautiful blond gal, with the blue eyes, it's her baby that's being killed. And it's not being killed tomorrow; it's being killed within the next 15, 20 minutes. It's a horrifying thing to be that close to that.

Only a few women sat-in on impulse (9%); more said they became active after having suddenly become a changed person (21%). Many more women were compelled to sit-in by the logic or "rightness" of direct action, regardless of its effectiveness (41%).

Women often formed intense commitment to activism, interweaving many of the themes discussed above. For example, one woman reasoned that, "I'm out there to save babies, and that is making a statement, that is lifting up Christ, but when I do it, it's to save a baby's life. It's one in all the same." Another woman mingled guilt, divine direction, intense desire to save a life, and the sensitization picketing produced. She explained that,

> This was after about a year of picketing. It just got to where I was so desperate I had to do more . . . because the babies were dying and I wasn't stopping them from dying. I wasn't saving anybody's life. I was just too comfortable out there picketing without trying to save a life. I knew I had to do more. I believe it was the holy spirit pulling at my heart to tell me to do it.

Women often sat-in in response to visceral conceptions of abortion. One woman remarked that,

> It got under my skin as a mother . . . I was horrified that somebody could take a baby and chop it up into little bitty pieces . . . It sent chills through me. I had a physical reaction thinking about it. It wasn't just an ideology. It was a very personal feeling.

Sometimes women started off with similar assessments of activism, but arrived at opposite conclusions. Like men, most women explained their withdrawal from direct action by noting its ineffectivness. In contrast, others responded by intensifying their commitment. One women concluded that,

> I just hate it when the police drag us away in five minutes and they're back to their killing again. I just think, why was I in there? It just seems so fruitless. So we have to chain ourselves [to furniture inside clinics].

WOMEN'S LEVELS OF PARTICIPATION

Most women explained their activism as an outgrowth or mainfestation of their Christianity and a response to pro-life rhetoric. The majority remarked on the rewarding social experiences that accompanied their activism. Despite their prevalence, none of these three themes indicated women's levels of participation. However, two metanarratives (conviction and instrumental rationality) and one narrative theme (saving lives) *were* significantly related to women's levels of activism (Maxwell and Jelen 1995b). The same two metanarratives related to men's participation; however, the influence of the narrative theme was unique to women. Women who reported conviction experiences engaged in significantly more sit-ins than women who did not describe conviction experiences. Women who attached primarily instrumental meanings to their activism were much more likely to persist in direct action than those whose motivation was primarily symbolic or religious (Maxwell and Jelen 1996). Finally, among women only, a large difference arose around the theme of saving lives. Respondents who explicitly articulated the desire to save babies exhibited substantially more extensive participation in sit-ins than those who did not (Maxwell and Jelen 1995b).[4] The effects of conviction, instrumental values, and the desire to save babies are primarily additive, that is, each independently influenced participation. If an individual experienced all three, they all exerted an influence, but one did not require the others to be influencial.[5]

---

[4] No interaction term between the thematic predictors of sit-in frequency attained statistical significance (Maxwell and Jelen 1995b).

[5] These findings contrast with Ginsburg (1989) who found procreation a dominant theme in women's narratives. However, Jelen and I found that the only demographic variable that correlated with levels of participation in sit-ins was the number of activists' children. A correlation analysis showed for the sample as

This analysis presents something of a mixed picture regarding the role of religious belief in accounting for the extent of women's sit-in activity. Conviction experiences often had religious overtones. Thus, to this extent, the supposition that pro-life direct action has a theological basis is confirmed. However, reducing anti-abortion activism to a religious activity or an outgrowth of religiosity masks the political nature of this activism, and overlooks the inherent connections between politics, law, economics, culture, and religion (cf. Marty and Appleby 1993; cf. Nelson and Chowdhury 1994).[6] The narrative themes discussed above illustrate the complex motivations underlying women's involvement in direct action.

One widespread method of erasing women's activism has been to define it as moral rather than political behavior (West and Blumberg 1990). Historically, much of women's activism has been tied to religious institutions and beliefs. For example, religious convictions sustained and justified black women opposing slavery and lynching, and seeking civil and welfare rights. Such considerations also girded white Victorian women campaigning against racial, class, and other injustices (West and Blumberg 1990:10). In a similar vein, anti-abortion activism has gained ideological support from theology. Individuals justified their participation as God-mandated, and churches organized pro-life voluntarism. Historically, voluntarism has been a major avenue into political activism for women.

The St. Louis data suggest that attributing the intensity of pro-life activism to religious motivations does not tell the entire story, despite the prominent association women drew between their Christianity and their

a whole, a statistically significant correlation of .27 (significant at .018) between the number of children activists had and the number of sit-ins they joined. This was a strong correlation, given the homogeneity of this sample (that is, most people in the sample did sit-in). However, as noted above, procreation did not dominate activists' conviction stories. This omission probably was not due to men's reluctance to express sensitivity; men expressed a wide range of emotions during interviews and several wept openly as they described experiences prior to, or entailed in their activism. Reproductive issues, in general, simply did not characterize men's narratives.

[6] These findings contrast with analyses that show the prominent role economic, social, and psychological deprivations play in overtly religious fundamentalist movements (Marty and Appleby 1993; Nelson and Chowdhury 1994). The political climate of the 1990s encouraged activism of many stripes to arise within conventional organizations, such as churches (Nelson and Carver 1994), potentially leading analysts to confuse political and religious motivations.

activism (Maxwell and Jelen 1995b). As the previous chapter demon-
strates, persistent rescue activity has substantial secular roots. Instrumental goals are strongly and positively related to the extent of protest
activity. While the general shift in anti-abortion rhetoric toward more
temporal, less religious forms of discourse may be strategic (cf. Grindstaff
1994), the strong effects of the very specific "save babies" theme suggest
that persistent rescuers focused on clearly defined secular goals. Women's
unconventional anti-abortion activism represents, from their perspective, active, rational attempts to address concerns and achieve desired
ends.

Indeed, female direct activists' objectives constitute a quintessential
theme in traditional women's activism, which is often defined as an extension of the nurturing and caring roles they play in the home. Scholars
recognize a pervasive, underlying theme in women's activism that has
been called "the politics of survival" – not a politics of self-interest, but
"a politics of love and caring that has propelled women to break out of
their boundaries and to confront or enlist the forces of the state" (West
and Blumberg 1990:14–15). The salient concern with survival and with
saving lives in women's anti-abortion activism reiterates the topical and
geographic breadth of this theme.

This movement presents an enigma. On one hand, the anti-abortion
movement opposes a core element in what might be broadly construed as
"the feminist agenda." On the other hand, challenging received notions
of women's activism (including the presumption that women are apo-
litical) has been a feminist project. This situation creates a tension that
demands careful self-examination on the part of analysts and rigorous
attention to empirical data. An experience-distant analysis recognizes
in anti-abortion activism an effort to regain a previous status quo and, so,
to protect a patriarchal social order. Analysts often describe traditional
or right-wing women as auxiliaries to men's activism. Presuppositions
about pro-life direct activists may distort some analyses, such as Faux's
(1990) and Faludi's (1991) representations of female direct activists as
quiescent followers. Such analyses disregard women's own discourse regarding their activism.

Women described highly personal motivations and intense personal
commitment to activism. The importance of "saving babies" to women
in this movement, that is, the importance of responding to another's
need – protecting, nurturing, and caring – connects their activism with
the underlying foundations of many women's movements, including that
of their own opposition.

Men's Narrative Themes and Levels of Participation

Most men explained their activism as a manifestation of their Christianity, their desire to belong to a group, and their need to act on their beliefs. In addition, most men used war imagery to describe their activism and considered themselves to be countering a threat to our nation. All but one man used at least one of these five themes to explain why they participated in direct action, most used several.

While these five themes helped explain why men entered direct action, only two were significantly related to the number of sit-ins men joined. Men who used martial imagery to describe their entry into direct action were significantly more likely to engage in extensive direct action than those who did not ($F = 6.85$, $p < .02$) (Maxwell and Jelen 1995a). Men who joined direct action as a consequence of strong bonds they either felt or sought with some group (typically fellow religionists) were significantly less active in sit-ins than those who used different themes to explain their participation ($F = 2.49$, $p < .04$) (Maxwell and Jelen 1995a).

Almost three-fourths of the men in the sample linked their activism to their Christian identity or to their relationship to God (72%). One man explained,

> I began to see that as a Christian I had a responsibility to defend people who couldn't defend themselves. That could be injustice or oppressed people anywhere, but there's nobody who is less capable of defending themselves than an unborn child.

Like women in the sample, many men explained that they sat-in to express their love for God or Christ. Literally paraphrasing a woman quoted above, one man reasoned that,

> Being there to keep a woman from killing her child would be the same as lifting up Christ. They would say the two are synonymous. It's their Christian duty to do that. The reason they are there is because they love Christ. That's why. That's the logic behind it. But if you ask them what are you doing here, they'll answer, I'm here to keep a woman from killing her child. Why do you do that? Well, because I love Christ and I want to show him my love. Those things are somewhat connected, or maybe completely connected, depending on the person.

Many men also spoke of the sense of duty they felt, as Christians, to protect people in danger. Some men argued that their sacrifice was necessary to prick the conscience of their fellow citizens. Men argued that both their actual suffering, and the commitment their civil disobedience confirmed, served this purpose. One man remarked that, "If those policemen were Christian, they'll never forget the Our Father" he shrieked as they twisted his arms, "They'll never forget what they did to another Christian." Another man explained,

> Because, to the extent that supposedly good citizens, who are not criminal in the rest of their lives, showed solidarity with the victim . . . When that happens, then it has a tendency to draw in the rest of the moral community that isn't the activist. Because if I'm a friend of yours and you know me to be a good person and to have a strong sense of morality, and you see me going to jail, and you know that I'm in jail this week, because I tried to do something that you say is right . . . you're going to be motivated in a way that you're not motivated if I'm not in jail.

In one rather extreme case, a man undertook regular, direct activism to affirm his decision to value himself, reconcile himself to God, and express gratitude to God for helping him survive a childhood of physical and emotional abuse. This man explained that,

> Even a year ago I was sayin', 'Why didn't He just abort me out?' . . . Why didn't God let me die like them in there? The babies in the abortion clinic.' I was sayin', 'How come they didn't have that modern technology back then? And if they would have, would my mother have done that? Would she have aborted me? Because I still had a score to settle between God and I. When you lose trust in those who is closest to you, you feel if I can't trust my relatives, I can't trust no one out there. And if I can't trust those who I can see, how can I trust someone I can't see? So through His word and through time, the things that He was callin' me to do that I just learned that in spite of what happened in the beginning, He took me away from all that, He gave me a reason to be here, to quit murmurin' about, 'Why? Why? Why?' like a little kid says, but to turn it over and to say, 'Thanks be to God that I am here, that He is gettin' me through this.' And I decided to come down [to the clinic] because of that I thank God that I wasn't aborted.

Another man struggled to formulate a clear concept of his place in a divine order, saying,

> I don't know if I can say this or not, but in a sense, am I an extension of God's justice? I do believe that God works through us if we allow Him or cooperate. For me to involve myself, I'm almost answering this question, 'Am I an extension of God's justice?' I guess, maybe I am.

This sense of immersion in a larger plan brought these men joy, despite the sometimes painful consequences of activism. One man linked the elation he felt after sitting-in to being immersed in a Christian role. He explained that, "It's fun to be a Christian in the trenches where it's happening, and to ask God to use you to bring the light into darkness."

Some men described joining direct action as taking a side, clarifying ambiguity in a diverse society, declaring their position and, so, reinforcing their identity as Christians. After sitting-in, one man explained,

> What hit me was that I'm against abortion, not only because it's wrong because it kills babies, but because I'm a Christian. That's the conviction it came out of. For me, fighting abortion comes out of my Christian principles . . . taking a stand for the Lord, raising up a standard of righteousness, because in the world there's no standards, everything is relativistic, you know. It's just what you feel is right and who can say it's wrong . . . So, when [I] tied it with the Lord, that's what convicted me.

Men frequently recounted the exhilaration of "taking a stand" and the relief of resolving their position on abortion. One man remembered,

> I felt like, 'Boy, what a privilege to be able to take a stand like I was taking.' It was a controversial stand, and yet it was a clear stand. I took a stand like that in the world and I felt the presence of God with me in just a real strong way. So it's a clear battle line that you are drawing . . . and people either give you the finger or they honk and they wave at you, but it's one or the other. It's not neutral ground. I was glad to take a stand where there was no neutrality.

The "lack of standards" in American society was a common theme among male and female activists alike. Some men situated abortion in a world in which people had to choose either a "God-centered" way of life defined by Biblical standards, or a "self-centered" approach dependent on the individual's wishes with "no accountability to any authority higher." This dichotomy drew a clear line between hierarchical and egalitarian orientations. Like female activists, many men lamented what they described as a general trend away from a God-centered society, and warned that this "shift" would create spiritual deprivation and its incumbent moral chaos. Men argued that, "The real key in the whole thing is the church," that the church should "rise up" as a whole and "take a stand." Like women, men were drawn to the evangelical potential of this activism. As one man commented, referring to the influence an earlier activist had on him,

> The thing that hit us so, was not just his fighting abortion, but that, because he was a Christian, he was leading people to Christ at the same time when he'd go into jail.

Given the strong role men's Christian identity played in their motivation, the Biblical principle that "faith without works is dead" privileged an action ethic. Sixty-six percent of men said they were compelled to participate because they realized that they had to act on their beliefs. One man explained that, "If you believe in something, you should be acting upon it . . . It left me in a place of repentance that, I needed to change not so much my opinions as my actions." Another man remarked that he,

> saw people were actually not just talking about the word of God, they were doing the word of God . . . I think God blesses people who are actually out doing good works, as opposed to talking about them. It was a breath of fresh air.

While most men vociferously rejected the notion that salvation depended on "good works," they adamantly argued that one must act on one's beliefs. This ethic was unequivocally stated by most men in the sample. As one man argued, "Those of us who see what is going on can't sit on the sidelines because there's a moral imperative that when you see truth, you have to act." Men insisted that action denoted the veracity of belief; one man asserted that "If you believe something, you don't really believe it unless you do it. You do what you believe."

Some men contended that this congruence of thought and behavior was not only a moral responsibility, but a necessity for personal well-being. They sat-in, in part, to resolve inner turmoil and attain a sense of wholeness through consistency and integration. As one man explained,

> If I want to be intellectually honest and integrated, consistent between my actions and my thoughts, my belief and how I live my life . . . then I can't just sit around and do nothing.

In other words, they sat-in to avoid cognitive dissonance caused by disunity between their beliefs and their behavior (cf. Festinger 1957).

Although some men argued that all people should take action against abortion, others felt personally called to "come against" it. Still others spoke as if they were somehow fated to accept the "responsibility" to "stand up for what was right."

Over half the men in the sample conceptualized abortion as a threat to American society (56%). As discussed in the chapter on conviction, many activists feared that socially sanctioned abortion would bring about a divine judgement on the nation. Some men feared an imminent catastrophe. As one man put it,

> I think that God brings back his own protection in time, usually through judgement, if we don't take action . . . I'm concerned because I fear that the hours are passing and . . . you're asking me about my reasons for activism, I would say that's the single most compelling reason that I've got is that.

Some men described abortion as a literal battle between good and evil, in which God and Satan struggled against one another, but through people. One man explained,

> Just like I believe that God inspires and works in people's hearts, the holy spirit works in people's hearts to protect the unborn, there's also an evil influence that works in people who are on the other side of the issue, not necessarily to their knowledge.

Another man told me that, "These children are being killed as Satan's attempt to bastardize the one blood sacrifice." He was not alone in this interpretation.

Other activists feared abortion would bring social degeneration. Like women, men feared that high rates of abortion would skew U.S.

demographics and either cause social security to fail, the economy to falter, or euthanasia to be implemented. One man argued that,

> No society can continue to exist with that kind of devastation. We've got over 26 million since Roe versus Wade... What's happening to the demographic shift? The graying of America. Who's going to pay all those social security checks?... The demographics are going backwards... Taking 1/3 of our children out... We're self-destructing.

Some men feared heightened contention over the legal status of abortion would lead to open conflict. One man warned, "It's going to rip this country apart. It's going to polarize people." Quite a few activists feared lethal conflict years before it occurred, but they did not expect pro-lifers to murder doctors and clinic staff. They predicted that pro-lifers would need to carry guns to defend themselves against murderous pro-choicers.

Many direct activists, both male and female, feared that socially condoned abortion would deteriorate society's morality. They argued that the moral conflict entailed in abortion pit personal liberty and "the pursuit of happiness" against the value of the individual and the "right to life," and that legalized abortion privileged the former. Direct activists insisted that the "right to life" preceded and superseded all other rights because, "You don't have any other rights if you're dead." They reasoned that the law enforcement, judiciary, and legislative systems that had opted for the "lesser right" were "in conflict with themselves," and so would erode. They argued that widespread acceptance of abortion was an "immoral" norm that would distort the "moral structure" of individuals in our society. The dread these concerns created was a powerful impulse to direct action for some men.

Two thirds of the "convicted" men felt impelled to participate in direct action either because a peer group with which they identified was engaging in it or because leaders they respected modeled this response to abortion. Such peer groups could be either imagined or actual.

Pro-life media presented an image of ordinary people doing what they had to do: "counting the costs" and "paying the price" of obedience and decency. The apparent pain of peers impelled men to join them in their trials. Referring to a direct action video, one man remembered that,

> The rescuers I saw were in serious pain ... they were really putting their life on the line. They were screaming and yelling and their arms were being twisted; they were being beaten.

Such images resonated with recruits' action ethic. The same young man continued, saying,

> I thought, man, they must really believe what they are doing. And they looked like everyday people . . . You don't see regular people doing that all the time, and in such mass.

This type of image was a potent factor in several men's convictions. The importance of a promised and longed-for unity was evident in one man's account of a large pro-life rally. He remembered that,

> Here on the platform was a Roman Catholic priest, and the Greek Orthodox priest, the Orthodox Jewish rabbis, the Protestants, and someone said there was Muslims, too . . . Now we'd have the biggest fight in the world if someone said, 'Let's talk doctrine,' but what they said was, 'Let's stop this atrocity'! That touched me!

Other men sat-in with an actual peer group – whether one with which they were already affiliated (such as a church congregation or study group), one that attracted them (such as a group of fellow students, friends, or colleagues), or a group of strangers with whom they shared some social characteristic. For example, veterans, pastors, and "victims of abortion" held their own sit-ins. One man described the rally preceding a Veteran's Rescue where he met and bonded with a stranger. He remembered that,

> As the meeting progressed he and I were both weeping. The simultaneous reality of God's grace in our lives. Here were two old military officers, we're both retired colonels . . . just the liberty and the gratitude of knowing that God had captured both of us and here we are standing together in a different battle, but still in the battle, in a more important battle – perhaps the last battle that God's got in his scheme for us – to restore us into completeness. Just the bonding, this guy, we just hugged each other. That's the kind of bonding, whether it's in a jail cell or on the street.

The allure of belonging induced some men to *join* groups that were sitting-in, despite their initial reticence toward direct action. Other men overcame their reluctance to sit-in in order to *retain* affiliation in groups that turned toward direct action. Peer involvement was contagious and encouraging. One man remembered thinking, "If those people can do it, I can do it." Another explained,

> Even though there may be 200 of you, it's kind of scary... Then you see someone going in there and you hear a person with a big booming voice saying, 'It's murder!' And it's kind of scary. Then you see someone else going in there and you hear yourself yelling, 'Don't go in there, Honey, they'll kill your baby. That's murder!'

Men warmed to the idea of belonging, drawn together by their commonalities. One man remembered the formation of a peer group within his church, recalling that,

> It seemed like we teamed up, we met a few other people in the church that felt strong about it. I remember coming in contact with them and it seemed like there was a likeness of hearts ... there was somethin' there that clicked.

Direct action groups' attraction built on (and sometimes superseded) the satisfaction men found in church participation. One man voiced a common theme among direct activists when he remarked that,

> The enthusiasm of rescuers and their commitment to Christ was really contagious, too. It was kind of like going to church every time you rescued. In fact, it was better.

Over half the men used war imagery to describe the attraction of belonging to direct action groups, convey their understanding of prolife direct action, or express their opinion on abortion (59%). One man described his decision to sit-in in vivid military terms, saying,

> I'm in blood covenant with these pastors. When my Commander-in-Chief says to follow him to war, I don't question that. I'm in blood covenant with them. I don't leave the flock ... When civil law differs from God's law, you go to war.

Similarly, another man explained that, "God said, 'I've got an assignment for you that I've been trying to show you for some time. Now here are your marching orders ... I've got a mission for you.'"

Some men's emphasis on "saving lives" (rather than "opposing abortion") lent a sense of mission to direct action that was enhanced by their war imagery. Other men used war imagery to describe their gratitude for being included in God's plan. One man remembered, "I felt like I was really in a war . . . So I felt, 'Well, boy, what a privilege to take a stand where you're on the battle line. You're on the front lines." Another direct activist echoed this sense of mission in the military imagery he used to describe a large, troubled sit-in his church conducted, saying,

> I feel like our church was like a battalion of warriors that went out to meet the enemy. And we went through the battle and I think we had a victory . . . We met the responsibility that we felt in our consciences. And we took injuries. There were many casualties – spiritually, relationally . . . As a body, the church, we had our dead and wounded, so to speak. So we all had to pull away from the battle and regroup . . . We have the moral high ground.

Although more men used war imagery than described abortion as a spiritual problem (59% and 38% respectively), most who used martial imagery, also spoke of abortion as being a spiritual problem. Many echoed the words of one man who said, "This is a war against Satan; it's not just a moral issue . . . It has to be fought like a war." If men were in battle, God was their Commander-in-Chief. As one man put it,

> These people, everyone of them that I know, had a very strong sense that God was the boss . . . They were taking their marching orders from God . . . It wasn't at all a lark.

Like women, men wove numerous themes into a complex fabric of motivation. One man's narrative illustrated the connections he made between his decision to sit-in and social degeneration, his own ethnic and religious identity, the need to act, and his desire to save "babies." He explained that,

> Part of the reason I got involved is, back when I was 14, I read The Rise and Fall of the Third Reich, and . . . I'm half German. And this was documented . . . and it showed that these people really knew they were killing these Jews . . . I got real upset because, ah, I mean, the most wonderful people in all the world to me are Germans . . . I know Germans are, they just are, they're a lovely,

lovely people, wonderful people. And so I saw this [long pause, very emotional voice] They were evil! There was a, there was a evil! ... There were thousands of people that knew about it! And they each did their part and they all killed these people ... But them Germans, I knew one thing, I knew the German people are as good and decent and law-abiding and everything as any other people. And here they were guilty of this. I thought, anybody else could do this, the Italians ... the French, the British, the Americans, anybody is capable of doing this ... That was part of why I got involved in the pro-life, because I understood how, see it's the same thing happening now as then. It's the same thing happening to these babies. It's a holocaust ... This is absolutely awful. But you can take the average Christian, a saved person, and he's just real blasé about it ... I remember thinking real strong, 'What would I have done if I were there?' at the end of the book. It was a real process I went through and I realized I would have done the same thing. I'm out there for me because I know the truth. If I don't do anything I've got to live with me ... You get involved and you confront it. You get informed and you tell the truth ... We're out there witnessing. I can go out to the mill and tell the truth and get spit on and yelled at and punched a couple times and come home and feel real good because we're out there telling the truth. That's what they didn't do in Hitler's time. I was free-er in jail, I mean, it's hard to explain. Because you see, I'd done what God wanted and I just had a sense of peace, you know?

This man spurned sit-ins as counterproductive until he "saw" that they were not only effective, but sometimes the only way to "save a baby." He recalled that, when he accepted this perspective on direct action, he felt impelled to act. He remembered that,

One day Dylan had went in there and I had saw this gal. She was a young gal and Dylan went in after her and she turned around and spit in his face and cussed him out, and ahh! She was just vicious. Kicked him and everything. And here comes the police and they're haulin' Dylan out, and I looked at this gal, and she was sitting over there and it was a transformation. And tears were rolling down her face and this got me because for the first time I saw ... the truth about what he was doin'. I says, 'Where are you going?' She says, 'I'm leavin' ... They're not going to kill my baby.' I says, 'What are you talking about?' Because I had watched her cuss Dylan out and swing at him and punch him and everything. And she says, 'He loved my baby more than I did.' . . . See she was under conviction because he went in there. And I realized that, it just hit me, it was like God told me, all of a sudden. I was adamantly against the rescues up til then, but I thought, she said it for me, she saw it. I didn't see it. But here's this gal, she was convicted because he was willing to put his life on the line for this baby. And it convicted me . . . Because that's the only way that baby would have been saved . . . What he did saved that baby . . . And so, boom! It hit me. And I knew then I was going to do it. I thought, if that's what it takes.

Unlike women in Ginsburg's (1989) sample, men did not explain their activism as a response to life-cycle changes, reproductive issues, or even distress over changing gender roles. However, like Ginsburg's women, many men addressed their own self-identities through activism by taking a stand that either resolved ambiguity or fortified an existing role trait. Many men also intended to shape society along the lines they preferred, but they aimed at larger dynamics that subsumed gender roles.

Prominent among their goals was fortifying a hierarchical, God-centered worldview. The action ethic that men endorsed did not represent an egalitarian, individual-centered moral order or relational strategy. Remember that most men explicitly stated that people must act on their beliefs, that is, that thinking and saying the "right" thing was insufficient, doing them was requisite, and the sheer fact of taking action brought satisfaction. Men qualified this ethic by saying that people had to act on Biblical principles, neither mouthing agreement nor acting on their own volition or beliefs. In this way the need to act was subordinated to a need to obey. The pre-eminence of obedience, and the merging of duty and action were illustrated by one man, who concluded that, "To be obedient to what God had told me, I had to rescue . . . I was just convicted by the Holy Spirit."

Men overwhelmingly acknowledged a desire to belong, to be part of a group of peers. Men responded to group dynamics both by overcoming a reluctance to sit-in and by capitulating to group norms that required them to cease sitting-in when they themselves would rather have persisted. One man explained, "I'm a team player. I can't be out there doing my own thing." This aspect of their motivation highlights the value they placed on community, again illustrating a hierarchical relational strategy.

Men's sense of Christian duty fed on the compassion aroused by their vivid concepts of fetuses. Although only 38% of "convicted" men said they joined direct activism upon "realizing the humanity of the unborn," most men expressed compassion inspired by the imagined suffering of "tiny, little babies" and their "mothers." Once aroused, this compassion helped sustain the sense of duty or mission men's Christian identity encouraged. As one man explained,

> I began to see in the scripture that you didn't just condemn a situation, you had a responsibility. In fact, if you didn't do anything, then actually part of the blame was on yourself... There's things the Lord shows you and once you became aware, then you were responsible. I didn't really need any convincing once I became aware [of what abortion entails].

However, the force of religious convictions was tempered by the strong urge to affiliate. Since direct action brought penalties, church groups tended to abandon it quickly. In this way, gregariousness led men away from sit-ins. Men also came to "recognize" that formulaic action, such as sitting-in, was inadequate to fulfill the role they had given it. The discrepancy between the symbolic act and the practical end they had prescribed for it helped some men withdraw from direct action. As one man reasoned,

> Why am I sitting in my office?... I haven't fully answered this question... Integrity can be shown in a lot of different ways, and even the most active of the activists, you could raise the question as to whether that person is doing all he or she can. Is he truly treating the unborn child as a human being? Because if you were, you might do something even more radical than sitting-in. So it's a continuum of questioning about our integrity.

Men used 17 themes to describe the events, experiences, conditions, beliefs, understandings, values, feelings, yearnings, and meanings surrounding their decisions to join direct action. The five predominant themes do not alone explain the decision to join direct action. Many Christians undoubtedly employ martial imagery when discussing a perceived threat, subscribe to an action ethic, or make decisions based on their desire to affiliate with a reference group, but do not sit-in (cf. Granberg 1982). These themes became potent when they resonated with a particular configuration of the myriad details of each individual's life – the constraints and opportunities career and family circumstances offered, the idiosyncratic psychological tasks individuals addressed through activism, and the evolving value system and ideology individuals used to interpret the world and their place in it. The specifics involved in this delicate interplay of factors varied with the individual, as previous chapters demonstrate.

Conclusion

Men and women wove together numerous themes explaining their participation in direct activism. Both genders clearly addressed their own self-identities through rescue. They resolved ambiguous aspects of their own natures and clarified their beliefs regarding the proper ordering of social relationships. They "took a stand" for a hierarchical, God-centered worldview in resistence to egalitarian, individual-centered social trends. Through direct activism they found ways to fulfill their "duty to God" and to respond to the needs of others, satisfying their personal urges and establishing social roles they desired. Both genders feared legal abortion would deteriorate our society's morality, generate economic collapse and social conflict. Both genders feared divine judgement for condoning abortion; some of each gender conceived of this as a battle between good and evil, God and Satan.

While men and women pointed to similar motivating concepts, they did so in somewhat different voices. Women emphasized affect and personal experiences when explaining their involvement in direct action. They spoke more often than men of the frustration with conventional activism that led them to risk arrest, the horror that preceded their commitment to direct action, the shock of videos that made them "realize what abortion did," their guilt, the distress that grew from watching women enter abortion clinics, and their desire to "save a life." Women also explained their activism as a response to others, to God, the "babies," and the "mothers." They spoke of the role of abortion in their own lives, or the lives of people they knew, and explained that they risked arrest to prevent other women from harming themselves or from being coerced into a self-destructive act. They pointed out that their activism was a message, a form of communication with the public and with lawmakers.

Men tended to explain their involvement in direct action by focusing on the reasoning behind their decisions. They carefully articulated the threat abortion posed to society and explained why that threat demanded action on their part. They expanded, in detail, on the basis of their need to act. Men also emphasized the role "belonging" played in their activism. Many men risked arrest to obtain or retain ties to a peer group and couched their discourse in martial imagery – with its implicit group, replete with "unbreakable" bonds and established relations and duties.

This is not to say that men were not impelled to risk arrest as a consequence of affect, or that women did not reason through their participation decisions. But the ways they described their decisions differed. If I were to generalize, I would say that men explained that they "sat in for this purpose . . . ," while women told me that they "sat in as a consequence of this relationship . . ." The one theme that pervaded both men's and women's narratives was the strong role religion played in their activism.

Both men and women spoke of risking arrest because they were called by God to do so, or because rescue gave them a chance to express their love of God, or fulfill their duty to God; they called it a way to act as a Christian – to *be* a Christian. Some of both genders hoped to realize the evangelical potential of direct action or to revive "the church" through it. But beyond that, their references to the religious nature of their activism differed in tenor. Compared to women, men spoke more of their *duty* to protect others, of sacrificing in order to prick consciences, and of the exhilaration and peace they found in taking a stand. Men said they risked arrest to *find* their own place in the divine order or to immerse themselves in God's larger plan. They seemed to emphasize seeking a relationship with God, while women seemed to act *upon* that relationship. Women spoke of pleasing God, serving God, showing their gratitude to God, or upholding God's righteousess. They spoke of their activism as an expression of their commitment to God, a reciprocal sacrifice for God, or a response to God's leading or command.

CHAPTER NINE

Individual Choices within Shifting Social, Legal, and Political Environments

Each of St. Louis's three rescue organizations formed a cohort. The first cohort created PAZ, drawing mainly from a broad base in the local Catholic community. The second cohort formed DAL, blending Catholics and Protestants. The third cohort formed around FSM and was mainly nondenominational. Each organization changed as it passed through various stages in its own lifecycle, even as each organization constituted a new stage in the pro-life movement as a whole.

The first pro-life direct activists coalesced in 1978 to initiate a "progressive, innovative movement" that sought to instill *new* values in society (cf. Stewart et al. 1989). They blended often intense anti-establishment liberalism and utopian yearnings with opposition to abortion. This group hoped to engage their community in a mass movement, feeling that their time had come, and success would inevitably follow because of the "logic" of their position and the "naturalness" of their response.

The second wave of activism, clearly distinct by 1984, constituted a "resistance movement," focused on stemming pervasive social changes (cf. Stewart et al. 1989). They believed their activism would shame and inculpate onlookers and promote incremental change through individual conviction. This group hoped to awaken (what appeared to them to be) a mysteriously unresponsive audience and cause them to see "the evil of abortion," and turn against it. These activists spoke of changing individual hearts.

The third group formed in the late 1980s as an essentially "revivalistic movement," oriented toward controlling abortion, but more explicitly toward instituting a return to "traditional Christian values" (cf. Stewart et al. 1989). They addressed their own personal religious issues and, simultaneously, "witnessed" to a society they believed had gone wrong. This group hoped to bring themselves in line with God's will and promote regeneration in society by reviving "the church."

Through direct action, experienced pro-lifers intensified their involvement in activism, entrenched their commitment to pro-life ideology, and extended the tactical repertoire of the modern pro-life movement toward the end of its first decade. These early direct activists created, in essence, a radical flank movement (cf. Haines 1988). Characteristic of an "enthusiastic mobilization" (a typical early stage in the life of a movement), they sat-in because of frustration and disaffection with "the institutions and their ability to change" (Stewart et al. 1989:25). Their approach to activism must be understood in relation to the larger, older conventional pro-life movement. Direct action offered immediate relief from the stress created by pro-lifers' failure to recriminalize abortion, despite years of activism. However, rescue also was the beginning of a new activist movement, replete with philosopher-agitators, novice activists, and a fresh sense of uniting to act upon newly recognized moral commitments. Over time, this new movement accumulated diverse components, but did not harmonize them. One long-time Catholic activist expressed this hostility in her dismay at evangelicals' self-castigating cries to "repent for having done nothing to stop this Holocaust." She voiced some contempt, remarking that,

> It is kind of disgusting when some of these people repent because we haven't done anything, and you say, 'Hey, I've been trying to tell you for eighteen years. What do you mean?' Not that I think I'm perfect and I shouldn't repent, but, I'm not sure I need to repent on this issue!

The high-pitched emotional interactions sit-ins entailed, combined with activists' intense commitment to their cause and their skeletal organizations, left direct action groups liable to internal clashes of personality or strategic philosophy. Their low level of bureaucracy made direct action groups dependent on leadership-by-personality and, so, vulnerable to individuals' weaknesses and open to divisive factionalization. This combination of 1) emotion-wrought experience, 2) a low level of official organization, and 3) emphasis on leaders' moral lives, not only facilitated fissioning, but encouraged obsessive participation by some activists, and eventually depressed broad participation.

Individual commitment to direct action was part of a complex, interactive process.[1] People made their decisions within larger social dynamics (such as the contest between egalitarian and hierarchical relational strategies, national trends in support of legal abortion, local socio-political environments, and the life-cycle stages of various rescue organizations). The specific individuals participating in an organization, their ideologies, personal relationships, and existing organizational structure affected the choices made among potential strategic alternatives (cf. DeNardo 1985). Such choices affected how the public responded to direct action. In this way, activism helped shape its own environment. Nonetheless, private symbolism, previously established ethics, shifting approaches to moral reasoning, and personal circumstances played determinative roles in activists' decisions, and consequently in this instance of direct action.

Participation depended on the meanings individuals gave to rescue, but these meanings were not static. Meanings derived from the personal objectives individuals pursued through activism. However, sometimes participation satisfied the drive created by such personal quests, alleviating the impulse to sit-in. Other times, participation aggravated that drive, and so intensified one's activism. Individuals also redefined these meanings in response to changes in their assessment of the "costs" of activism. Such costs were a function of their sociopolitical environments (which were, in turn, altered by institutional, community, family, and peer responses to direct action).

The impact of the meanings activists gave to rescue, that is, the effect personal interpretations had on participation decisions, was modified by three factors: 1) individuals' own particular circumstances, 2) their personal ethics, and 3) their broader ideologies. These factors defined the implications of the meanings, that is, they identified the actions that should flow from the meanings.

Consequently, the constraints and opportunities provided by one's personal circumstances, the interpretability of specific ethics, and the perspectives on self and others provided by ideology and style of moral reasoning, mediated between meanings and decisions. But each person's own participation also altered their personal circumstances and sociopolitical contexts. In this way, participation altered both the initial impulse to join direct action and the circumstances within which continued

---

[1] The dynamics entailed in this model are not necessarily tied to abortion activism per se, and may pertain to participation in direct action, more generally.

activism would occur. As such circumstances changed, personal ethics and ideology dictated alterations in individuals' commitment to activism.

Commitment to direct action often arose from distress created by the interaction of life experiences, patterns of moral reasoning, and exposure to abortion (whether empirical or imagined). Such distress or grief shaped – and often amplified – individuals' responses to pro-life rhetoric so that rhetoric not only aggravated, but channeled distress into activism. Then again, as life experiences, individuals' responses to abortion and to pro-life rhetoric helped define their patterns of moral reasoning, their personal ideology. This connection may not be unique to pro-life direct activism; activism in general may serve to construct meaning for potentially liminal stages in a person's life by affirming a correct moral order for society and one's place in it, much as conversion resolves conflict and anxiety by restructuring the convert's self-world concept.

Personal circumstances shaped individuals' responses to changes in activism's environment. Key elements in the objective environment of activism included: 1) the infrastructure of the organization with which an individual affiliated, 2) its resources (such as the number of people it could draw together and the legal support available to it), 3) its relationships with other similar organizations (either collaborative or conflictive), 4) institutional responses (ranging from community encouragement to police violence), and 5) opportunities (which arose from such external events as the U.S. Supreme Court's Webster decision or the Freedom of Access to Clinic Entrances Act). Family and job considerations, and the availability of social support played important, if subordinate, roles in individuals' commitment to activism. Activists' personal circumstances challenged and reworked their patterns of moral reasoning, which in turn, interpreted their personal circumstances.

While personal quests dominated individuals' decisions to *engage* in direct action, cost evaluation dominated their decisions to *withdraw* from activism. Personal quests created private symbolism that subjectively defined the costs and benefits of participation. While intent on pursuing personal quests and suffused with a sense of responsibility to intervene, individuals appeared to discount the notion of safety in numbers and disparage alternative avenues for opposing abortion. The more pressing the quest, the less daunting the costs. When activists began to resolve their personal quests, participation had less value to them. Once the initial impulses faded, discussion of rescue's costs and potential for success entered into discourse. Sooner or later such considerations gained prominence.

This fluid understanding of rescue altered not only the relative weight of costs, but redefined what was considered to be a cost. For example, the meaning an individual gave to suffering mediated its perceived cost so much that personal sacrifice could be considered either a benefit or a cost of participation. Hirschman (1982) argues that costs can only be assessed correctly when allowance is made for the benefit activists receive from the actual struggle to reach their goals, and cannot be assessed according to those goals alone. This held true among rescuers. Some activists framed suffering as a sacrifice that they could "offer up" to benefit "the babies" or fellow activists in jail. This approach made suffering seem more a benefit and less a cost of participation. Other activists framed suffering not only as a personal trial but as a burden on their family members. From this perspective, suffering seemed a heavy cost.

Activists tended to interpret their ethics by determining what the ethics implied in particular situations involving specific individuals. Conviction experiences directed activists toward the "needs" of fetuses, their mothers, or God. Conviction allowed one's ideological and affective opposition to abortion to converge. This convergence clarified ambiguity in activists' perspectives and created ideologically consistent logical, moral, and social strategies. This simplification brought relief and energized individuals, providing them a clear, unidirectional impulse. But this clarity appeared to dissipate over time as the complexity of life forced compromises that curtailed individuals' participation in direct action. Withdrawal from participation usually entailed redefining whose needs would receive attention, rather than refuting the principles impelling participation. This particularism is an approach that Gilligan described in her alternative to the impartialist morality described in Kohlberg's model of moral reasoning.

Many studies note that individuals tend to employ varying amalgams of impartialist (justice) and particularist (care) orientations to moral reasoning. Direct activists' narratives illustrated the social and political contexts that surrounded: 1) individuals' changing interpretations of the implications of persistent moral orientations, 2) shifts in the types of moral orientations individuals employed, and 3) the interpretive and moderating functions particularistic moral reasoning performed, even in the application of an impartialist morality. Jan's narrative demonstrated the varying implications one individual can derive from a persistent particularist moral orientation. Dylan's narrative demonstrated the shift from an impartialist to a particularist orientation. Men's narratives illustrated the blending of an impartialist orientation toward duty with the careful consideration of social contexts that characterizes particularist reasoning. In their narratives, *particularist* approaches defined the practical implications of *impartialist* ethics such as the "need to act," the "need to aid others," and the "duty to obey God."

When examining the behavior of the sample as an aggregate, value-rational motivations, which might be presumed to connect personal quests to persistent, fanatic activism, actually correlated with low levels of participation. Conversely, instrumentally rational motivations, which might be associated with risk evaluation and weak commitment to activism, correlated instead with high levels of participation.

A fairly clear scheme emerged. Individuals who were convinced of the value of sitting-in, but pursued some objective other than stopping abortions, were readily dissuaded from persisting. Such value-rational actors could find equally valid alternative methods for attaining their ends when the costs of participation became onerous. Costs had only to *redirect* the impulse-to-act in order to dissuade such individuals. In contrast, instrumentally rational actors, who thought sitting-in was the most effective tolerable means available to stop abortions, and felt personally responsible to do so, persisted. In order to dissuade such individuals, the costs of participation had to *outweigh* the obligation to act. These divergent motivations created a disjunction between individuals' discourse regarding commitment to direct action and their actual participation.

Activists' narratives illustrated the influence of individuals' life histories, regional backgrounds, and self-identities on their moral reasoning and behavior. Although an aggregate view showed people falling rather neatly into types, individuals did not remain so. Activism had a dual nature. It was both instrumental and symbolic – a political tool and a personal experience that expressed and refined activists' self-identities. Individuals' lives were integrated into diverse contexts and their self-identities altered as those contexts changed. Such changes rearranged the practical constraints on interviewees' self-expressions, and so reconfigured the moral considerations they addressed. Interviewees adjusted their behavior in response to the reasoning generated by new conditions to avoid conflicts that threatened to harm them. In regard to moral reasoning, such interdependent processes may provoke a spiraling rather than a linear developmental progression.

The structure and ideology of this activism were mutually supportive in some ways. For example, the sporadic nature of direct activism provided a format for individuals to pursue private quests intensely for brief periods and then return to their normal lives. Women who addressed past abortion experiences through rescue provided other direct activists with truncated exposure to damaging abortion sequelae, perpetuating activists' beliefs about abortion. However, the movement's ideology did not cope well with fluctuations in the level of participation. Large sit-ins and strong community support not only ensured political success and reduced the likelihood of severe penalties, they also created inspiring, satisfying social contexts. But high levels of participation only arose sporadically and usually were quelled by penal sanctions. While the Lambs' strategic philosophy addressed jail and court time, the broader pro-life direct action movement did not.[2] Without this affective component to offset the costs of participation, ideology and personal quests usually did not sustain activism.

In the long run, direct action organizations failed to sustain the perspective and commitment conviction evoked. While pro-life rhetoric was crucial to some individuals' decisions to participate in direct action, the role rhetoric played usually hinged on other circumstances in the individual's experience. For example, Loren had heard pro-life rhetoric her whole life. As long as she lacked a personal motive to address the abortion issue, that rhetoric did not move her to activism. Even when she made a personal link to abortion through her daughter's near death, her impulse to act lay dormant until her material circumstances provided both the freedom to act and an available avenue into activism. Pro-life rhetoric, potent when an individual was ripe for its message, proved inadequate to sustain commitment once individuals' personal quests were resolved or if their personal circumstances drew them away from activism.

The chronological point of entry into direct action, and the consequent manner in which individuals were socialized as activists, appeared to be more important determinants of their commitment to rescue than their denomination. In St. Louis, evangelicals' introduction to direct action was a virtual inversion of early Catholics' adoption of it. Long experience in conventional activism formed the emotional basis (the frustration and personal commitment to stop abortion) that underlay

---

[2] Camaraderie and inspiration turned jail time into a great strength for other direct action movements, as well (cf. Epstein 1991).

most Catholics' decisions to sit-in. In contrast, evangelicals were not responding to earlier frustrated attempts, but rather to an initial sense of responsibility regarding abortion. They had not established a personal commitment to recriminalizing abortion long in advance of their foray into direct action.

Direct action was disruptive to both Catholic and evangelical congregations, but not in the same ways. Among Catholics, the Archbishop censured those under him – priests and lay people. Catholic activists felt personally criticized by their peers and, to varying degrees, betrayed by their leadership, but their religious institution was essentially undisturbed by their activism. Those who persisted in direct action argued that the Archbishop's edict was a personal interpretation handed down dictatorially. They, as lay members, contested his position, charging that it contradicted official church policy, and especially the Pope's stand on abortion. The layers of authority in the Catholic church provided both the opportunity to exercise authority and the basis for resisting authority (cf. Maxwell and Spickard 1993).

By contrast, direct action created crises in evangelical congregations that were dealt with in a collective manner, redefining (to a small degree) their institutions. Duncan recruited among evangelicals new to political action of any sort. He introduced direct action as the only logical and moral response to legal abortion. Evangelical pastors seemed to wake to "the sin of abortion and the even greater sin of having done nothing to oppose it." They led their followers to the clinic doors, and into jail. Congregations recoiled from the negative effects (the costs) of direct action and demanded reconsideration of their involvement. Pastors were forbidden to risk arrest; conventional activism was adopted and direct action was "tabled." Evangelical pro-life committees organized regular pickets and sporadic joint-church prayer vigils and rallies, much as Catholic pro-lifers had done years *before* initiating direct action. Evangelicals did not renounce, reject, or officially abandon direct action; it simply was not made to recur, at least not as a church activity. In essence, evangelical leaders forged into activism; followers balked, then recalled the leaders. The compromise policy each evangelical congregation developed was binding on members, but it was also their collective voice.

The differences in St. Louis's Catholic and evangelical perspectives on pro-life direct action were not solely attributable to their theology or church organization. As Himmelstein found, the "influence of religion on attitudes toward . . . abortion . . . cannot be understood purely or primarily in terms of differences in church doctrines" (1986:7). Broadly speaking, Catholics and evangelicals occupied different niches within the historical flow of this movement. These different historical positions exposed recruits to particular concepts and experiences of direct action, varying the perspectives of individuals in different faiths. The resulting correlation between religious affiliation and approach to direct action probably stemmed more from historical exposure than from religious doctrine. The three cohorts were shaped no more by the intrinsic qualities of the various religious factions within them than by historically derived qualities of the organizations each religious faction joined.

Changes in the conditions under which direct action was pursued or in the way it was conducted highlighted ideological differences among activists and precipitated "defections." When a narrow array of options was available, people who disagreed on basic political strategy agreed on the relative value of specific tactics. When a less restrictive political environment arose, people of different stripes continued to pursue the strategy that seemed most appropriate according to their own style of reasoning, but in the changed political environment, their definitions of "appropriate" differed. In this way underlying differences in political strategy surfaced and quickly created factional schisms when the environment changed.

The two general approaches to activism that individuals evinced suggested the sources of Rosa Luxemburg's dilemma. Individuals who persisted in direct activism tended to pursue narrowly targeted goals best served by their assertive tactics. Their motivations appeared to be instrumentally rational and the meanings they gave rescue were essentially secular. This hard-core remnant formed what Luxemburg likened to a sect, much criticized by observers, both pro-choice and pro-life. However, the majority of direct activists responded initially to powerful, but diffuse evanescent inspiration, then drifted toward either conventional activism or nonparticipation. They acted on apparently value-rational motivations and tended to give sacred meanings to their activism that could be satisfied through activities other than direct action. This orientation inclined them toward what Luxemburg denigrated as bourgeois social reform – the conventional activities that Stewart and colleagues lauded as the only avenue to sustained activism! Together, these two factions produced the thriving direct action movement of the 1980s. Luxemburg's dilemma arose from the need to maintain a synthesis of two distinctly different approaches to activism. Neither faction constituted a middle ground between what were to both the radical philosopher and the political scientist, two undesirable poles. Ultimately, these activists were unable to negotiate the twin dangers Luxemburg identified: They could not build their base of support while maintaining their identity, and they could not sustain a movement without a sufficient base of support.

Sample Description

This appendix provides a detailed description of the St. Louis sample, a description of the sampling method I used in Wichita, and selected comparisons between the two samples.

St. Louis

Because of the explanatory power attributed to abortion activists' socio-economic characteristics (Luker 1984) and the presumed influence of such characteristics on direct activists (Faludi 1991; Faux 1990; Ginsburg 1993; Tribe 1990), I will provide a demographic profile of St. Louis's "rescuers." This description is based on standard measures that include those in Luker's (1984) and Ginsburg's (1989) studies. These are sex, age, education and income levels, occupational and marital status, ethnicity, and family size. I will also describe the relative intensity of sample members' activism and the distribution of sample members across the history of the movement. I determined the intensity of individuals' activism by the number of times they sat-in, and based distribution on the date individuals first sat-in.

INTENSITY

I distinguished between those who never sat-in, those who joined one to three sit-ins, and those who sat-in four or more times. I chose these breaking points partly because most people did not know exactly how many times they sat-in, but they could distinguish at these levels. Some people perceived themselves to have sat-in very frequently, but actually had done no more sit-ins than other people who felt they only sat-in a few times. For example, one activist reiterated, "That's what I did every Saturday for three years," and later estimated more concretely that she participated in 12 or 15 sit-ins altogether. (Several people kept records of their direct action, aiding this comparison.) I could not rely on activists' subjective statements or feelings about how frequently they sat-in to quantify their experiences.

In St. Louis, evangelicals' rush into direct action entailed three local sit-ins. This foray culminated in a massive protest in nearby Granite City. Anyone doing more than three sit-ins participated outside that narrow window of activity, either because they began direct action prior to that series of sit-ins, or because they persisted beyond the Granite City event. I wanted to be able to distinguish people who had exposure to the movement outside that church-focused experience.

The 15 people whose activism did not involve sitting-in were integral to pro-life direct action in St. Louis, taken as a whole. Some of those people were "sidewalk counselors" who acted in conjunction with the "sitters"; others regularly enacted unique forms of activism. While "sidewalk counselors" were readily recognized by "sitters" as important or even essential to rescue, the other people had a more ambiguous status in the movement. I will refer to them as "independents," a term I occasionally heard affiliated activists use for them. Most "sidewalk counselors" and independents were arrested at least occasionally. "Sidewalk counselors" generally understood they were risking arrest; independents usually did not intend to risk arrest.

I designated people as "still rescuing" if I observed them sitting-in, saw their participation reported in news articles, or if they named a date on which they had risked arrest within nine months of their interviews. People actively sitting-in when interviewed tended to have participated in a high number of rescues, suggesting that those I term "still rescuing" tended to be persistent in their activism rather than neophytes accidently captured by the sample at the time of their first and only sit-in.

Very few people said they had stopped "rescuing," even when several years had passed since their last active involvement in sit-ins. I do not think they were trying to deceive me by implying they were active; they just did not think of themselves as having quit. Instead, "rescue just wasn't right, now," or they "would do it again if circumstances were right," or "if God told" them to. In any case, they continued to identify themselves as rescuers.

Distinguishing between people who were active in sit-ins and those who were not was highly problematic, and I chose to be conservative in designating people as "still rescuing." Some interviewees had withdrawn from direct action for a year or more, then returned and participated intensely for years afterwards. I could not distinguish between people who would eventually return to direct action and those who had left but preferred not to acknowledge that fact (whether to me or to themselves). Consequently, I chose to include only those whose activism was empirically evident.

Of the 80 people in this sample:

PARTICIPATION IN SIT-INS

15 (18.75%)   never sat-in
24 (30.00%)   sat-in up to three times
41 (51.25%)   sat-in four or more times
16 (20.00%)   were "still rescuing" when I interviewed them

DISTRIBUTION

I sorted dates of entry into time periods that corresponded to salient events in the movement. These were as follows: prior to April 1980; April 1980 through 1983; 1984 through 1987; 1988; and 1989 through 1990. Chapter 2 describes the events and transitions associated with these periods. Although many people could not determine exactly when they undertook direct action, I was able to associate their initial activism with a date by connecting events they mentioned with dates that were confirmed in news articles or other activists' narratives. By sorting dates of entry according to important events in the movement's history, I had chronological points of reference that were likely to occur in narratives. Also, by grouping activists according to these time periods, I was able to relate individuals to the larger environmental contexts they experienced while active.

People who adopted direct action prior to April 1980 began before Archbishop May denounced sit-ins, inhibiting community participation. Those who joined between April 1980 and 1983 engaged in direct action when its timing and location were shifting due to injunctions, and the sense of a community-in-action was challenged. People adopting direct action between 1984 and 1987 joined as (or after) the Direct Action League (DAL) and Family Support Ministries (FSM) formed and before Operation Rescue (OR) rose to prominence. Those beginning direct action in 1988 began as OR made its national debut. Those beginning between 1989 and 1990 were exposed to the local evangelical venture into direct action as well as the two older groups (DAL and FSM), and they adopted direct action after it had received national attention.

The 80 individuals in the sample began direct action in the following time periods:

DATE OF FIRST ACTIVISM

11 (13.75%) began direct action before April 1980
6 (7.5%) began between April 1980 and 1983
19 (23.75%) began between 1984 and 1987
17 (21.25%) began in 1988
27 (33.75%) began between 1989 and 1990

SEX AND ETHNICITY

The St. Louis sample was composed of 48 women (60%) and 32 men. One interviewee referred to her former lesbian identity, however, I did not ask interviewees to identify their sexuality. The sample included the only nonwhite individual anyone remembered participating in St. Louis's sit-ins. She described her mother as white and her father as African American. Only one self-identified African American, a man, regularly demonstrated at clinics during my two years of fieldwork; he was an independent who did not risk arrest. All other pro-lifers I interviewed or observed would be described as "white," echoing the ethnic makeup both Luker and Ginsburg described. Several individuals emphatically identified themselves as Irish or German – not unusual given St. Louis's ethnic heritage. However, since St. Louis was 51% African American, the preponderance of white activists is noteworthy.

AGE

Direct activists in St. Louis did not appear to group in the low and high age ranges Ginsburg found among pro-lifers in Fargo. Given the time span of this activism, developing a profile of activists' ages (the range, mean, and so forth) was problematic. I tried to estimate the age range active in the past by asking long-time activists to estimate the ages of people listed on injunctions, and reviewing newspaper articles that listed names and ages of activists current at particular periods. These tentative snapshots of activism suggested that people in a wide range of ages sat-in at any given period in this movement. The range of ages in this sample at the time I interviewed is similar to that of activists listed in injunctions in the early 1980s, a time when direct action drew widely from the pro-life community.

This sample draws from discrete phases of the pro-life direct action movement, phases that differed demographically, to represent a composite of the whole 14-year period. At the time I interviewed them, activists ranged in age from 21 to 77:

AGE AT TIME OF INTERVIEW

 2 (2.5%)   were between 21 and 25 years of age
 5 (6.25%)   were between 26 and 30 years of age
26 (32.50%)   were between 31 and 40 years of age
25 (31.25%)   were between 41 and 50 years of age
16 (20.00%)   were between 51 and 60 years of age
 4 (5.00%)   were between 61 and 70 years of age
 2 (2.50%)   were between 71 and 80 years of age
(N = 80)
Median Age Range = 41 to 50 years of age

Of the 16 people currently active in rescue when I interviewed them:

AGE OF THOSE STILL RESCUING

1 (6.25%)   was between 21 and 25 years of age
1 (6.25%)   was between 26 and 30 years of age
4 (25.00%)   were between 31 and 40 years of age
6 (37.50%)   were between 41 and 50 years of age
3 (18.75%)   were between 51 and 60 years of age
1 (6.25%)   was between 61 and 70 years of age

The group "still rescuing" constitutes St. Louis's entire direct action population during a two-year period. The ages represented in this group are similar to those of the larger conglomerate sample of 80, and to activists' recollections of past phases of rescue. Consequently, I assume the larger sample is not a gross distortion of the age range of people who engaged in pro-life direct action in this city over time. The sample probably presents a reasonable approximation of the demographics of various phases of pro-life direct action, excepting the first few sit-ins that were conducted in other states by college-aged activists only.

EMPLOYMENT

Most people in the sample, including the women, were employed and the majority were employed full-time. Two people classed as being employed part-time were students. One was employed almost full-time in addition to his studies; the other was a full-time student and had little formal employment. Otherwise, part-time employment meant working 20 hours or less a week, or working sporadically but on an on-going basis. For example, one woman classed as part-time surveyed gas stations throughout a section of the state for a large corporation; she also did bookkeeping for a family business. Survey work was intense, but occurred only several times a year. Bookkeeping was sufficiently sporadic to allow her to homeschool her five children.

RATES OF EMPLOYMENT

54 (67.50%)   were employed full-time
 9 (11.25%)   were employed part-time
13 (16.25%)   were homemakers
 4 (5.00%)   were either retired or temporarily
                unemployed
($N = 80$)

I categorized activists' occupations according to the major occupational groups recognized by the U.S. Bureau of Labor Statistics. I added "homemakers, homeschoolers" to these groups, because several activists identified their occupations in these terms.

OCCUPATIONS DEFINED BY U.S. BUREAU OF LABOR STATISTICS
WITH HOMEMAKERS AND HOMESCHOOLERS ADDED

37 (46%)   Managerial and professional speciality:
  12   Executive, administrative, managerial
  25   Professional speciality

14 (17%)   Technical, sales, administrative support:
  2   Technicians and related support
  5   Sales occupations
  7   Administrative support, including clerical

8 (10%)   Service occupations:
  4   Private household
  4   Service, other

5 (6%)   Precision, production, craft, repair:

4 (5%)   Operators, fabricators, and laborers:
   1   Machine operators, assemblers, inspectors
   3   Helpers, laborers, others

12 (15%)   Homemakers, homeschoolers
($N = 80$)

MARITAL STATUS

Most direct activists were married and almost all couples were in a first marriage for both partners; 15% of the sample was single, never married. The sample included nine married couples. Each individual was interviewed in full, and spouses' direct action experiences tended to be quite distinct. Marital status in the sample was as follows:

MARITAL STATUS
54 (67.5%)   were married
26 (32.5%)   were single
($N = 80$)

In more detail:

42 (52.50%)   were currently in their first marriage
 3 (3.75%)   had a spouse die, then remarried
 9 (11.25%)   divorced, then remarried
11 (13.75%)   were single and divorced
 3 (3.75%)   were single and widowed
12 (15.00%)   were single, never married
($N = 80$)

Faludi (1991) asserted that direct activists tended to be single, downwardly mobile men, thwarted by women. Her characterizations have been cited by other authors (Ginsburg 1993; Tribe 1990 [citing Faludi 1989]) but are not reflected in St. Louis's demographics. Most direct activists, both male and female, were married. Twenty-four men (75%) were married; 3 (9%) were single and divorced, and 5 (16%) were single and never married. This is a much higher rate of marriage than the national average. Nationally, 64.3% of men in 1990 were married,

7.2% were single, divorced, and 25.8% were single, never married (U.S. Bureau of Census 1996). Nor did data gathered on direct activists' parents' occupations and educations suggest a trend of downward mobility among male activists.

INCOME

I gathered information on household, rather than personal, income.[1] All interviewees sharing a household income were married to one another. The income levels reported here are conservative. Some individuals' income had recently dropped significantly (sometimes by $40,000 or more) due to various factors, such as retirement, varying partnership distributions, a change in occupations, self-employment, or employment on commission. I used the current figures in such cases. Most interviewees who preferred reporting a range of income did so because their income varied from year to year due to commissions.

St. Louis's five poorest direct activists reported an annual income under $10,000. Two of these were women living on either alimony or a stipend from an estranged husband. One, previously a partner with her husband in entrepreneurial ventures, had lived on a household income of over $100,000 most of the time she was participating in direct action. One man was self-employed; he remarked that he had to keep his business small to accommodate his activism. The fourth person was a self-supporting college student. The fifth was supported solely by Social Security and Supplemental Security Income.

The sample contained 69 households with calculable incomes; 25 households (36% of the sample) received less than the median income for households in the United States in 1989. This sample contradicts Faludi's (1991) and Ginsburg's (1993) characterization of pro-life direct activists. Faludi asserted that among the group she observed "the vast majority belonged to the lower income brackets" and "were downwardly mobile sons . . . hurting from severe economic and social dislocations"

---

[1] I asked interviewees to calculate their household incomes for the year preceding their interview, which was generally 1989. People interviewed toward May of 1991 reported 1990 income. The incomes reported by two people were unscorable. Those two people were willing only to state whether their 1989 income was over or under the national median for that year ($28,900). One of these two people made much less than the national median and the other made substantially over the national median.

(1991:401–2). However, Faludi cites no objective source of data. Ginsburg (1993) adopted Faludi's characterization uncritically.

Almost everyone in the St. Louis sample, whether male or female, had worked in the wage labor market at some point in their lives. Most worked many years. Very few interviewees fit the image studies of conventional pro-life activists depict of homemakers excluded from the wage labor market (Faux 1990; Luker 1984; Tribe 1990).

Household incomes in the sample were as follows:

HOUSEHOLD INCOME

5 households (7.24%)	under $10,000
10 (14.5%)	10,000 to 19,999
10 (14.5%) (12 interviewees)	20,000 to 29,999
16 (23.0%) (17 interviewees)	30,000 to 39,999
8 (11.6%) (10 interviewees)	40,000 to 49,999
3 (4.3%) (4 interviewees)	50,000 to 59,999
6 (8.7%) (7 interviewees)	60,000 to 69,999
4 (5.8%)	70,000 to 79,999
2 (2.9%)	80,000 to 89,999
2 (2.9%)	90,000 to 99,999
2 (2.9%) (3 interviewees)	100,000 to 200,000
1 (1.5%)	over 200,000

(N = 69 households, 78 interviewees)
Median Income Range: $30,000–39,999

EDUCATION

All but three activists completed four years of high school and most (65 people, or 81% of the sample) had at least some formal education or training beyond that level. The three people who did not complete four years of high school were not simply drop-outs, and in fact, they either completed all available grades or continued their educations beyond high school. Six people (7.5% of the sample) had done post-doctoral work or had earned multiple, but not successive degrees (that is, they had either two bachelors degrees or masters degrees in addition to those anticipatory of their terminal degrees). Several people were working on undergraduate or graduate degrees. Four interviewees were pastors, and a fifth was a youth minister. Three of the four pastors were ordained. St. Louis's educational profile was as follows:

16 (20.0%)	had at least some high school
23 (28.8%)	had some college but no degree
24 (30.0%)	had an undergraduate degree (AA, BA, or BS)
5 (6.3%)	had some graduate school or technical training beyond the undergraduate degree such as a nursing degree (RN, LPN)
12 (15.0%)	had at least one graduate degree (MA, PhD, JD, MSW, MBA, or MDiv)

$(N = 80)$

Median Educational Level: undergraduate degree

CHILDREN

Both Luker (1984) and Ginsburg (1989) suggested that procreation played important roles in motivating pro-life activism. In addition, a correlation analysis of the St. Louis sample showed high levels of participation in sit-ins correlated with high numbers of children in one's family. To give some impression of activists' exposure to procreation, I will describe the number of children in their families, including adopted, step, and deceased children.

The average number of children per family was 3.54 (N of children = 79; N of adults = 69, adjusted to account for married couples parenting the same children). Some of the people without children were past childbearing age, others were young and planned to bear children in the future. Interviewees grew up in families that averaged 4 children (N of adults with data on siblings = 56).

Family sizes in the sample were as follows:

FAMILY SIZE

13 (16%)	had no children	(62% were women)
28 (35%)	had 1 or 2 children	(64% were women)
14 (17.5%)	had 3 or 4 children	(50% were women)
20 (25%)	had 5 or 6 children	(60% were women)
4 (5%)	had 7 or more children	(75% were women)
1 (1%)	(datum was missing)	

$(N = 80)$

Median Family Size: 3 or 4 children

All of the people who were single and had never married were also childless, and one married woman had not had children (although she intended to interrupt her career to do so). Men and women were roughly equally represented in each family-size category, although men were slightly overrepresented among those with three or four children. In other words, the sample was not characterized by childless men, adults separated from their offspring, or women with huge families. Perhaps the only unusual characteristic of the sample was the high number of people with five or six children. Two of these were blended families.

RELIGIOUS AFFILIATION

All of St. Louis's direct activists said they were affiliated with a religious group and most activists reported high involvement with their churches. Most activists implied that their religiosity was crucial to their self-identity and guided their feelings and decisions in important ways.

Activists were raised with the following religious affiliations:

RELIGION RAISED

41 (51.25%)	were raised Catholic
31 (38.75%)	were raised in a Protestant denomination
1 (1.25%)	was raised nondenominational
1 (1.25%)	was raised Jewish
6 (7.50%)	were raised without a religion
(N = 80)	

Many interviewees had changed religious affiliation at some point prior to joining direct action. Only two activists changed religious affiliation after beginning activism; one of these two was still "rescuing." Activists' religious affiliations at the time of their interviews were as follows:

CURRENT RELIGION

23 (28.75%)	were Catholic
14 (17.50%)	were in a Protestant denomination
43 (53.75%)	were nondenominational
0	were Jewish
0	lacked religious affiliation
(N = 80)	

Religious conversion was often either central to interviewees' positions on abortion or relevant to their activism. Religious experiences suggested tendencies in interviewees' responses to stress or change. Altogether 51 people (64% of the sample) experienced religious conversions. Five of those explained they had experienced two significant religious conversions, the second returning them to the religion of their childhood. One man was raised nondenominational, became a devout and active Mormon for several decades, then left the Mormon church and joined a nondenominational church quite different from his childhood congregation. Two women were raised in a liberal Protestant denomination which they rejected as teenagers, joined nondenominational churches, rescued, then joined a conservative Baptist congregation. Two more women left liberal Protestant denominations and joined conservative Protestant churches. Of the 51 people who experienced religious conversions, 43 (54% of the sample) became nondenominational; only 2 people converted to Catholicism. Another 29 people (36% of the sample) retained their childhood religious affiliations. Of those, many participated in the Catholic charismatic renewal movement.

Patterns of religious conversion were as follows:

RELIGIOUS CONVERSION

51 (63.75%)   underwent religious conversions
29 (36.25%)   did not
($N = 80$)

PATTERNS OF RELIGIOUS AFFILIATION

21 (26.25%)   were lifelong Catholics
2 (2.50%)   left a denominational church to become Catholic
19 (23.75%)   left Catholicism to become nondenominational
17 (21.25%)   left a Protestant denomination to become nondenominational
5 (6.25%)   became nondenominational, no previous religion
1 (1.25%)   left Judaism to become nondenominational
1 (1.25%)   began, left, then returned to nondenominational religion
8 (10.00%)   were lifelong Protestant denominationals
4 (5.00%)   began, left, then returned to some Protestant denomination
1 (1.25%)   left Catholicism, became denominational Protestant
1 (1.25%)   joined a Protestant denomination, no previous religion

($N = 80$)

WICHITA

In order to place the St. Louis sample in perspective, I will compare it to a random sample of people present at a large pro-life direct action event in Wichita, Kansas in 1991. That event was called the "Summer of Mercy '91," and was widely recognized as an Operation Rescue event. This perception was not entirely accurate. An older local rescue group spent three years trying to convince OR to come to Wichita, and many such groups, groups associated with PLAN – like DAL – participated in the Wichita event.

I surveyed activists over a period of six days at the three abortion clinics under protest. I divided the time I sampled proportionately between the three clinics, spending more time at the clinic most heavily protested. At each clinic, I divided the area protestors occupied into four-foot segments and attempted to recruit three people located in each segment. Very few people declined to participate in the survey. In all, 178 people agreed to participate, and all but 15 answered all questions on the survey form. The remaining 163 people comprise the Wichita sample.

GENDER, INTENSITY, ABORTION EXPERIENCES

Women constituted 60% of both the St. Louis and Wichita samples. However, 83% of the St. Louis sample actually sat-in, while only 51% of the Wichita sample had done so. This difference is not surprising considering that in St. Louis, I sought out people who sat-in. The preponderance of women in both samples calls into question Faludi's (1991) assertion that Operation Rescue was predominantly male. Faludi provides no numbers and does not describe the basis of her assessment.

In the Wichita sample, 83 people had rescued; 46 (55% of those who sat-in) were women. In the St. Louis sample, 66 people sat-in; 40 (61% of those who sat-in) were women. In St. Louis, a slightly higher percentage of women sat-in, compared to men (83% of women sat-in, while 81% of men did so). In the Wichita sample 47% of women and 56% of men sat-in.

The greater proportion of men risking arrest in Wichita may relate to the high proportion of evangelicals to Catholics in this movement in the late 1980s and early 1990s. Catholics tended to both tolerate and encourage women's participation in direct action, while many evangelicals were uncomfortable with women's participation. The higher proportion of women risking arrest in the St. Louis sample may reflect the greater proportion of Catholics involved in early sit-ins there and their persistence in local direct action groups.

These two samples compare as follows:

RATES OF RESCUE BY SEX

Wichita ($N = 163$)

37 men sat-in	(56% of sex, 23% of sample)
46 women sat-in	(47% of sex, 28% of sample)

St. Louis ($N = 80$)

26 men sat-in	(81% of sex, 33% of sample)
40 women sat-in	(83% of sex, 50% of sample)

Although the sheer numbers and percentages of activists who had aborted or paid for partners' abortions in either city were modest, the relative proportion of men to women was suggestive. Rosenblatt and Burns (1986) found that mothers were significantly more troubled by perinatal and abortive losses than were fathers, and direct activists' narratives reflect this dynamic. Past abortions were crucial factors in women's activism, but not so in men's activism. Rates of abortion in the two samples were as follows:

ACTIVISTS WHO ABORTED

Wichita ($N = 163$)

2 men	(3% of sex, 1% of sample) aborted "own child"
10 women	(10% of sex, 6% of sample) aborted "own child"
($N = 12$)	(7.4% of sample)

St. Louis ($N = 80$)

1 man	(3% of sex, 1% of sample) aborted "own child"
6 women	(12.5% of sex, 7.5% of sample) aborted "own child"
($N = 7$)	(8.8% of sample)

References

AGI (Alan Guttmacher Institute)
1997 *The Limitations of U.S. Statistics on Abortion.* New York: Alan Guttmacher Institute.
1998 *Facts in Brief: Induced Abortion.* New York: Alan Guttmacher Institute.

Alder, Nancy E., Henry P. David, Brenda N. Major, Susan H. Roth, Nancy F. Russo, and Gail E. Wyatt
1990 Psychological Responses After Abortion. *Science* 248: 41–4.
1992 Psychological Factors in Abortion. *American Psychologist* 47:10:1194–204.

Andrews, Joan, and John Cavanaugh-O'Keefe
1989 *I Will Never Forget You: The Rescue Movement in the Life of Joan Andrews.* San Francisco: Ignatius Press.

Armsworth, Mary W.
1991 Psychological Response to Abortion. *Journal of Counseling and Development* 69:377–9.

Arthur, Joyce
2001 [1997] Psychological After-Effects of Abortion: the Real Story. *The Humanist* 57:2:7–9.

Bailey, F. G.
1983 *The Tactical Uses of Passion.* Ithaca, NY: Cornell University Press.

Bellah, Robert N., Richard Madsen, William M. Sullivan, Ann Swidler, and Steven M. Tipton
1985 *Habits of the Heart: Individualism and Commitment in American Life.* New York: Harper and Row Publishers.

Bentley, G. Carter
1987 Ethnicity and Practice. *Society for Comparative Study of Society and History* 29:1:24–55.

Berger, Joseph
1998 Slaying Spotlights Fear as Abortion Access for Poor Is Cut. *The New York Times*, p. B8.

Berger, Peter L., and Thomas Luckmann
1966 *The Social Construction of Reality: A Treatise in the Sociology of Knowledge*. New York: Anchor Press, Doubleday.

Berk, Laura E.
1989 *Child Development*. Boston: Allyn and Bacon.

Blanchard, Dallas A.
1994 *The Anti-Abortion Movement and the Rise of the Religious Right: From Polite to Fiery Protest*. New York: Twayne Publishers.

Blanchard, Dallas A., and Terry J. Prewitt
1993 *Religious Violence and Abortion: The Gideon Project*. Gainesville: University Press of Florida.

Blum, Lawrence A.
1993 Gilligan and Kohlberg: Implications for Moral Theory. In *An Ethic of Care: Feminist and Interdisciplinary Perspectives*. Mary Jeanne Larrabee, ed. pp. 49–68. New York: Routledge.

Bracken, Michael B., M. Philip Moshe Hachamovitch, and Gerald Grossman
1974 The Decision to Abort and Psychological Sequelae. *The Journal of Nervous and Mental Disease* 158:2:154–62.

Brown, Lyn Mikel, and Carol Gilligan
1992 *Meeting at the Crossroads: Women's Psychology and Girls' Development*. Cambridge, MA: Harvard University Press.

Burnett, Andrew
1993 Tiller Shot: Oregon Woman Accused. *Life Advocate* October.

Callahan, Cecilia M.
1988 *Post-Abortion Syndrome, a Form of Post-Traumatic Stress Disorder*. Unpublished.

Chafetz, Janet Saltzman, Anthony Gary Dworkin, and Stephanie Swanson
1990 Social Change and Social Activism: First-Wave Women's Movements Around the World. In *Women and Social Protest*. Guida West and Rhoda Lois Blumberg, eds. pp. 302–20. New York: Oxford University Press.

Clarke, Alan
1987 Moral Protest, Status Defence and the Anti-Abortion Campaign. *The British Journal of Sociology* 38:2:235–53.

Clifford, James, and George E. Marcus, eds.
1986 *Writing Culture: The Poetics and Politics of Ethnography.* Berkeley: University of California Press.

Cohen, Abner
1974 *Two-Dimensional Man.* Berkeley: University of California Press.

Cohen, Larry, and Susan Roth
1984 Coping with Abortion. *Journal of Human Stress* 34:140–4.

Cohn, Norman
1961 *The Pursuit of the Millennium.* New York: Harper.

Coles, Robert, and Jane Hallowell Coles
1978 *Women of Crisis: Lives of Struggle and Hope.* New York: Dell Publishing Company, Inc., Radcliffe Biography Series.

Condit, Celeste Michelle
1990 *Decoding Abortion Rhetoric.* Chicago: University of Illinois Press.

Cook, Elizabeth Adell, Ted G. Jelen, and Clyde Wilcox
1992 *Between Two Absolutes: Public Opinion and the Politics of Abortion.* San Francisco: Westview Press.

Cowden-Guido, Richard, ed.
1988 *You Reject Them, You Reject Me: The Prison Letters of Joan Andrews.* Manassas, VA: Trinity Communications.

Cucchiari, Salvatori
1988 Adapted for Heaven: Conversion and Culture in Western Sicily. *American Ethnologist* 15:3:417–41.

[DAL] Newsletter
1991 Defense Funds Request. December:1–2.

David, Henry P., Niels Kr. Rasmussen, and Erik Holst
1981 Postpartum and Postabortion Psychotic Reactions. *Family Planning Perspectives* 13:2:88–92.

Davis, Henry L.
1998 The Abortion Squeeze: Slaying Puts Spotlight on Increasing Difficulty of Getting an Abortion. *The Buffalo News*, November 1, p. H1.

DeNardo, James
1985 *Power in Numbers: The Political Strategy of Protest and Rebellion.* Princeton, NJ: Princeton University Press.

deParrie, Paul
1989 *The Rescuers.* Brentwood, TN: Wolgemuth and Hyatt Publishers.

Devereux, G.

1979[1955] A Study of Abortion in Primitive Societies. New York: International Universities Press, Inc.

Ehrenreich, Barbara

1983 The Hearts of Men: American Dreams and the Flight from Commitment. Garden City, NY: Doubleday Press.

Epstein, Barbara

1991 Political Protest and Cultural Revolution: Nonviolent Direct Action in the 1970s and 1980s. Berkeley: University of California Press.

Faludi, Susan

1991 Backlash: The Undeclared War Against American Women. New York: Crown Publishers, Inc.

Faux, Marian

1990 Crusaders: Voices from the Abortion Front. New York: A Birch Lane Press Book by Carol Publishing Group.

Festinger, Leon

1957 A Theory of Cognitive Dissonance. Stanford, CA: Stanford Unversity Press.

Festinger, Leon, Henry W. Riecken, and Stanley Schachter

1956 When Prophecy Fails. Minneapolis: University of Minnesota Press.

Flanagan, Owen, and Kathryn Jackson

1993 Justice, Care, and Gender: The Kohlberg-Gilligan Debate Revisited. In An Ethic of Care: Feminist and Interdisciplinary Perspectives. Mary Jeanne Larrabee, ed. pp. 69–88. New York: Routledge.

Forrest, Jacqueline, and Stanley Henshaw

1987 The Harrassment of U.S. Abortion Providers. Family Planning Perspectives. 19:1:9–13.

Galanter, Marc

1982 Charismatic Religious Sects and Psychiatry: An Overview. American Journal of Psychiatry 139:12:1539–48.

Gamble, Nicki Nichols

1997 Testimony of Nicki Nichols Gamble to the Subcommittee on Courts and Intellectual Property, Committee on the Judiciary, U.S. House of Representatives Oversight Hearing on "Judicial Misconduct and Discipline" [online], available http://www.prochoice.org/violence/gamblew.htm 12/7/99.

Garton, Jean Staker

1979 Who Broke the Baby? Minneapolis, MN: Bethany House Publishers.

Geertz, Clifford

1973 *The Interpretation of Cultures: Selected Essays by Clifford Geertz.* New York: Basic Books.

Gilligan, Carol

1982 *In a Different Voice: Psychological Theory and Women's Development.* Cambridge, MA: Harvard University Press.

1993 Reply to Critics. In *An Ethic of Care: Feminist and Interdisciplinary Perspectives.* Mary Jeanne Larrabee, ed. pp. 207–14. New York: Routledge.

Ginsburg, Faye

1989 *Contested Lives: The Abortion Debate in an American Community.* Berkeley: University of California Press.

1991 Gender Politics and the Contradictions of Nurturance: Moral Authority and Constraints to Activism for Female Abortion Activists. *Social Research* 58:3:653–78.

1993 Saving America's Souls: Operation Rescue's Crusade Against Abortion. In *Fundamentalism and the State: Remaking Polities, Economies, and Militance.* Martin E. Marty and R. Scott Appleby, eds. pp. 557–88. Chicago: University of Chicago Press.

Ginsburg, Faye, and Anna Lowenhaupt Tsing

1990 *Uncertain Terms: Negotiating Gender in American Culture.* Boston: Beacon Press.

Glick, Mario, and Edward Zigler

1985 Self-Image: A Cognitive-Developmental Approach. In *The Development of the Self.* Robert L. Leahy, ed. pp. 1–54. New York: Academic Press, Inc.

Goldstein, Amy

1995 U.S. Abortion Services Drop: Fewer Doctors Performing Procedure, Study Says. *The Washington Post,* January 22, p. A1.

1999 Antiabortion Violence: Faced with Threats, D.C. Physician Quits Practice. *The Washington Post,* November 11.

Granberg, Donald

1981 A Comparison of Members of Pro- and Anti-Abortion Organizations in Missouri. *Social Biology* 28:239–52.

1982 Family Size Preferences and Sexual Permissiveness as Factors Differentiating Abortion Activists. *Social Psychology Quarterly* 45:1:15–23.

Grindstaff, Laura

1994 Abortion and the Popular Press: Mapping Media Discourse from *Roe* to *Webster.* In *Abortion Politics in the United States and Canada:*

Studies in Public Opinion. Ted G. Jelen and Marthe A. Chandler, eds. pp. 57–88. Westport, CT: Praeger Publishers.

Gulden, Cameron
1994 Taking the Battle Home. *Life Advocate* February, 10–13.

Guth, James, Corwin Smidt, Lyman Kellstedt, and John Green
1993 The Sources of Antiabortion Attitudes: The Case of Religious Political Activists. *American Political Quarterly* 21:1:65–80.

Haines, Herbert H.
1988 *Black Radicals and the Civil Rights Mainstream, 1954–1970.* Knoxville: University of Tennessee Press.

Halliday, M. A. K.
1976 Anti-Languages. *American Anthropologist* 78:570–84.

Harding, Susan
1981 Family Reform Movements: Recent Feminism and Its Opposition. *Feminist Studies* 7:1:57–75.
1987 Convicted by the Holy Spirit. *American Ethnologist* 14:1:167–81.
1990 If I Should Die Before I Wake: Jerry Falwell's Pro-Life Gospel. In *Uncertain Terms: Negotiating Gender in American Culture.* Faye Ginsburg and Anna Lowenhaupt Tsing, eds. pp. 76–97. Boston: Beacon Press.

Hart, Daniel, and William Damon
1985 Contrasts between Understanding Self and Understanding Others. In *The Development of the Self.* Robert L. Leahy, ed. pp. 151–78. New York: Academic Press, Inc.

Harter, Susan
1985 Competence as a Dimension of Self-Evaluation: Toward a Comprehensive Model of Self-Worth. In *The Development of the Self.* Robert L. Leahy, ed. pp. 55–73. New York: Academic Press, Inc.

Heilig, Steve, and Therese S. Wilson
1999 The Need for More Physicians Trained in Abortion: Raising Future Physicians' Awareness. *Cambridge Quarterly of Healthcare Ethics* 8:485–88.

Heirich, Max
1977 Change of Heart: A Test of Some Widely Held Theories about Religious Conversion. *American Journal of Sociology* 83:3:653–80.

Henshaw, Stanley K.
1998 Abortion Incidence and Services in the United States, 1995–1996. *Family Planning Perspectives* 30:6:263–87.

Hill, Paul J.
1993 Who Killed the Innocent – Michael Griffin or Dr. David Gunn? *Life Advocate* August, 40–3.

Himmelstein, Jerome L.
1986 The Social Basis of Antifeminism: Religious Networks and Culture. *Journal for the Scientific Study of Religion* 25:1:1–15.

Hirschman, Albert O.
1982 *Shifting Involvements*. Princeton, NJ: Princeton University Press.

Hoffer, Eric
1951 *The True Believer*. New York: Mentor.

Jelen, Ted G.
1993 *The Political World of the Clergy*. Westport, CT: Praeger Publishers.

Kaiser, Donn L.
1991 Religious Problem-Solving Styles and Guilt. *Journal for the Scientific Study of Religion* 30:1:94–8.

Kass, Jared D., Richard Friedman, Jane Leserman, Patricia C. Zuttermeister, and Herbert Benson
1991 Health Outcomes and a New Index of Spiritual Experience. *Journal for the Scientific Study of Religion* 30:2:203–11.

Kegan, Robert
1985 The Loss of Pete's Dragon: Developments of the Self in the Years Five to Seven. In *The Development of the Self*. Robert L. Leahy, ed. pp. 179–204. New York: Academic Press, Inc.

Kelly, G. A.
1955 *A Theory of Personality*. New York: Norton.

Kent, Ian, R. C. Greenwood, Janice Loeken, and W. Nicholls
1978 Emotional Sequelae of Elective Abortion. *British Columbia Medical Journal* 20:118–19.

Kidahl, J. P.
1965 The Personalities of Sudden Religious Converts. *Pastoral Psychology* 16:37–45.

Klatch, Rebecca E.
1987 *Women of the New Right*. Philadelphia: Temple University Press.

Kolata, Gina.
1990 Under Pressures and Stigma, More Doctors Shun Abortion. *New York Times*, pp. 1,11.

Lake, Randall A.
1984 Order and Disorder in Anti-Abortion Rhetoric: A Logological View. *Quarterly Journal of Speech* 70:425–43.
1986 The Metaethical Framework of Anti-Abortion Rhetoric. *Signs: Journal of Women in Culture and Society* 11:3:478–99.

Larrabee, Mary Jeanne, ed.
1993 *An Ethic of Care: Feminist and Interdisciplinary Perspectives*. New York: Routledge.

Leahy, Robert L.
1985 *The Development of the Self*. New York: Academic Press, Inc.

Lee, Ellie, and Anne Gilchrist
2001 [1997] Abortion Psychological Sequelae: The Debate and the Research. Paper given at conference titled Issues in Pregnancy Counseling: What do Women Need and Want? Oxford, England, May 1997. National Abortion Federation website [online], available http://www.prochoice.org 1/26/01.

Lo, Clarence Y. H.
1982 Countermovements and Conservative Movements in the Contemporary U.S. *Annual Review of Sociology* 8:107–34.

Luker, Kristin
1984 *Abortion and the Politics of Motherhood*. Berkeley: University of California Press.

MacKay, H. T., and A. P. MacKay
1995 Abortion Training in Obstetrics and Gynecology Residency Progams in the United States, 1991–1992. *Family Planning Perspectives* 27: June: 112–15.

Maehr, Martin L.
1989 Thoughts about Motivation. In *Research on Motivation in Education*, Volume 3. Carole Ames and Russell Ames, eds. pp. 299–316. New York: Academic Press, Inc.

Marty, Martin, and R. Scott Appleby, eds.
1993 *Fundamentalisms and the State: Remaking Politics, Economies, and Militance*. Chicago: University of Chicago Press.

Maslow, Abraham H.
1970[1954] *Motivation and Personality*, Second Edition. New York: Harper and Row Publishers.

Maxwell, Carol J. C.
1995 Save Them Lord or Slay Them Dead: Violence, Religion, and Anti-Abortion Activism. Paper presented at the 94th Annual Meeting of the American Anthropological Association in Washington, DC, November 15–19.

Maxwell, Carol J. C., and Ted G. Jelen
1994 Religious and Secular Objectives for Pro-life Direct Action. Paper presented at the Annual Meeting of the Society for the Scientific Study of Religion, Albuquerque, NM. November 4–6.

1995a Commandos for Christ: Narratives of Male Pro-life Activists. *The Review of Religious Research* 37:2:117–31.

1995b Saving, Not Salvation: Meaning and Motivation Among Female Pro-Life Direct Activists. Paper presented at the Annual Meeting of the Society for the Scientific Study of Religion, St. Louis, October 27–29.

1996 Symbolic and Instrumental Objectives for Pro-life Direct Action. *Journal for the Scientific Study of Religion* 35:1:65–70.

Maxwell, Carol J. C., and James V. Spickard

1993 Catholic Activists' Narratives: Commonalities and Divergences in the Peace-and-Justice and Pro-Life Movements. Paper presented at the Annual Meeting of the Society for the Scientific Study of Religion, Raleigh, NC, October 29–31.

McCombs, Harriet G.

1985 Black Self-Concept: An Individual/Collective Analysis. *International Journal of Intercultural Relations* 9:1–18.

Mohr, James C.

1978 *Abortion in America: The Origins and Evolution of National Policy, 1800–1900.* New York: Oxford University Press.

MSFC (Medical Students for Choice)

1999 *Abortion Training in U.S. Obstetrics and Gynecology Residency Programs: A Guide for Medical Students.* Berkeley, CA: Medical Students for Choice.

Murphy, William P.

1990 Creating the Appearance of Consensus in Mende Political Discourse. *American Anthropologist* 92:24–41.

NAF (National Abortion Federation)

2001 Incidents of Violence and Disruption Against Abortion Providers, 1999. National Abortion Federation website [online], available http://www. prochoice.org 1/26/01.

1997 Anti-Abortion Violence and Harassment, 1997: An Analysis of Trends. National Abortion Federation website [online], available http://www.prochoice.org 1/6/00.

NAS (National Academy of Sciences, Institute of Medicine)

1975 *Legalized Abortion and Public Health.* Washington, DC.

Nelson, Barbara J., and Kathryn A. Carver

1994 Many Voices But Few Vehicles: the Consequences for Women of Weak Political Infrastructure in the United States. In *Women and Politics Worldwide.* Barbara J. Nelson and Najma Chowdhury, eds. pp. 737–57. New Haven, CT: Yale University Press.

Nelson, Barbara J., and Najma Chowdhury
1994 *Women and Politics Worldwide.* New Haven, CT: Yale University Press.

Ney, Philip G., and Adele Rose Wickett
1989 Mental Health and Abortion: Review and Analysis. *The Psychiatric Journal of the University of Ottawa* 14:4:506–16.

Nice, David C.
1988 Abortion Clinic Bombings as Political Violence. *American Journal of Political Science* 32:1:178–95.

Noonan, John, ed.
1970 *The Morality of Abortion: Legal and Historical Perspectives.* Cambridge, MA: Harvard University Press.

Official Catholic Directory, The 1999 *Overview and Profiles of the Dioceses. Anno Domini 1999.* New Providence, NJ: P.J. Kennedy.

Ohlhausen, Golden, and Cathy Ramey
1993 Rescue and "Use of Force" Debate. *Life Advocate* August, p. 24.

Oliner, Samuel P. and Pearl M. Oliner
1988 *The Altruistic Personality: Rescuers of Jews in Nazi Europe.* New York: Free Press.

Olson, Mancur
1971 *The Logic of Collective Action.* New York: Schocken Books.

Pearlin, Leonard
1992 Conference on Social Policies and Research on Human Values April 3–5, St. Louis, MO.

Peterman, Jean
1991 *The Abortion Decision: Women Tell Their Stories.* Unpublished.

Plutzer, Eric
1987 Attitudes toward Abortion: A Study of the Social and Ideological Bases of Public Opinion. Ph.D. dissertation, Department of Sociology, Washington University, St. Louis, MO.

Reardon, David C.
1987 *Aborted Women: Silent No More.* Westchester, IL: Crossway Books.

Risen, James, and Judy L. Thomas
1998 *Wrath of Angels: The American Abortion War.* New York: Basic Books.

Rodman, Hyman, Betty Sarvis, and Joy Walker Bonar
1987 *The Abortion Question.* New York: Columbia University Press.

Rogers, Ann Gaile
1987 Gender Differences in Moral Reasoning: A Validity Study of Two Moral Orientations. Ph.D. dissertation, Department of Education, Washington University, St. Louis, MO.

Rose, Thomas, ed.
1969 *Violence in America: A Historical and Comtemporary Reader.* New York: Random House.

Rosenblatt, Paul G., and Linda Hammer Burns
1986 Long-Term Effects of Perinatal Loss. *Journal of Family Issues* 7:3:237–53.

Rosenblatt, Paul C., R. Patricia Walsh, and Douglas A. Jackson
1976 *Grief and Mourning in Cross-Cultural Perspective.* Human Relations Area Files, Inc.

Rosenthal, Elisabeth
1995 Finances and Fear Spurring Hospitals to Drop Abortions. *The New York Times*, p. A1.

Rylko-Bauer, Barbara
1991 Abortion From a Crosscultural Perspective: An Overview. Paper presented at the 90th Annual Meeting of the American Anthropological Association, Chicago, IL.

Sanchez, René
1999 Abortion Foes' Internet Site on Trial: Doctors Fear of Violence Collides with Radical Opponents' Right to Free Speech. *The Washington Post*, January 15, p. A3.

Schneider, David M.
1980 [1968] *American Kinship: A Cultural Account.* Second Edition. Chicago: University of Chicago Press.

Sears, David O., Richard R. Lau, Tom R. Tyler, and Harris M. Allen, Jr.
1980 Self-interest vs. Symbolic Politics in Policy Attitudes and Presidential Voting. *American Political Science Review* 74:670–84.

Segers, Mary C., and Timothy A. Byrnes, eds.
1995 *Abortion Politics in American States.* New York: M. E. Sharpe.

Seymour, Romney L.
2000 Statement issued to the press, supplied to me by Physicians for Reproductive Choice and Health.

Sherif, M.
1936 *The Psychology of Social Norms.* New York: Harper and Brothers.

Simmonds, R. B.
1977 Conversion as Addiction: Consequences of Joining a Jesus Movement Group. *American Behavioral Science* 20:909–24.

Simon, Nathan M., and Audrey G. Senturia
1966 Psychiatric Sequelae of Abortion. *Archives of General Psychiatry* 15:378–89.

Snow, David A., and Richard Machalek
1984 The Sociology of Conversion. *Annual Review of Sociology* 10:167–90.

Speckhard, Anne
1985 Post Abortion Stress: The Psycho-Social Outcomes of Abortion. Unpublished dissertation, University of Minnesota.

Stark, Rodney, and William Sims Bainbridge
1980 Networks of Faith: Interpersonal Bonds and Recruitment to Cults and Sects. *American Journal of Sociology* 85:6:1376–95.

Stark, Trisha A., Robert William Blum, Michael D. Resnick, and Linda Bearinger
1986 Research Update: Social and Psychological Factors Associated with Pregnancy Termination. Paper presented at the 94th Annual Convention of the American Psychological Association, August 22–26, Washingtion, DC.

Steinauer, Jody E., Teresa DePineres, Anne M. Robert, John Westfall, and Philip Darney
1997 Training Family Practice Residents in Abortion and Other Reproductive Health Care: A Nationwide Survey. *Family Planning Perspectives* 29:5:222–27.

Stewart, Charles J., Craig Allen Smith, Robert E. Denton, Jr.
1989 *Persuasion and Social Movements*, Second Edition. Prospect Heights, IL: Waveland Press, Inc.

Stromberg, Peter G.
1990 Ideological Language in the Transformation of Identity. *American Anthropologist* 92:42–56.
1993 *Language and Self-Transformation*. New York: Cambridge University Press, Publications of the Society for Psychological Anthropology.

Taylor, Bryan
1976 Conversion and Cognition: An Area for Empirical Study in the Microsociology of Religious Knowledge. *Social Compass* 23:1:5–22.

Terry, Randall A.
1988 *Operation Rescue*. Springdale, PA: Whitaker House.

Thomas, Judy
1996 Fear Lingers at Abortion Clinics: Many Facilities Enhance Security Effort. *The Kansas City Star*, March 10, p. A4.

Tribe, Laurence H.
1990 *Abortion: The Clash of Absolutes.* New York: W. W. Norton and Company.

Ullman, Chana
1982 Cognitive and Emotional Antecedents of Religious Conversion. *American Journal of Personality and Social Psychology* 43:1:183–92.

U.S. Bureau of the Census
1990 Census of Population and Housing, Supplementary Reports, Metropolitan Areas as Defined by the Office of Management and Budget, June 30, 1993. Publication code CPH-S-1-1.
1996 Statistical Abstract of the United States: 1996 116th edition. Washington DC.

Vanderford, Marsha L.
1989 Vilification and Social Movements: A Case Study of Pro-life and Pro-Choice Rhetoric. *Quarterly Journal of Speech* 75:166–82.

Waters, Mary-Alice, ed.
1970 *Rosa Luxemburg Speaks.* New York: Pathfinder Press.

Weber, Max
1978 *Economy and Society: An Outline of Interpretive Sociology.* Guenther Roth and Claus Wittich, eds. Berkeley: University of California Press.

West, Guiday, and Rhoda Lois Blumberg, eds.
1990 *Women and Social Protest.* New York: Oxford University Press.

Wikan, Unni.
1990 *Managing Turbulent Hearts: A Balinese Formula for Living.* Chicago: University of Chicago Press.

Whorf, Benjamin Lee.
1956 *Language, Thought, and Reality: Selected Writings of Benjamin Lee Whorf.* John B. Carroll, ed. Cambridge, MA: MIT Press.

Wills, Garry
1990 *Under God.* New York: Simon and Schuster

Woolf, Virginia
1936 *Three Guineas.* New York: Harcourt, Brace & World.

Index